# FIRST LOVE

# TRANSMISSION

Transmission denotes the transfer of information, objects or forces from one place to another, from one person to another. Transmission implies urgency, even emergency: a line humming, an alarm sounding, a messenger bearing news. Through Transmission interventions are supported, and opinions overturned. Transmission republishes classic works in philosophy, as it publishes works that re-examine classical philosophical thought. Transmission is the name for what takes place.

# FIRST LOVE
A PHENOMENOLOGY OF THE ONE

Sigi Jöttkandt

re.press Melbourne 2010

# re.press

PO Box 40, Prahran, 3181, Melbourne, Australia
http://www.re-press.org
© Sigi Jöttkandt 2010
The moral rights of the authors have been asserted

This work is 'Open Access', published under a creative commons license which means that you are free to copy, distribute, display, and perform the work as long as you clearly attribute the work to the authors, that you do not use this work for any commercial gain in any form whatsoever and that you in no way alter, transform or build on the work outside of its use in normal academic scholarship without express permission of the author (or their executors) *and* the publisher of this volume. For any reuse or distribution, you must make clear to others the license terms of this work. For more information see the details of the creative commons licence at this website:
http://creativecommons.org/licenses/by-nc-sa/3.0/

British Library Cataloguing-in-Publication Data
*A catalogue record for this book is available from the British Library*

Library of Congress Cataloguing-in-Publication Data
*A catalogue record for this book is available from the Library of Congress*

**National Library of Australia Cataloguing-in-Publication Data**

Jottkandt, Sigi.
First love : a phenomenology of the one / Sigi Jöttkandt.

9780980544053 (pbk.)
978-0-9806683-0-8 (ebook)

Series: Transmission.

Notes: Bibliography.
Subjects: Love. Love in literature.
Psychoanalysis. Philosophy.

152.41

Designed and Typeset by A&R

This book is produced sustainably using plantation timber, and printed in the destination market reducing wastage and excess transport.

# CONTENTS

| | |
|---|---|
| *Acknowledgements* | *vii* |
| 1. A IS FOR ANNA, OR 'THERE IS SOME ONE': SAMUEL BECKETT | 1 |
| 2. FORFEITS AND COMPARISONS: IVAN TURGENEV | 37 |
| 3. IN THE SELF'S TEMPORARY LODGINGS: EUDORA WELTY | 59 |
| 4. I MARY YOU: JOHN CLARE | 87 |
| 5. 'THE FIRST LOVE IS THE TRUE LOVE AND ONE ONLY LOVES ONCE': SØREN KIERKEGAARD WITH EUGENE SCRIBE | 121 |
| *Afterword* | *161* |
| *Bibliography* | *167* |

# ACKNOWLEDGEMENTS

If every book has its secret co-author, or at least its one intended reader, here that person is Justin Clemens whose intellectual generosity and creative suggestions have kept me unfailingly aware of how the process of writing is always implicitly a 'scene of Two'. The book's inevitable 'other reader', then, is Dominiek Hoens, in whose sympathetic company many of the ideas explored here took on their early shape. A portion of the first chapter appeared as 'The Narcissism of Small Differences: On Beckett's First Love' in *(a): the journal of culture and the unconscious*, vol. 3, nos. 1-2, 2003, pp. 117-26. The second chapter appeared as 'Forfeits and Comparisons: Turgenev's First Love' in *Lacan: the Silent Partners*, Slavoj Žižek (ed.), London, Verso, 2006. I thank the editors for permission to reprint this material. I would also like to take this opportunity to thank the Flemish Fund for Scientific Research and Ghent University for financial assistance during the writing of this book, and to express my gratitude to the members of the research project, A Critique of Literary Ethics: Gert Buelens, Ortwin de Graef and Benjamin Biebuyck. I am also very grateful to the Jan van Eyck Academy for support in the final stages of this writing, as well as to Paul Ashton, Lorenzo Chiesa, Tom Cohen, Joan Copjec, Marc de Kesel, Oliver Feltham, Chris Gemerchak, Gary Hall, Lieven Jonckheere, Juliet Flower MacCannell, J. Hillis Miller, Ed Pluth, Tom Toremans, and the current and former researchers at the Jan van Eyck Circle for Lacanian Ideology Critique.

Brussels, 2009

*for D.O.*

# 1. A IS FOR ANNA, OR 'THERE IS SOME ONE': SAMUEL BECKETT

> 'A is for Anna like L is for Liv. Aha hahah, Ante Ann you're apt to ape aunty annalive! Dawn gives rise. Lo, lo, lives love! Eve takes fall. La, la, laugh leaves alass! Aiaaiaiai, Antian, we're last to the lost, Loulou! Tis perfect'
> —James Joyce, *Finnegan's Wake*

Let me begin with a claim that must sound astonishing to many ears, John Robert Keller's assertion of the 'primacy of love' in Beckett's work.[1] Clearly intended as a provocation to contemporary Beckett studies, Keller's book, *Samuel Beckett and the Primacy of Love*, counters a long-running strain in Beckett criticism that has painted Beckett as an unrelentingly pessimistic figure, whose bleak vision of humanity is mitigated only by the blackest of black humor. While Keller doesn't deny what he calls the 'primal catastrophe' that many readers have detected shaping the contours of the Beckettian narrator's world, he finds Beckett's fiction to be powerfully inflected by a courageous attempt at love, at whose center 'is an attempt to connect to the mother'.[2] With this, Keller swiftly and economically confirms what Freud has reportedly taught us all along, such that it has become a truism of psychoanalytic criticism, namely, that the mother is the child's 'first love'. Keller's thesis, worked out through sustained readings of *Murphy*, *Watt*, *Waiting for Godot* and several texts from the short fiction (although, surprisingly, not the short novella *First Love*), is that by writing, by telling stories, Beckett's narrator attempts to mend

---

1. John Robert Keller, *Samuel Beckett and the Primacy of Love*, Manchester, Manchester University Press, 2002.
2. Keller, *Samuel Beckett and the Primacy of Love*, p. 12.

the gap that has separated him from the 'loving otherness' that is the maternal being. Writing, Keller asserts, is a desperate 'plea for connection, by a self that is unifying, then fragmenting under the weight of non-recognition'.[3]

Although Keller's is probably not a Beckett many of us would recognize at first sight, his assessment of the writer as a thinker of utmost perseverance and fortitude would likely gain an appreciative nod from Alain Badiou. Badiou's lifelong engagement with Beckett is recorded in a series of essays, recently translated in Alberto Toscano's and Nina Power's useful volume, *On Beckett*.[4] In this collection, Badiou speaks of the urgent need to put distance between ourselves and the Sartrean or 'existentialist' Beckett that has dominated Beckett studies for much of the past half century (although, as Andrew Gibson points out in his thoughtful afterword to the volume, Badiou seems largely unaware of the challenge to this characterization posed by more recent studies in the deconstructive vein). Badiou invites us to rediscover a writer whose fundamental 'lesson' is one of 'measure, exactitude and courage'.[5] Badiou thus shares Keller's conviction that the Beckettian subject is nothing if not powerfully engaged with one of the philosophical 'conditions' Badiou identifies as love. But the philosopher, I suspect, would likely retreat from Keller's more expansive claim regarding love's primacy or 'firstness' for Beckett. Love is, after all, only one of the four conditions that Badiou identifies under which truths can emerge, and the Beckett that Badiou encounters is just as deeply engaged with politics (his work in the French resistance), with science (the Cartesian 'Method') and of course with art (writing), as he is with love.

With respect to these last, an important strand of critique has surfaced in tandem with the appearance of the English translation of Badiou's magnum opus *Being and Event*. Badiou, this critique alleges, is not as responsive as he might be to the *preconditions* under which an event and its truth procedure might occur.[6]

---

3. Keller, *Samuel Beckett and the Primacy of Love*, p. 23.

4. Alain Badiou, *On Beckett*, ed. and trans. Alberto Toscano and Nina Power, Manchester, Clinamen Press, 2003.

5. Badiou, *On Beckett*, p. 40.

6. This is in essence Jean-Luc Nancy's critique of Badiou, expressed in his essay 'Philosophy Without Conditions'. He writes there is 'a precondition which is at once and indissociably historical, technical and transcendental'. In *Think Again: Alain Badiou and the Future of Philosophy*, Peter Hallward (ed.), London, Continuum, 2004, pp. 39-48, p. 47. For a good overview of some of these

An event is always a rare, aleatory occurrence, but the challenge posed by this critique is whether we can think a situation's own implication in an event—that is, whether any of its local aspects or historical features can colour or play a more or less defining role in the way, or even *if,* the event occurs. Recent cases in point include Sam Gillespie's persuasive call for the need to identify the affect that 'grips' the subject in the truth operation that makes it susceptible to and capable of recognizing an event, and Peter Hallward's continuing critical appraisal of what he calls 'despecification' implicit in the Badiouian system whose anti-relational subtraction, he claims, 'effectively proscribes thought from considering the *production* of an event'.[7] To this, one would want to add Adrian Johnston's instructive summation of the difficulties Badiou confronts in formulating a consistent theory of historical temporality that arises as a result of the philosopher's adherence to the theme of discontinuity and insistence on rupture as the privileged figure for the event.[8] Troping his query through a concept of evental time,

---

arguments, see Adrian Johnston, 'The Quick and the Dead: Alain Badiou and the Split Speeds of Transformation', *International Journal of Zizek Studies*, vol. 1, no. 2, 2007, <http://zizekstudies.org/index.php/ijzs/issue/view/4> [accessed 20 February, 2008].

7. Sam Gillespie, 'Giving Form to Its Own Existence: Anxiety and the Subject of Truth', in *The Praxis of Alain Badiou*, Paul Ashton, A. J. Bartlett and Justin Clemens (eds.), Melbourne, re.press, 2006, pp. 180-209; Peter Hallward, *Badiou: A Subject to Truth*, Minneapolis, University of Minnesota Press, 2003, p. 371. For an excellent itemization of his and others' problems with Badiou's philosophy around these points, see also Hallward's 'Introduction: 'Consequences of Abstraction' in *Think Again*, pp. 1-20.

8. Johnston summarizes it thus: 'Such a theory must succeed at envisioning processes of transformation as immanently arising from a given situation, rather than being imposed upon "what is" from a mysterious external Elsewhere. As per the latter formulation from *Logiques des mondes*, evental time emerges out of (and then separates itself off from) other historical-temporal currents (this could be described as an immanent genesis of the thereafter-transcendent *qua* subsequently independent in relation to its evental site as a situational point of origin). And yet, Badiou's other above-cited insistence that one must think "discontinuity as such" appears to pull him away from stressing the immanence to broader stretches of historical time of the event's engendering of another time, perhaps based on the worry that this would amount to a concession to the "cult of genealogies" (Badiou, 2006, p. 531) (i.e. historicist orientations in post-modernism that compulsively re-inscribe all occurring phenomena back within overdetermining streams of historical continuity) resulting in the inability to think genuine newness per se due to the implicit denial that utter and complete ruptures with what comes before are possible'. Johnston, 'The Quick and the Dead', pp. 6-7. Also see Alain Badiou, *Logiques des mondes: L'être et l'événement 2*, Paris, Seuil, 2006.

Johnston probes whether it is possible for something to be 'related to a situation or world without, for all that, being entirely determined and dominated by such relations', noting how 'although evental time is produced on the basis of the materials of non-evental time, the former nonetheless achieves a self-defining, auto-constituting autonomy that distances and separates it from the preceding background of temporal currents from which it branched off as what might initially have appeared to be a tributary'.[9]

Andrew Gibson's magnificent study, *Beckett and Badiou: The Pathos of Intermittency*, advances the most intricate and sustained version of this critique.[10] Gibson's central claim here is that, owing to his unabashedly affirmative philosophy, Badiou allows no place in his system for what the critic, following Beckett, terms 'the remainder' (*le reste*). Clearly with this term, Gibson intends to marshal a prominent tradition in contemporary philosophy that over the past fifty odd years has been dedicated to empowering 'the Other' to enter discourse. The key figures of this philosophy of alterity—difference, history, multiplicity, contingency, materiality—have lately congealed around another figure, *pathos*, which is also the privileged figure for Gibson's Beckettian critique of Badiou. Contending that in *Being and Event* Badiou is remiss in failing to theorize the remainder as such—the concrete historical situations into which events erupt—the literary critic, through Beckett, will direct us to a certain pathos subtly perforating the steely Badiouian universe, which he names the 'pathos of intermittency'. Gibson writes, 'however liberated from "the pathos of finitude", a universe structured in terms of actual infinity and event cannot be immune to a pathos of its own'.[11]

Despite their varying points of incision, the common thread of this critique can be phrased thus: what Badiou is lacking (albeit for stringent philosophical reasons, it transpires[12]) is a place in his philosophy for the *aesthetic* as such—the dimension of sensation, affect, perception in general and, with respect to art, the faculty of

---

9. Johnston, 'The Quick and the Dead', p. 7.
10. Andrew Gibson, *Beckett and Badiou: the Pathos of Intermittency*, Oxford: Oxford University Press, 2006.
11. Gibson, *Beckett and Badiou*, p. 19.
12. Badiou asserts that because philosophy is conditioned by art, because art is one of philosophy's 'conditions', it can never become an object for philosophical speculation. For a full account of the need for an 'inaesthetics' as opposed to an aesthetics, see Badiou's *Handbook of Inaesthetics*, trans. Alberto Toscano, Stanford, Stanford University Press, 2005.

judging or, in Badiou's term, of 'liking'.[13] In its stead, Badiou proposes a 'new schema' to describe the relation between art and philosophy, one that, unlike classical philosophical aesthetics, makes *no* claim, 'to turn art into an object of philosophy'. To the contrary, as he explains in his introductory note to the *Handbook of Inaesthetics*, his term 'inaesthetics' is intended solely to recount 'the strictly intraphilosophical effects produced by the independent existence of some works of art'.[14]

As a number of critics have already pointed out, however, the direct result of this refusal to admit a place for the aesthetic is the ambiguous role that language, as one of the possible loci of the event's preconditions, is obliged to play in the Badiouian 'set-up'. Gibson, for one, has previously taken the philosopher to task for seemingly neglecting the possibility that language may serve as a potential eventful site in its own right.[15] Gibson's critique emerged from his keen literary sensitivity to how, the emphasis Badiou places on the act—and ethics—of naming notwithstanding, the author of *Being and Event* remains in essence unconvinced by the part art, and more specifically language, might play in the evental schema. One sees how Badiou in fact wavers on this point. In his essay, 'What is a Poem?' Badiou refers to a 'power' inherent in language that appears to convoke the void in a way that bears close similarities to his classical description of the catastrophe of presentation he calls an event. According to Badiou, 'Every poem brings a power into language, the power of eternally fastening the disappearance of what presents itself'.[16] Continuing, Badiou—again quite classically—identifies this power as something 'unnamable' within the situation [of the poem]. He says,

> this power of language is precisely what the poem cannot name. It effectuates this power, by drawing upon the latent song of language, upon its infinite resource, upon the novelty of its assemblage. But poetry cannot fasten this infinite because it is to the infinite of language that the poem addresses itself in order to direct the power of language toward the retention of a disappearance.[17]

---

13. Badiou, *Handbook of Inaesthetics*, p. 4.
14. Badiou, *Handbook of Inaesthetics*, p. xiv.
15. Gibson has in the meantime amended this critique with his recognition of Badiou's concept of *événamentalité*, the logic of the event or 'event of the event' that appears to satisfy this concern. See chapter 3 of *Beckett and Badiou*.
16. Badiou, *Handbook of Inaesthetics*, p. 24-25.
17. Badiou, *Handbook of Inaesthetics*, p. 25

Badiou concludes, 'language as an infinite power devoted to presence, is precisely the unnamable of poetry'.[18] Earlier however, in the opening essay of the *Handbook of Inaesthetics*, 'Art and Philosophy' that evidently serves as a sort of manifesto for his concept of inaesthetics, Badiou appears to retreat from this position, insisting that 'it is impossible to say of the work [of art] *at one and the same time* that it is a truth and that it is the event whence this truth originates'.[19] 'Art *itself*', he explicitly states in this essay, 'is a truth procedure' and as such can only be faithful to an event, rather than an event itself.[20]

No particular astuteness is required to see why Badiou might find it problematic to entertain the possibility of a specifically linguistic 'event'. This derives from how language ineluctably traverses *all* of the generic procedures—politics, science, art and love—through the critically vital role nomination plays in his set-up. Recall how, for Badiou, an event only obtains existence through a subject's recognition and naming of it as an event. Thus every act of naming, Badiou claims, is 'in essence poetic' in the sense that it 'eternally fasten[s] the disappearance of what presents itself'.[21] By his logic, naming a poetic event would necessarily entail a second order 'poeticization' of a poem, but this, says Badiou in 'What is a Poem?' is strictly forbidden. Following Stéphane Mallarmé's lead, Badiou indicates 'there could never be a poem of the poem, a metapoem'.[22] The reason is that such a 'metapoem' would not so surreptitiously reintroduce an uncounted One or Whole into Badiou's system and on this point Badiou will always stand firm: '*it is an essential property of being qua being*', he reiterates again in his recent work, '*that there cannot exist a whole of beings, once beings are thought solely on the basis of their beingness*'.[23]

Still, the unintentional outcome of this fundamental theorem of the non-existence of being as a whole is the way art and particularly literature are reduced to playing an essentially allegorical role for Badiou. 'It often seems', Elie During remarks, 'as if philosophy finds in art simply the effect or local verification of its own opera-

---

18. Badiou, *Handbook of Inaesthetics*, p. 25.
19. Badiou, *Handbook of Inaesthetics*, p. 11.
20. Badiou, *Handbook of Inaesthetics*, p. 9.
21. Badiou, *Handbook of Inaesthetics*, p. 26, pp. 24-5.
22. Badiou, *Handbook of Inaesthetics*, p. 25.
23. Alain Badiou, *Theoretical Writings*, ed. and trans. Ray Brassier and Alberto Toscano, London: Continuum, 2004, p. 169 (Badiou's emphasis).

tions'.[24] Gibson similarly observes how Badiou's tendency to read literature as though it were philosophy inevitably occludes how art and aesthetic experience 'might modulate [his thought], temper it, lend it other intonations'.[25] My suspicion is that if one was to permit these 'other intonations' that aesthetic or, in this case, literary experience, lends to Badiou's philosophy to surface, they may prove the source for possible answers to certain lingering questions that persist in Badiou's work as a result of the philosopher's conflicted attitude to what Gibson has called art's 'double contingency': art's—and particularly literature's—unique positioning within the four truth procedures as being both 'produced by events and capable of reflecting on them'.[26] Included among these questions are the following which I propose to allow as our guides in the following exploration: what permits the count-as-One to count itself in the sudden gear-change through which presentation becomes representation? Or, how can something *inside* presentation come to act in a meta-presentational way? Furthermore, does the way an event *appears* affect how it is taken up in a truth procedure of fidelity? And, anticipating my concerns in this first chapter, what is the origin of the creative power that enables a future subject of truth to name an event?

This is the complex of questions that will occupy us in our effort to trace the efflorescence of a certain One as it hides in open sight in the literary tradition of First Love. By this latter I am referring to the striking cluster of texts that, traversing a variety of historical and generic boundaries, share the same title 'First Love'. I have singled out five of these texts to discuss here, the *First Love* of Samuel Beckett, Ivan Turgenev, Eudora Welty, John Clare, and Søren Kierkegaard. But a quick word of explanation is in order first. My intention in this book is not to offer a careful point-by-point analysis of the places in Badiou's philosophy where he dispenses with or erases the autonomy of the aesthetic, which these literary texts would be privileged to reveal. This is not so much a book on Badiou as one inspired by him and by the possibility of what, to the extent of my knowledge, he has so far failed to fully think: the existence of an *uncounted One* as named and held faithful to by the literary tradition of First Love. One might thus

---

24. Elie During, 'How Much Truth Can Art Bear?', trans. Laura Balladur, *Polygraph*, no. 17, 2005, 143-55, p. 147.
25. Gibson, *Beckett and Badiou*, p. 116.
26. Gibson, *Beckett and Badiou*, p. 178.

consider this book an analytic attempt to listen to what literature is saying when it claims insistently through this repeated title that love is indeed (as Keller claims) 'first' for Beckett—and for our other four writers as well. To grasp what is entailed in this primacy, and to approach what is at stake in the 'One' that literature speaks about so gracefully and persistently, will require the suspension of everything Badiou has told us about the One's 'inexistence'. In good phenomenological form, it will demand we bracket the ontological claims of the philosophical tradition, including the incisive challenge posed to it by Badiou, and attend to literature's reiterated attestations through its myriad stories, poems and plays titled *First Love* that, contra Badiou, the One *is*.[27] Literature maintains that a One exists that is *not the result of a count*. There is (some)One, in Lacan's phrasing (*Y de l'un*[28]), that—or perhaps *who*—is not purely an effect of structure.

As we move forward, it should quickly become apparent that the One of first love bears little in common with the One that lies at the foundation of what Badiou elegantly calls the 'the portico of the ruined temple' that is ontology since Parmenides.[29] For this literary One is neither posited *a priori*, nor a product of addition; neither a meta-structure, nor an element of the situation. Even less, as we will see in a subsequent chapter, is it another name for the Two, the scene of the investigations or 'inquiries' about the world and its 'common practices' that comprises the truth procedure of love for Badiou. Of the writers discussed in this book, it is Beckett who provides the most rigorous, 'mathematical' deduction of this One's existence, which is why I have chosen to open this study or 'phenomenology' of love's One with a discussion of his novella *First Love*. Additionally, more than any of the other writers discussed here, Beckett has lent himself particularly felicitously to psychoanalytic interpretations, in part emerging from his much-discussed analysis with Wilfred Bion, but also because, under the capture of the psychoanalytic myth of first love as mother love, many psychoanalytic critics—John Keller included—have found

---

27. In the opening pages of *Being and Event*, Badiou lays out the groundwork of his philosophy: 'What has to be declared is that the one, which is not, solely exists as operation. In other words, there is no one; only the count-as-one', *Being and Event*, trans. Oliver Feltham, London, Continuum, 2005, p. 24.

28. See Jacques Lacan, *The Seminar of Jacques Lacan, Book XX, Encore: On Feminine Sexuality, The Limits of Love and Knowledge, 1972-73*, Jacques-Alain Miller (ed.), trans. and notes Bruce Fink, New York, Norton, 1998, p. 66.

29. Badiou, *Being and Event*, p. 23.

his work rich in Oedipal dramas.³⁰ Beckett thus offers a particularly fertile base for mapping out the stakes of my other chief concern in this book, which is to revisit, through the literary tradition of First Love, the traditional psychoanalytic narrative of first love as the love of the mother. This ostensibly psychoanalytic myth takes its inspiration from Freud's famous pronouncements about the mother although, as I will be arguing in the following pages, it derives from a crucial misreading of what Freud actually said. If there is one thing these five, profoundly different texts titled *First Love* have in common, it is their unreserved rejection of the purportedly Freudian myth of first love as mother love. In not one of the texts under discussion does 'first love' have anything remotely to do with the mother, and especially not as the child's fantasmatic Ideal that he will dedicate his entire adult life to attempting to restore. Note that by saying this, I am not in any way denying the critical locale the mother occupies in the subject's structure of desire. However, this place has for too long erroneously been designated the child's 'first love' which, as we will see, entails something of a completely different order and about which the critical psychoanalytic tradition has been remarkably silent up till now.

\*\*\*

Samuel Beckett's *First Love* is a short, semi-autobiographical novella that was written in 1946 but remained unpublished until its appearance in 1970 (as *Premier amour*).³¹ In it, Beckett's narrator recounts the events following the death of his father: his eviction from the family home, his subsequent homelessness, his meeting with the woman Lulu with whom he shares a penchant for the same bench, their unlikely union which leads to the narrator's moving in with Lulu and the birth of what appears to be his child. The story ends with the narrator being driven out of Lulu's house by the baby's incessant crying—such is the sequence of events the narrator dryly calls 'my marriage'. From even such a minimal summary, it is already apparent that Beckett's *First Love* dethrones many of the key tropes and tenets of the psychoanalytic myth of first love as mother love. For starters, it is not from a blissful

---

30. A classic example of such an Oedipal reading is Phil Baker, *Beckett and the Mythology of Psychoanalysis*, Basingstoke, Palgrave Macmillan, 1998.
31. Samuel Beckett, *Premier amour*, Paris, Les Éditions de Minuit, 1970; *First Love*, London, Calder and Boyars, 1973.

maternal but a *paternal* universe that the narrator is summarily ejected. And instead of tracing a narrative of return to the mother (through one or more substitute objects, more about which in a moment), the key narrative events are *separations* and *expulsions* rather than reunifications. It strikes me as a little unaccountable, therefore, how in his Jungian reading of the tale, Paul Davies still succeeds in retrieving the classical features of the psychoanalytic narrative from this disconcerting text. In line with a respected vein of Beckett criticism, Davies regards the narrator as suffering the 'spiritual emergency' of the Cartesian subject, excised both from itself and from the sensible world, who is thereby forced to inhabit the purely symbolic, deathly world of pure thought.[32] Davies accordingly attributes the well-known negative affective features of the Beckettian internal landscape to a yearning for what the critic, following Coleridge, calls the 'I AM, the Identity that predates the fatal divide into I and not-I'.[33]

Davies' invocation of Coleridge is revealing insofar as it prompts recognition of the not-so-hidden literary Romanticism implicitly powering the psychoanalytic myth of mother love, whose mother-child unity shares many of the features of the philosophical tradition Coleridge is referencing. As pre-lapsarian fantasies of an originary unity (or One), both Coleridgean 'Identity' and the psychoanalytic myth of mother love have eminent forebears in the Greek and Christian traditions, a story that typically begins with Aristophanes' fable of the original humans being cut in two by the gods. The spectre of this original One has long served to anchor the history of Western philosophy that Badiou ultimately has in his sights as it sculpts and finally secures the gatherings, ascents, mergings and returns that make up the master tropes of this philosophical idealism. Central to this tradition of course is love, which acts as the 'glue' (as one strand of the medieval tradition has it) that binds the lovers together, and, ultimately, the lover with the One. As one of the great lovers of history, Abelard, memorably put it, love is 'a particular force of the soul, existing not for itself nor content by itself, but always pouring itself into another with a certain hunger and desire, wanting to become one with the other, so that from two diverse wills one is produced without

---

32. Paul Davies, 'Three Novels and Four Nouvelles: Giving Up the Ghost to be Born at Last', in *The Cambridge Companion to Beckett*, John Pilling (ed.), Cambridge, Cambridge University Press, 1996, pp. 43-66, p. 45.

33. Davies, 'Three Novels and Four Nouvelles', p. 63.

difference'.³⁴ The master narrative of psychoanalysis, as traditionally told, cannot be divorced from this history. Exemplarily, it relates how the child enjoys an original state of union with the mother, from which it becomes severed by the paternal prohibition, known in psychoanalysis as 'castration'. Under 'normal' (that is, neurotic) circumstances, the child submits to this Name/No by which the Law of the Father makes its presence felt, and consoles him or herself for the loss of the original 'first love' by seeking the mother out in the later, substitute objects of desire. The child thus gives up its 'being' for 'having' the phallus, wagering that it will recoup its forfeited *jouissance* symbolically, on the 'inverse scale of the Law of desire' as Lacan famously puts it.³⁵ When Freud says the mother, as lost object, can only ever be 're-found', one typically understands him as meaning that in the object of desire we re-find the primordial maternal object. Our entire desiring trajectory aims at recovering—finding once more—the original One, or condition of unity, we have lost.

As venerable as this Parmenidean philosophical tradition is, from which Freud also famously and explicitly draws, it is nevertheless impossible to reconcile with Beckett's *First Love*. The narrator's problem, as far as I can tell, lies not so much in his tragic inhabiting of a purely symbolic world cut off from a primordial unity, as Davies has it, but in the way he is not inscribed in that world *satisfactorily enough*. Evidence of this lack of symbolic anchoring is discovered in the much-discussed way our hero, like many other Beckettian narrators, persistently blurs all symbolically-marked distinctions, up to and including Coleridge's 'fatal divide' separating I from Not-I. Indeed the narrator's self-composed epitaph reads as an ironic parable of his congenitally lapidary condition: 'Hereunder lies the above who up below/So hourly died that he lived on till now'.³⁶ In this compressed sequence of paradoxes, Beckett's narrator exposes the fundamental predicament proper not only to his own situation but to that of every speaking subject: the same language that purports to deliver us from (real) death, causes us to be in a sense symbolically 'dead' to ourselves.

---

34. *The Lost Love Letters of Heloise and Abelard: Perceptions of Dialogue in Twelfth-century France*, Constant J. Mews (ed.), trans. Neville Chiavaroli, Basingstoke, Palgrave Macmillan, 2001, p. 67.

35. Jacques Lacan, 'The Subversion of the Subject and the Dialectic of Desire', *Écrits: the First Complete Edition in English*, trans. Bruce Fink, New York, Norton, 2006, p. 700.

36. Beckett, *First Love*, p. 11.

The 'I'—the subject whose personal history the stone epitaph records for posterity, thereby enabling it to 'live on'—can never be present in the instance it is spoken about, because language fundamentally divorces us from our being. Dying 'hourly' with each and every utterance, we inhabit a linguistic world that, while holding itself illusorily 'above' or over the real world, is really an 'up below'—an inverted, spectral 'copy' of an original that recedes with every step we take towards it.

As is well known, Lacanian psychoanalysis proposes the Name-of-the-Father or paternal signifier (S1) as the psychic entity that traditionally grounds the linguistic operation and prevents the spectral or Symbolic 'copy' from severing its last links to the material or 'real' world (the realm of Being). The S1 prototypically 'quilts' the registers of the Symbolic, Imaginary and Real together and binds them together in a more or less stable configuration. It accomplishes this by means of its ability to function as a *point de capiton*, an anchoring button or linguistic knot that checks language's endless metonymic slide. In Beckett's narrator's case, however, something seems to have happened to this stabilizing function. Death—precisely the 'real' death that symbolic or epitaphic language is supposed to forestall—has rendered the narrator's father, along with his protective 'paternal function', strangely impotent. Complaining that he was not allowed to see his father's will—the Law written in the paternal hand itself and intended to continue his reign after death—the narrator explains: 'It was he who wanted me in the house. [...] Yes, he was properly had, my poor father, if his purpose was really to go on protecting me from beyond the tomb'.[37] Thus while Daniel Katz, in one of the few extant sustained readings of the tale, regards the short story's trajectory as following an 'overly programmed Oedipal course',[38] the paternal demise in fact leads not to the anticipated joyous reunion with the lost maternal object as proposed by the traditional psychoanalytic myth of first love, but to an unwilling exile from the place the narrator had called home, including from 'all those lips that had kissed me, those hearts that had loved me [...], those hands that had played with mine and those minds that had almost made their own of me!'[39] 'Poor Papa', the narrator muses, 'a nice

---

37. Beckett, *First Love*, pp. 13-14.
38. Daniel Katz, 'Beckett's Measures: Principles of Pleasure in Molloy and 'First Love', *Modern Fiction Studies*, vol. 49, no. 2, 2003, pp. 246-56, p. 250.
39. Beckett, *First Love*, pp. 18-19.

mug he must have felt that day if he could see me, see us, a nice mug on my account I mean'.[40]

Orphaned by his father's inability to reach beyond death and continue to protect his son 'from beyond the tomb', the narrator is forced to pack his scanty belongings and leave his father's house. Here it is worth noting that, although up till now I have been emphasizing the differences between Beckett's *First Love* and the psychoanalytic narrative as most commonly told, such an expulsion from the paternal or 'symbolic' shelter is nevertheless not without its own precedent in psychoanalysis. As is also well known, for Lacan, each of the psychic structures, neurosis, perversion, psychosis, enjoys a very specific relation to the paternal signifier, the last of which—psychosis—entails a similar symbolic 'exclusion'. The psychotic is said to 'foreclose' the Name-of-the-Father, a statement that ought to be clarified by saying that foreclosure is not so much the *total absence* of knowledge of a paternal signifier but rather that the psychotic, 'refuses to be subject to this knowledge', as Joel Dor formulates it.[41] The effect of this refusal is to render the psychotic subject incapable of joining the Name-of-the-Father to a signified in a signifying process that would enable the paternal function to be psychically represented. As a result, the symbolic realm of the big Other manifests itself to the psychotic through predominantly imaginary relations, famously typified in the figure of the persecuting double whom one must either vanquish or be vanquished by in the eternal psychotic round of imaginary rivalry.

Nevertheless, a closer look at *First Love* reveals that this description manifestly does not describe Beckett's narrator's experience. The narrator is, after all, capable of establishing certain symbolically derived facts, such as the date of his birth and his age at the time of his 'marriage', even if these numbers are rendered unstable by persistent doubts as to their verifiability. Sharing the same obsession with measurement exhibited by other Beckettian narrators, leading Hugh Kenner to his haunting description of Beckettian man's 'fate' as the pathos of being destined to 'inscribe the figures of plane geometry on a spherical surface', the narrator of *First Love* seems to suffer not so much from the total absence

---

40. Beckett, *First Love*, p. 19.
41. Joel Dor, *Structure and Perversions*, trans. Susan Fairfield, New York, Other Press, 2001, p. 154. Lacan's preferred phrase for this subjectivation of the phallus is 'historicization', which I discuss in more detail in chapter 3.

of the quilting provided by the Name-of-the-Father, as from a certain *shortfall* in its operation.[42] This is the shortfall that must accompany all symbolizing or 'measuring' attempts, and this for the simple reason that the 'topography' we are trying to measure—the field of signification—is not flat, as Kenner observed, but curved.[43] Describing the Beckettian subject, Kenner poignantly explains how, 'From over [the narrator's] shoulder, we may be heartened by his sureness and finesse. It is when we get a sufficiently distant view of the sphere that we can discern pathos in his illusion that he is accomplishing straight lines and right angles, drawing an accurate map or plotting a reliable course'.[44]

Let us now take a closer look at this shortfall in the big Other's quilting or 'structuring' function as it is given to us through the narrator's language. The novella opens with a tentative attempt at correlation: 'I associate, rightly or wrongly, my marriage with the death of my father, in time. That other links exist, on other levels, between these two affairs, is not impossible. I have enough trouble as it is in trying to say what I think I know'.[45] Many critics have observed the striking way Beckett's narrators seem constitutively unable to state a thing definitively, giving themselves over to qualifying and endlessly re-qualifying revisions. Steven Connor has suggested that this feature of the Beckettian narrator's language is symptomatic of a defense against what Connor, following Melanie Klein and Walter Bion, calls failed projective identifications: a child's early attempts to divide the world into good and bad objects, the latter of which he or she attempts to deposit ('project') in the mother.[46] If such projective identifications are unsuccessful (if the mother is unable or unwilling to serve as a 'container', as Bion phrases it), all the negative affects of terror, horror, envy, hatred associated with the bad object persist in the child, who deals with these feelings by viciously turning on the

---

42. Hugh Kenner, *Samuel Beckett: A Critical Study*, New Edition with a Supplementary Chapter, Berkeley, University of California Press, 1973, p. 74.

43. The 'curve' in the topography of language is the 'topological' effect introduced by the object *a*. For an extended discussion of this topology see Lacan's unpublished Seminar XIII, *The Object of Psychoanalysis* (1965-66). See also later in the Identification seminar.

44. Kenner, *Samuel Beckett*, p. 74.

45. Beckett, *First Love*, p. 7.

46. Steven Connor, 'Beckett and Bion', a paper delivered at the *Beckett and London* conference, Goldsmith's College, London, 1998. <http://www.bbk.ac.uk/english/skc/beckbion/> [accessed October 2, 2008].

attempted link itself in what Bion theorized as an 'attack on linking'. If the attempted link fails, then the link itself must be negated, and since language is one of the means by which a link can be initiated, language must be 'pulverized' and 'morcelized' until every last remaining connection with the persecutory object (now embodied as the mother) is destroyed. Yet, as Connor notes, every act of destroying a link negatively reaffirms that link, leading to the endless vicious spiral that characterizes one very conspicuous aspect of Beckettian speech.

Connor's suggestion is intriguing, all the more in how it enables him to arrive at the opposite conclusion to Keller, who employs the same Kleinian and Bionian object relations theory to explore Beckett's narrators' psychic dilemmas. Despite their differences in valuation—for Keller, the mother as the loved but absent object, for the Connor, the mother as the all too present, persecutory figure—both critics nevertheless share the same belief in the centrality of the maternal phantasm in the subject's first love. Accordingly, for both critics the distinctive quality of the narrator's language is reflective of the subject's relation to *her*. Yet one could just as easily, and more convincingly I think, regard this aspect of Beckett's style as symptomatic not of either a deficit or surplus on the maternal side but as a sign of a disturbance in the paternal function, namely, a loss of the anchoring point in language ordinarily supplied by the $S_1$. Not so much refusing or 'foreclosing' this mooring point as re-membering it in all the melancholy of its loss, Beckett's narrator appears unable to perform the crucial act of forgetting that permits us to mourn. This is the process Freud describes in 'Mourning and Melancholia' as a gradual narcissistic flight from the thought of one's own death that the other's demise inevitably conjures up.[47] Mourning, as it transpires in Freud's paper, is not so much a mature acceptance of the reality principle that enables us to take leave from a loved object through a painful process of 'hypercathection'. It is rather a *retreat into fantasy*, spun by what Freud calls 'the sum of the narcissistic satisfactions [the ego] derives from being alive' which enables the subject to deny for itself the 'fate' suffered by the loved dead one. Crucially, what I was calling 'epitaphic' or symbolic language plays an important role in this process, assisting the bereaved one with bringing up 'the

---

47. 'Mourning and Melancholia', *Standard Edition of the Complete Psychological Works of Sigmund Freud*, vol. 14 (1914-16), trans. James Strachey, London, Hogarth, 1968, pp. 243-58.

memories and expectations in which the libido is bound to the object', and enabling us to give the loved object the names that allow him or her to 'live on' in the symbolic universe, untouched by time and death ('he was a good husband', 'she was a loving wife', a 'darling child', etc.). Melancholy, on the other hand, entails a refusal of this flight into fantasy. Rather than detaching from the loved object, the melancholic internalizes it in what Freud hypothesizes is a 'regression' from object-love to narcissistic identification, which Freud also calls the 'earliest and original form of emotional tie'.[48] Identification, he writes, 'is a preliminary stage of object-choice, [...] the first way—and one that is expressed in an ambivalent fashion—in which the ego picks out an object'.[49]

We will have reason to come back to the question of identification shortly, but let me first note how Freud's description of melancholia also does not seem to entirely tally with the narrator's experience. In melancholia, the loved object is maintained in the full extent of its libidinal power even after it becomes internalized. This is evinced by the well-known denigration of the melancholic ego which, having become the psychic representative of the lost object, is bitterly reproached by the melancholic. Freud notes the ease with which love—always an ambivalent emotion—transforms in such cases into hate, even as the original libidinal cathexis is retained.[50] Beckett's narrator, on the other hand, seems bereft even of this internal support (small comfort as indeed this is). Following the father's death, the Beckettian narrator has been definitively shut out of the paternal 'home', whether housed inside or outside the ego. Death has definitively stripped the father's signifier of its sheltering powers, with the result that the narrator finds himself cast adrift in a linguistic world that still bears traces of its former meanings but which has inexplicably lost its center. Detached from their anchoring points

---

48. 'Group Psychology and the Analysis of the Ego (1921)', *Standard Edition of the Complete Psychological Works of Sigmund Freud*, vol. 18 (1920-22), trans. James Strachey, London, Hogarth, 1968, pp. 65-144, p. 107.

49. Freud, 'Mourning and Melancholia', p. 249.

50. Freud notes how 'The loss of a love-object is an excellent opportunity for the ambivalence in love-relationships to make itself effective and come into the open' and 'If the love for the object—a love which cannot be given up though the object itself is given up—takes refuge in narcissistic identification, then the hate comes into operation on this substitutive object, abusing it, debasing it, making it suffer and deriving sadistic satisfaction from its suffering'. Freud, 'Mourning and Melancholia', p. 251.

in the symbolic weave, words begin to exhibit a doubleness or semantic instability, leading not only to the previously discussed chipping-away of their content through the play of statement and counter-statement, but their very form, too, becomes subject to strange mutations. This second, again much-discussed, characteristic of Beckett's prose is found in what are known as the 'portmanteau' words that come to dot his heroes' recitations of events. Reminiscent of a literary version of Tourette's-syndrome, these unexpectedly uttered, apparently nonsensical combinations of words coalesce to form neologisms such as 'Catch-cony life!' or 'Omnidolent!' that we find spread liberally throughout Beckett's work, including *First Love*.[51]

Accordingly, the psychoanalytic concept that best describes the Beckettian hero's well-documented assaults or 'attacks' on language—the narrator's ferocious turning on every constative statement—is neither psychosis, nor the 'paranoid-schizophrenic position' (or 'borderline psychosis') suggested by a Kleinian-Bionian analysis, nor even melancholia, but depression, although this is not a state that has been elaborated in any fully developed way by Lacan, whose famous dismissal of it in *Television* highlights what he considers the specifically ethical nature of its failure.[52] Depression, for Lacan, 'isn't a state of the soul, it is simply a moral failing, as in Dante, or Spinoza: a sin, which means a moral weakness, which is, ultimately, located only in relation to thought, that is, in the duty to be Well-spoken, to find one's way in dealing with the unconscious, with the structure'.[53] Despite Lacan's condescension, his pinpointing of depression in terms of a specific relation to language has recently been taken up by some Lacanian thinkers, notably Paul Verhaeghe and Stijn Vanheule, who deliver a less contemptuous judgment on this disorder. For Paul Verhaeghe, for example, depression is conceived in terms of a moment of passage whose role, similar to mourning, is to facilitate a process of 'de-identification'. Here depression is held out as possessing not only a similar 'ontological possibility' as the psychoanalytic cure, but in many cases is the very sign of the analytic work itself that serves to detach the subject from its primary identifications—its fundamental fantasy—and hurl it into the void of 'subjective destitution'.[54]

51. Beckett, *First Love*, p. 27.
52. Jacques Lacan, *Television: A Challenge to the Psychoanalytic Establishment*, Joan Copjec (ed.), trans. Dennis Hollier, Rosalind Krauss and Annette Michelson, London, Norton, 1990.
53. Lacan, *Television*, p. 22.
54. Paul Verhaeghe, *On Being Normal and Other Disorders: A Manual for Clinical*

What is most striking for our purposes is the way, in an illuminating study of the structural position of neurotic depressive complaints within the Lacanian difficulty/movement matrix introduced in Seminar X, *Anxiety* (1962-63), Verhaeghe's colleague at Ghent University, Stijn Vanheule, portrays the depressive subject's relationship to language. In a recent essay, Vanheule contrasts phenomenological theories of depression by Ey, Minowski, and Sartre that stress various kinds of subjective 'deficits'—whether of energy (or, in Sartre's case, of moral duty)—with Lacan's insistence that depression concerns a deficit 'at the level of the signifier and/or of the Other'.[55] Calling the depressive state 'symbolically immobile' in relation to anxiety, Vanheule locates depressive problems on the left hand side of Lacan's 'Difficulty/Movement' matrix:

Difficulty →

| Inhibition | Impediment | Embarrassment |
|---|---|---|
| Emotion | Symptom | Passage-à-l'acte |
| Dismay | Acting-out | Anxiety |

↓ Movement

Figure 1. The difficulty/movement matrix

As he explains in his seminar on Anxiety, Lacan created this matrix to illustrate the way the three Freudian terms, Inhibition, Symptom and Anxiety from the essay of that title, are not on the same psychic 'level' with respect to the twin forces of difficulty and movement. The vertical Movement axis displays the degree of the drive's thrust, with the bottom row expressing the greatest amount of tension. The horizontal Difficulty axis expresses the relative difficulty with which the subject is able to symbolize what it is experiencing. Vanheule points out how the left- and right-hand sides of the grid track the distance between the subject and the Other, where the right-hand side indicates the over-proximity

---

*Psychodiagnostics*, trans. Sigi Jöttkandt, New York, Other Press, 2004. Verhaeghe notes how 'Depression can [...] be conceived as the reverse of identity acquisition, the loss of an identificatory anchoring point in the Other', Verhaeghe, p. 275. See also his comment on p. 278 about how both Lacan and Klein conceive of the end of the treatment in terms of depression.

55. Stijn Vanheule, 'Neurotic Depressive Trouble: Between the Signifier and the Real', *Journal for Lacanian Studies*, vol. 2, no. 1, 2004, pp. 34-53, p. 37.

of the Other while the left-hand side represents the Other's relative absence. Vanheule explains,

> The right side of the difficulty vector hereby indicates a situation where the Other is far too present (*'signifiant en trop'* [Lacan, 1962-63, 19 December 1962]). In that case, there is a lack of lack in the relation between subject and Other (*'défaut du manque'* [Lacan, 1962-63, 5 December 1962]), which implies that the insisting presence of the Other will be experienced as threatening. The left side of the vector on the other hand implies a situation of 'not enough' (*'signifiant en moins'* [Lacan, 1962-63, 19 December 1962]), where there is only a minimal structuring by the signifier and where the Other appears as distant and deteriorated.[56]

Vanheule then goes on to employ the matrix in a way that Lacan did not envision, that is, as a way of representing where the depressive subject is positioned in relation to the drive (object *a*) and to the Other (language). As mentioned, Vanheule locates 'depressive trouble' on the left hand side of the matrix, that is, as far away from the Other as possible. However, lest one imagine that depression thereby represents a subject's inward turn away from the Other—a 'moral failing'—we must keep in mind Vanheule's striking and original formulation that, in depressive trouble, it is the Symbolic Other, not the subject, *who is depressed*, and this has far-reaching implications for how a subject navigates language.[57] We hear how, in depression,

> The circulation of signifiers and the signifying capacity of the Other is suspended and language loses its metaphoric value in organizing subjective reality. [...]. A major consequence is that the Real of being remains profoundly unstructured. [...]. [The subject's] being is signified only poorly and suffering is largely felt at the bodily level. Indeed, the depressed subject is only loosely integrated into the Other: it stands quite apart from the Other's structure and, as a result, order more generally gets lost. Consequently, from a Lacanian perspective, the depressed subject is correct in its impression that it is an outcast of the Other and that it lives in a senseless world. After all, sense can only be acquired by means of the Other's signifying system. In the end, speech itself and more specifically the associated object a, voice, is affected (e.g. monotonous speech).[58]

---

56. Vanheule, 'Neurotic Depressive Trouble', p. 39.
57. Vanheule, 'Neurotic Depressive Trouble', p. 40.
58. Vanheule, 'Neurotic Depressive Trouble', p. 41.

Vanheule's summary could easily serve as a clinical description of the linguistic idiosyncracies of the narrator of *First Love*. For him, like for the depressive subject, the formerly structuring properties of language appear to have been lost or abandoned, leaving the Beckettian hero adrift in a sea of language whose words still carry the traces of structure and signification but which, having 'lost their metaphoric value' as Vanheule phrased it, now float like abandoned pieces of driftwood from a shipwreck. Wrested from their embedding in the big Other—the Symbolic life-support system that gives them their rosy back-lighting and imbues them with meaning—words continue to circulate but are no longer chained to any stable anchor or 'point de capiton'. The effect is precisely the loss of mooring Vanheule pinpoints, since it is through language that one is 'hooked', as it were, into the Symbolic weave. As Vanheule notes of the depressive patient,

> No longer structured by the Other, nor affected by the flux of movement, the subject risks being reduced to the nothingness and the numbness of an object a that is cut off from any dialectical relation. In that case, the subject occupies the radical position of shit, the position of the outcast (*déchet*).[59]

This second feature of the depressive subject position then recalls nothing so much as the other marked characteristic of the Beckettian narrator's speech: sudden explosions of the linguistic *jouissance* that has been building up over the course of the linguistic drift. Such *jouissance* is normally channeled through the banks and canals cut by the paternal signifier but here our narrator seems continually in danger of being drawn under the symbolic surface by treacherous whirlpools and rip currents of *jouissance* that belch out of him in peculiar, half-sense/half-nonsensical sounds.

However, something occurs that disrupts this state of affairs. The woman, Lulu, joins him on his bench by the canal. Together they spend a number of wordless evenings, punctuated only by Lulu's singing. One night an apparently involuntary sexual encounter on the narrator's part ensues, after which the narrator decides he can no longer bear her presence. He abandons the bench, although less on account of her, he says, than because it is now failing to meet his particular needs. Installing himself next in a cowshed, he discovers to his horror that he cannot stop thinking of Lulu, whose name he finds himself inexplicably

---

59. Vanheule, 'Neurotic Depressive Trouble', p. 42.

inscribing in the cowpats of his field among the nettles. He calls this feeling 'love':

> Yes, I loved her, it's the name I give, alas, to what I was doing then. I had nothing to go by, having never loved before, but of course had heard of the thing, at home, in school, in brothel and in church, and read romances, in prose and verse, under the guidance of my tutor, in six or seven languages, both dead and living, in which it was handled at length. I was therefore in a position, in spite of all, to put a label on what I was about when I found myself inscribing the letters of Lulu in an old heifer pat or flat on my face in the mud trying to tear up the nettles by the roots.[60]

Next comes a short digression on the nature of his 'love' where the narrator deliberates whether what he is feeling is 'Love-passion? Somehow I think not'. 'Perhaps I loved her with Platonic love? But somehow I think not. Would I have been tracing her name in old cowshit if my love had been pure and disinterested? And with my devil's finger into the bargain, which I then sucked'.[61] Eventually, having exhausted his 'philosophical' resources, the narrator concedes that his thoughts 'were all of Lulu' when suddenly, without warning, he changes her name:

> Anyhow, I'm sick and tired of this name Lulu, I'll give her another, more like her, Anna for example, it's not more like her but no matter. I thought of Anna, then, I who had learnt to think of nothing, nothing except my pains.[62]

To my mind, this is a genuinely remarkable moment in the novella, although it is glossed over by the narrator in his usual deadpan fashion. What makes it remarkable is the radical change it indexes in the narrator's linguistic abilities. In renaming Lulu 'Anna', the narrator is not canceling out an earlier constative statement with its opposite, in the manner of his other symbolic waverings. But nor does this impress us as one of his neologisms, formed through collapsing together unrelated words. To the contrary, the name 'Anna' appears to have been generated through a wholly different process, and whatever this process is, it evidently occurred in the course of the narrator's obsessive writing of Lulu's name in the cow pats. What in this lover's graffiti could create such a change in the narrator's linguistic abilities?

---

60. Beckett, *First Love*, pp. 31-2.
61. Beckett, *First Love*, pp. 32-33.
62. Beckett, *First Love*, p. 33.

I find the best way of understanding what has just occurred is through reference to what Lacan calls the 'unary trait'. This is a term he obtains from Freud's discussion of identification in *Group Psychology and the Analysis of the Ego*. We saw already how for Freud, identification is considered the earliest emotional tie, occurring prior to any object-choice. It takes place as part of what Freud calls primary narcissism. Identification, Freud explains, occurs when a child takes

> a special interest in his father; he would like to grow like him and be like him, and take his place everywhere. We may say simply that he takes his father as his ideal. This behaviour has nothing to do with a passive or feminine attitude towards his father (and towards males in general); it is on the contrary typically masculine. It fits in very well with the Oedipus complex, for which it helps to prepare the way.[63]

Freud goes on to attach identification to the adoption or 'incorporation' of a single trait (*Einziger Zug*) from the other. This trait, which it transpires is typically nothing more than a certain look, a cough etc., lodges in the child's psyche as a foreign object, and operates there as the first point or 'seed' around which the narcissistic ego subsequently grows.

Although it originates in Freud's theories of identification and narcissism, the concept of the unary trait comes to acquire a far greater reach in Lacan. His most extended discussion of the unary trait occurs in Seminar IX, *Identification* where the trait is christened as nothing less momentous than the 'support as such of difference'.[64] Lacan's concern in this seminar is with the relationship of the subject to the signifier, a relation that is instrumental in the subject's emergence as a signifying subject. A minimal definition of a signifying subject is a subject that is capable of identifying with a signifier—for example, one's own name—which thus becomes empowered to represent that subject for another signifier, in Lacan's famous phrasing.

Much of the early part of the Identification seminar is taken up with exploring and developing the theoretical basis of the 'sameness' that this 'identity' of the subject with the signifier entails.

---

63. Freud never quite settles in this essay the question of the priority of identification and the creation of the love object but he is very clear that it occurs during what he calls the 'early history' of the Oedipal complex.

64. *The Seminar of Jacques Lacan, Book IX, Identification (1961-61)*, unpublished seminar (lesson of 13 December, 1961).

Lacan first quickly dispenses with the kind of identity proposed by imaginary similarities: the likeness discovered between the simple shapes, looks or sounds of things. The example Lacan employs in his lesson of 29.11.61 of the notches on a hunter's bone makes this very clear. It is not because the small cuts share an identical shape or size (they clearly don't) that they can be taken in the most profound sense as being 'the same'. What enables these little marks to be understood as signifying the same thing (a kill)—or, in Lacan's other example from this lesson, for his careful but unskilled copies of seven Chinese characters from a calligraph to be identifiable as 'the same seven characters' despite the fact that they by no means resemble the originals—is something he calls 'the essence of the signifier'. The essence of the signifier is difference as such, difference 'in the pure state' as he calls it.

In order to better understand what Lacan means by this, we can turn to an unexpected correlation Lorenzo Chiesa has discovered between Lacan's elaborated conception of the Freudian *Einziger Zug* and Badiou's count-as-One.[65] In this stunning reading, Chiesa forges a striking parallel between the trait and signifier in Lacan, and the count-as-One and its redoubling in what Badiou calls the 'second count' or 'count of the count' that serves to 'seal' the first count as the basis—the One—for a system of representation (literally, re-representation, the presentation of presentation). It is worth spending a little time with this parallel between the two thinkers because it helps to map out the problem facing the Beckettian subject in a surprisingly efficient way.

In a lucid explication of a particularly difficult section in Lacan's seminar, Chiesa notes how the unary trait and the signifier can be distinguished from one another by the fact that the trait merely *marks* difference, while the signifier is 'the one as difference'.[66] Much in the way representation, in Badiou's sense, is founded on and 'seals' the presentation that constitutes the first 'count', the signifier 'as difference' is 'supported' by the trait; the trait is what effectively founds one's 'identification' with the signifier. Prior to being able to say that one's name or even simply the shifter 'I' represents me, a 'One' or basic unity of a subject has to form, and this 'One' is produced by an operation. What is this operation?

---

65. Lorenzo Chiesa, 'Count-as-One, Forming-into-One, Unary Trait, S1', in *The Praxis of Alain Badiou*, Paul Ashton, A. J. Bartlett and Justin Clemens (eds.), Melbourne, re.press, 2006, pp. 147-76.

66. Chiesa, 'Count-as-One, Forming-into-One, Unary Trait, S1', p. 156.

For Lacan, as for Badiou, it is a matter of a mathematical operation of counting. The ability to count reaches into the heart of identification because it is the original and simplest form of evidence that a subject has successfully understood and become able to use a system of symbolic representation. Without this ability to count, the symbolic universe of language, and by extension the ability to give names (to allow a word to stand in for an object with which it has no relation other than a purely formal one) must remain off-limits to the subject. One remains stuck in the imaginary register, unable to see beyond the small, empirical or individual similarities and differences to the difference 'in the pure state' that enables one to add up 'oranges with apples, pears with carrots', as Lacan explains in the lesson of 6.12.61, that is, to form sets of disparate objects and yet regard them all as (signifying) the 'same'.

Chiesa illustrates the difference between these imaginary and symbolic 'counts' in the following way, using the notation / to signify the mark or trait in order to distinguish it from the 1 'identified with' the signifier:

> In order to stress how / + / + / is not the same as 1 + 1 + 1, Lacan goes as far as suggesting that a child may well be able to count up to two and three *without* being able to operate with numbers: two and three are in this case nothing but a repetition of the / produced by the unary trait, and should be distinguished from the number 2 and 3 understood as 1 + 1 and 1 + 1 + 1. This 'early' counting is ineffective when dealing with numbers higher than 3.[67]

Chiesa then clarifies the crucial difference between these two 'counts' by saying, 'What is at stake in the gap that separates these two counts is nothing less than the birth of the subject's identification as modern Cartesian subject split between consciousness and the unconscious'.[68]

The critical question is how the child accomplishes this remarkable act of identification? What allows her to move from / + / + / to the 1 + 1 + 1 that enables her to count beyond 3, that is, beyond the 'immanent' situation of the imaginary count, as Chiesa puts it? From what resource does she generate the concept of number that permits her entry into the symbolic realm of modern science, 'split between consciousness and the unconscious'? Lacan's

---

67. Chiesa, 'Count-as-One, Forming-into-One, Unary Trait, S1', p. 155.
68. Chiesa, 'Count-as-One, Forming-into-One, Unary Trait, S1', p. 155.

answer, peculiarly enough, will be *writing*. Writing is the cause or source of the origin of number.

A much earlier moment in Lacan's thinking offers a useful vantage point for explaining this, namely, the chapter on Poe's 'The Purloined Letter', in Seminar II, *The Ego in Freud's Theory and the Technique of Psychoanalysis (1954-55)*.[69] There Lacan refers to a game of coin toss to explain the idea of what he calls 'memory' as opposed to remembering.[70] This memory, which he terms 'internal to the symbol', is manifested when, in a series of random coin tosses, a pattern emerges that sees certain combinations of pairs prevented from forming.[71] In any one toss, the odds of a coin landing on either heads (+) or tails (-) are always 50-50. But once you begin to *group* a series of random coin tosses into pairs, something rather strange begins to happen. While possible sets of pairs continue to appear in completely random order, if one arranges these sets into overlapping pairs, it quickly becomes evident that certain future pair possibilities have been precluded by the last member of the pair that has immediately preceded them. If, for example, all possible pair types are two heads (++), two tails (--), one head/one tail (+-) and one tail/one head (-+), a coin toss that produces a pair of two heads (++) precludes there from ever occurring a subsequent overlapping pair made up of two tails (--), since the first member of that overlapping pair has already been established as a head (+). The only possible remaining toss for such an overlapping pair following two heads, must be either two heads again (++), or one head, one tail (+-).

If we return now to the lesson of 6 December in the Identification seminar, there is a remarkable moment when Lacan, part-way through his explanation of the unary trait, describes being overcome by 'emotion' by the sight of a fragment of a Cervide deer in the museum of Saint-Germain. He describes how, 'bending over one of these glass cases I saw on a thin ribbone [...] a series of little strokes: first two, then a little interval and afterwards five, and then it recommences. "There" I said to myself addressing my self by my secret or my public name, "this is why in short Jacques Lacan your daughter is not mute, this is why your

---

69. Jacques Lacan, *The Seminar of Jacques Lacan, Book II: The Ego in Freud's Theory and in the Technique of Psychoanalysis (1954-1955)*, Jacques-Alain Miller (ed.), trans. Sylvana Tomaselli, notes John Forrester, New York, Norton, 1991.

70. Lacan, *Seminar II*, p. 185.

71. Lacan, *Seminar II*, p. 193

daughter is your daughter, because if we were mute she would not be your daughter'".[72] Lacan's emotional response comes, I conjecture, from the evidence given in both of these examples how, from a simple, repetitively inscribed pattern, a self-organizing principle can nevertheless emerge that contains certain intrinsic laws. In both the coin toss and the marked bone, a simple repetition combined with what Manuel de Landa would call a certain 'selection pressure' (that is, the grouping that emerges as a function of being notated or *written*) succeeds in bringing to light an internal ordering mechanism that becomes instrumental in determining what can happen in later iterations of the pattern.[73] Note that the grouping or writing down in itself does not change anything about the odds themselves which continue, as we saw, to fall out in an entirely random sequence. The writing thus cannot be considered an externally imposed structuring device. It merely brings an *immanent* law into visibility. In Seminar II, Lacan called this internal ordering mechanism a 'symbolic memory' but it should be clear how what he is talking about is very different from the symbolic memory activated in epitaphic language, that is, a form of writing that enables a subject to defeat death and live on (in language and in the minds of those surviving one). The memory Lacan has in mind is unqualifiedly distinct from remembering, insofar as the former can never be the act of any 'subject' but entails rather a 'memory' recorded by notation or inscription itself. Writing, or at least writing in its most minimal and reduced form, as the trait or mark—the 'letter', as Lacan will also go on to call it—activates this other 'memory' and brings a concealed pattern literally into sight.

The conclusion is that an act of writing appears susceptible of having an effect on the Real in some way, drawing out from it an inherent or what we might a little unorthodoxly call a *pre-castrative Law* (or perhaps *laws*) that possess many of the characteristics of what we ordinarily call the Symbolic or the big Other. Writing compels this 'immanent' law to enter visibility. Without its activation in the repeated inscription of the hunter's notches, or the marking of the coin toss—or indeed the writing and re-writing of

---

72. Lacan, *Seminar IX* (lesson of 6.12.61).

73. 'The coupling of "variable replicators" with a selection pressure results in a kind of "searching device" (or "probe head") that explores a space of possible forms'. Manuel de Landa, *A Thousand Years of Nonlinear History*, New York, Swerve, 2000, p. 139.

the word 'Lulu' in the cowpats—this 'law' would never have become visible. Nor, perhaps, would it even actually 'exist', in the sense of being part of a situation in Badiou's terms. It is surely this Lacan has in mind when he states at the close of the following lesson in Seminar IX that repetition's goal is not, as we usually imagine, to return to an originary unity (as has been thematized ad infinitum in the traditional psychoanalytic narrative of 'first love' as mother love). The aim of repetition, rather, is to make 'the *original unary re-emerge from one of its circuits*'.[74]

The following, then, is the most convincing explanation I can find of the sudden change in the narrator of *First Love*'s linguistic abilities—and, to return to one of the questions posed at the beginning, how the Badiouian subject, ineluctably *in* the linguistic 'situation', is nevertheless capable of an act of naming (that is, of an ontological or transhistorical act). It may even offer the beginnings of an answer to the old chestnut of whether Beckett's writing itself, rather than his analysis with Bion, may have produced some sort of 'therapeutic' effect in the early days of his career, plagued by boils and unshakable colds, and suffering from acute panic attacks and feelings of suffocation as he was, following his father's death in 1933.[75] Repetitively inscribing Lulu's name—a sequence of grouped traits (lu lu lu lu, or even /u /u /u /u)—in the cowpats, the narrator has unwittingly created the formal or better *technical* conditions under which a signifying Law, can (re-)emerge. And with the recovery of this 'difference in the pure state' that can act as a basis for a count-as-One, the big Other emerges renovated and resuscitated—no longer 'depressed'—capable of quilting the Symbolic fabric once more. For the narrator at least, the implications of this return are profound: the return of the One endows him with the linguistic ability to name. Re-identified with the signifier, which is also to say split firmly again between conscious and unconscious, the narrator for the first time in the tale is able to form linguistic relations that are, in a sense, purely symbolic, based on a purely *abstract* conception of likeness:

---

74. Lacan, *Seminar IX* (lesson of 13.12.61) (emphasis added).

75. A number of psychoanalytic critics have weighed in on this question, beginning with the Lacanian analyst Didier Anzieu in 1983 when he suggested Beckett's formal style replicated something of the patterns and rhythms of the analytic sessions Beckett had engaged in with Wilfred Bion for a couple of years. Didier Anzieu 'Un Soi disjoint, une voix liante: l'écriture narrative de Samuel Beckett', *Nouvelle revue de psychanalyse*, no. 28, 1983, p. 80 (cited in Conner, 'Beckett and Bion').

> Anyhow, I'm sick and tired of this name Lulu, I'll give her another, more like her, Anna for example, it's not more like her but no matter.[76]

Deceptively minor in itself and largely passed over in the critical literature in favor of the other chief narrative event of the tale (the birth of Lulu/Anna's child), this act of (re)naming implies the regained ability to see beyond merely empirical or imaginary differences, and to begin to operate and play with difference 'in the pure state'. Needless to say, the effect on the narrator is profound. No longer sliding directionless through the signifying chain, Beckett's narrator is for the first time in the tale able to make a statement not plagued by doubt and dissension: he begins to count. 'I thought of Anna, then, long long sessions, twenty minutes, twenty-five minutes and even as long as half an hour daily. I obtain these figures by the addition of other, lesser figures. That must have been my way of loving'.[77] The reappearance of the One returns him a place, a 'home' in language that anchors his speech, curing the Other's 'depression'.

Am I suggesting, then, that in order to become a signifying subject, a One identified with one's name, a child first has to learn to write? That would of course be absurd. What I am suggesting is that writing, at least *writing of a certain kind*, reactivates or perhaps better recreates an operation that occurs in the act of primary identification. Beckett's and his narrator's own style gives us a clue to what this kind of writing might be, and it recalls own Lacan's reference in Seminar IX to the school pupil kept in after class and forced to 'write out a hundred lines of 1's' for the teacher.[78] And perhaps there is more to this punishment than meets the eye (we will want to come back to this question of first love's 'pedagogy' in the final chapter). For now, however, it is enough to say that a certain unconscious repetition of a trait picked up from the Other can 'engrave' itself onto the subject's psyche in a way that, like in the game of coin toss, a hidden law can be brought to light. Previously I described this a 'pre-castrative' law to emphasize the way it emerges seemingly spontaneously from the act of repetition, although one must remember that the trait itself originally derives from the Other. As we will see in later chapters, a complex relation inheres between the signifier and the subject which cannot be interpreted in terms of a simple inside/outside dichotomy,

---

76. Beckett, *First Love*, p. 33.
77. Beckett, *First Love*, p. 34.
78. Lacan, *Seminar IX* (lesson of 29.11.61).

where the subject is either entirely 'determined' by the castrating cut, or volunteers the original source for the representing law. The chapter on Eudora Welty's 'First Love' will go on to detail the way the castrating cut of the signifier is effective only insofar as it is 'historicized' by a subject. What Beckett lets us glimpse in the meantime are what one might think of as the *preconditions* of this 'historicization': the way a trait may be taken up and incorporated into the psyche such that it maps out the furrows where the phallic signifier can later take hold, enabling the subject to recognize the cut of castration as addressed uniquely to it. One could thus think of primary identification as a sort of primitive and earliest encoding of the possibility of a subject, a repetitive drumming or binary on-off switch—or indeed Fort-da game—that elicits our strange and, for Lacan, always wondrous ability to speak. Without primary identification, Lacan's daughter 'would not have been his daughter', not because she would not have borne his name, but because quite simply he would have had no word for 'daughter' (or for any other thing, for that matter).

At the end of the tale, Beckett's narrator leaves Lulu/Anna's house, driven out by the baby's cries. But differently from his previous expulsion, love's regeneration of the One appears to have had an additional effect, allowing the subject to unburden itself to some extent from the signifier and its inexorable law. Describing his final exit from the house, this time with the new-born baby inside, the narrator relates how 'I began playing with the cries, a little in the same way as I had played with the song, on, back, on, back, if that may be called playing'.[79] 'Playing' in this way with the voice in its most elementary state, the narrator searches in the sky: 'I looked among the stars and constellations for the Wains, but could not find them. And yet they must have been there. My father was the first to show them to me. He had shown me others, but alone, without him beside me, I could never find any but the Wains'.[80] I find it almost impossible to believe Lacan did not have Beckett's recently published *First Love* at least partly in mind when he makes his proviso in his celebrated session, 'Lesson on Lituraterre' in Seminar XVIII (1971) that 'the subject takes support from a constellated sky, and not merely from the unary trait, for its fundamental identification'.[81] The trait is two-faced. As the

---

79. Beckett, *First Love*, p. 62.
80. Beckett, *First Love*, p. 62.
81. 'C'est par là qu'il s'appuie sur un ciel constellé et non seulement sur le trait

signifier, it plunges the first yardstick into the real, enabling us to accede to Beckett's famous 'Cartesian' measure, the 'symbolic' or universe of science at whose seemingly miraculous appearance *ex nihilo* Lacan never ceases to marvel. As letter, the trait rounds out the symbolic's rigid lines from the inside with an imperceptible 'curve', for which no increase in symbolic precision will ever be sufficient to account. This curve in the signifier that Lacan calls the letter will prove the creative source of our capacity, even compulsion, to trace out myriad shapes, faces and figures in the luminary points of distant light that make up our universe. My argument in this book is that it will be literature, the sole discourse that 'would not be a semblance', that is uniquely capable of giving this creative power of the letter its proper name.

\*\*\*

By way of a conclusion, we can return to some of the questions that opened this chapter. Extrapolating a bit, we seem to have found in Beckett a way of thinking an event's *precondition*, that is, an indirect but nevertheless still somehow 'causal' relation that inheres between a situation and its absolute rupture that is required by Badiou's concept of event. When Beckett's narrator renames Lulu as Anna, he draws on something that is apparently immanent to the situation yet which nevertheless has the capacity to re-generate the founding Law upon which that situation is based. Something interior to the count thus provides the narrator with a foothold for an act that, in Johnston's formulation, has 'transhistorical' implications. Note that this is different from saying that the event is always fashioned out of elements of the situation, that it is always specific to a situation insofar as it is a situation that supplies an 'evental site' (the site being accordingly that (non)part of the situation which is on the edge of the void[82]). It is also different from the '*subjectivité de l'attente*' that Gibson, among others, has identified, as Badiou's acknowledgment that, in some rare cases, something within the situation may, if not 'cause' or 'conjure' the event, but at least prefigure it, anticipate it.[83] For Badiou, this attentive wait-

---

unaire, pour son identification fondamentale'. Jacques Lacan, Le *Séminaire de Jacques Lacan, Livre XVIII, D'un discours qui ne serait pas du semblant (1971)*, texte établi par Jacques-Alain Miller, Paris, Seuil, 2006, p. 125.

82. In *Being and Event*, Badiou explains how the evental site it is presented 'but "beneath" it nothing from which it is composed is presented', p. 175.

83. In *Handbook of Inaesthetics*, Badiou writes, 'we can say that every event admits

ing is typically thought through the figure of 'the poet'. However it also, famously, in Meditation 9 of *Being and Event*, is inhabited by the political subject who Badiou describes as a 'patient watchman of the void instructed by the event'.[84]

What I am proposing with Beckett, however, is not so much the quiet patient work of a militant-poetic subject, whose sentry duty 'clears the ground', as Gibson puts it, for an event that may or may not occur.[85] (Badiou's favorite instance of this kind of anticipatory work is Mallarmé). As we have seen in *First Love*, it is a question of something far more urgent: a compulsion or *drive to write*, whose origins apparently lie in 'first love', supplies the technical conditions under which the sole event in the tale occurs. The name 'Anna' is our evidence that an event occurred, that the absent paternal signifier was successfully regenerated—and to ensure we didn't miss this, Beckett even underlines what has happened by choosing a palindrome for the new name. In the word 'Anna', Beckett gives a formal reflection of the fact that the narrator has recovered a solid anchoring point in language, a tether in the shape of a linguistic 'buckle' that prevents him from floating back out into the depressive soup.

To help clarify this, as well as to pinpoint the difference between my reading of Beckett and Badiou's, we can compare the narrator's renaming of Lulu with the example the philosopher returns to several times in *On Beckett* as an instance of a nomination of an event. Towards the end of his remarkably illuminating account of the fundamental *dispositif* or 'set-up' of Beckett's work, 'The Writing of the Generic', Badiou identifies a change in Beckett's 'enterprise'. After 1960, Badiou sees Beckett's fundamental set of problems changing, with the emphasis no longer on 'description and narrative' but on 'the *figural poem* of the subject's postures'.[86] This change is announced as a new opening to alterity, the 'supplementation of being' provided by the Other that Badiou links to a new musicality in Beckett's prose. Badiou goes so far as to assert that the writer's prose comes 'to be governed by a latent poem' that regulates and unifies in a subterranean fashion the 'discontinuous interweavings' of the subject.[87]

---

of a figural presentation, that it always possesses a pre-evental *figure*', p. 120.
84. Badiou, *Being and Event*, p. 111.
85. Gibson, *Beckett and Badiou*, p. 112.
86. Badiou, *On Beckett*, p. 16 (Badiou's emphasis).
87. Badiou, *On Beckett*, p. 17.

For Badiou, Beckett's new concern with the Other is, significantly enough, reflected in a change in focus from his initial hermeneutics (which Badiou defines as 'an attempt to pin the event to a network of meanings'[88]) to the question of nomination, of naming. *Ill Seen Ill Said* is the work in which this change is primarily indexed for Badiou. He writes,

> The poetics of naming is central to *Ill Seen Ill Said*, starting with the very title of the text. [...]. 'Ill seen' means that what happens is necessarily outside the laws of visibility of the place of being. [...]. And what does 'ill said' mean? The well-said is precisely the order of established meanings. But if we do manage to produce the name of what happens inasmuch as it happens—the name of the ill seen—then this name cannot remain prisoner of the meanings that are attached to the monotony of the place. [...]. 'Ill seen ill said' designates the possible agreement between that which is subtracted from the visible (the 'ill seen'), and that which is subtracted from meaning (the 'ill said'). We are therefore dealing with the agreement between an event, on the one hand, and the poetics of its name, on the other.[89]

Up to this point I have absolutely no disagreement with Badiou, but what I find surprising is the passage he chooses from the Beckett text to illustrate his point. Badiou refers to a section from *Ill Seen Ill Said* that confronts the fundamental problem we have been considering—how it is possible from within a given (linguistic) situation to name an event such that this name can serve as the foundation, the Law of the count for a radically *newly structured* situation? Or in more Beckettian terms, how can Being acquire a 'measure' (in both senses) of existence without thereby inevitably falling into the old dialectic of the suffering cogito? Here is the Beckett passage in question:

> During the inspection a sudden sound. Startling without consequence for the gaze the mind awake. How explain it? And without going so far how say it? Far behind the quest begins. What time the event recedes. When suddenly to the rescue it comes again. Forthwith the uncommon noun collapsion. Reinforced a little later if not enfeebled by the infrequent slumbrous. A slumbrous collapsion. Two. Then far from the still agonizing eye a gleam of hope. By the grace of these modest beginnings.[90]

---

88. Badiou, *On Beckett*, p. 21.
89. Badiou, *On Beckett*, p. 21.
90. Badiou, *On Beckett*, p. 21.

In Badiou's reading, we are confronted in this passage with a classic case of poetic language—a text speaking about the impossibility of speaking about itself. Yet, despite this impossibility, the text nevertheless manages to accomplish this speaking in the form of a 'poetic' invention: the phrase 'slumbrous collapse' in which Badiou discovers an 'ill saying adequate to the ill seen of the noise'.[91] Badiou explains, 'the name of the noise-event is a poetic invention. This is what Beckett signals by the paradoxical alliance of "collapse" and "slumbrous", one "uncommon" and the other "infrequent". This naming emerges from the void of language, like an ill saying adequate to the ill seen of the noise'.[92] 'What is thus opened up', he goes on, 'is the domain of truth. In its separable origin, this is the domain of alterity. The naming guards a trace of an Other-than-being, which is also an Other-than-itself'.[93]

Let me state my suspicion baldly. I believe that here Badiou is making a formal claim that is in fact based on the text's *content*, which admittedly very beautifully and succinctly 'well says' just what he is wanting to say himself philosophically. I simply do not find in the construction 'slumbrous collapse' evidence of the kind of 'renovation' of the signifier I proposed must have been present in the 'event' that enabled Lulu to be renamed as Anna. Despite Badiou's claims for it, 'slumbrous collapse' does not testify 'poetically' to what Badiou is wanting it to say *because it is not 'ill said' enough;* it is not senseless in quite the same way that a proper name such as Anna is. As I have indicated, for me 'Anna' is evidence in language of the presence of a Law that is capable of structuring a *new* situation. Badiou's example of the portmanteau word does not permit this because it is not 'identified', in Lacan's specific sense of being arbitrarily glued or *sutured*, with the signifier, that is, with difference 'in the pure state'.

Not a name in the sense Lacan intends with his concept of identification—that is, a 'proper name'[94]—the portmanteau word in fact retains all the problems associated with what I, following

---

91. Badiou, *On Beckett*, p. 22.
92. Badiou, *On Beckett*, p. 22.
93. Badiou, *On Beckett*, p. 22.
94. See especially lessons 20.12.61 and 10.1.62 of the Identification seminar. See also Chiesa's comment how 'the proper name is closer to the letter than to the symbolic proper: it approaches the unary trait by redoubling its operation, the idiotic in-difference of its count, and in this way guarantees the consistency of the structure of language, the differentially phonematic chain of signifiers'. Chiesa, 'Count-as-One, Forming-into-One, Unary Trait, S1', pp. 161-2.

Vanheule, was calling 'depressive trouble'. As an extrusion of Real *jouissance*, the phrase has not been subjected to what Badiou has called the 'second count', namely, the representational forming-into-One that, submitting the count's presentation to a law, enables a name to found a (new) situation. To my mind, the portmanteau word embodies at best only a given situation's 'symptomal torsion', to employ Badiou's vocabulary, a point of excess in the situation that indicates that not everything in a situation has been 'counted'. Whereas in the proper name Anna, being appears to itself as void ('pure' difference), in the phrase 'slumbrous collapsion' I detect only the condensation we found previously making up one of the characteristics of the narrator's 'depressive' language, the defensive strategies of epitaphic language when it is confronted with the 'startling' discovery that it is itself the death of which it tries to speak (and hence deny). It is as if Badiou retreats here from his own (Lacanian) insight as stated unambiguously in the title of Meditation 4, that the Void is the 'proper name of being'.[95] The proper name, on which Lacan dwells at some length in his Identification seminar, is constitutionally different from all other symbolic names, he says, for the reason that it is uniquely defined by a relationship with 'something that is of the order of the letter'.[96]

Despite himself, then, I suspect Badiou has allowed himself to be too seduced by Beckett's content, that is, too seduced by precisely the 'description and narrative' he regards Beckett as successfully leaving behind after 1960, and this puts the philosopher at the risk of neglecting the evidence supplied by the text's formal qualities. But if this properly 'aesthetic' field of enquiry—literary *form*—were permitted into his philosophy (something which he precludes, as we saw, through his concept of inaesthetics) it might encourage greater alertness to occasions of precisely the type of change that he is profoundly interested in thinking through, namely, forms of change that are, in Johnston's phrasing, 'immanently generated from within the internal parameters of a specific situation and/or a given world'.[97]

In order to wrap things up quickly now, am I claiming we should take the name 'Anna' as an instance of the 'uncounted One' whose traces I will be dedicated in the following pages to uncovering? By no means. As I stated above, 'Anna' is merely—albeit

---

95. Badiou, *Being and Event*, p. 52.
96. Lacan, *Seminar IX* (lesson of 20.12.61).
97. Johnston, 'The Quick and the Dead', p. 2.

also, as I hope to have shown, remarkably—the textual attestation of the (in Beckett's case, renewed) presence of the Law of the signifier. As such, it is the mathematical result of, precisely, a 'count-as-One', that is, a *structured* or 'consistent' presentation of the inconsistent multiplicity. Consequently, if the uncounted, 'literary' One in fact exists, we will need to seek it elsewhere, although Beckett has already pointed us in the right direction: in the murky and as yet unfathomed regions of a certain imaginary space and time, a certain 'transcendental aesthetic' that is the haunt of the unary trait in its guise as 'letter'. Badiou repeatedly emphasizes the utter rareness of the event, its entirely aleatory appearance. Beckett, however, reminds us how the simple power to name—and thus to become the subject of the event's unique 'truth'—is arguably just as 'rare'. I mean this not in the quantitative sense—most of us do, after all, become 'signifying subjects', identified with our names and capable of counting beyond three—but in its connotation of something extraordinary, exceptional, singular. In *First Love*, Beckett demonstrates how our 'residence' in the symbolic is both unpredictable and precarious. The continuing presence of the master signifier in our psychic structures cannot be automatically assumed, while our comportment toward it, our 'identification' with it, can undergo any number of disturbances. I ventured 'first love' here as the name of a rare nominal power whose source lies in primary identification. In the following chapter, we will see how the initial furrows marked out on the subject's psyche by the unary trait are filled in with a *jouissance* that can provide traction to the later, consolidating cut of castration.

## 2. FORFEITS AND COMPARISONS: IVAN TURGENEV

Love has so honeycombed ethical discourse today it is as if we had been taken hostage by an Other whose escalating demands on our affection now carry the full force and weight of the original superegoic injunction from which Freud so famously recoiled.[1] Yet the proper answer to this loving impasse is not, as Slavoj Žižek has suggested, to respond with a fully 'ethical' violence that shatters the loving circle but, rather, *more* love.[2] Or to put it more accurately, as the recent spate of divorces attributed to the website Friends Reunited attests, the proper response to love's spiraling demands is to return to one's first love. Why our first love? Because by returning us to the originary, primary imbalance, the primordial experience of being seized by an other, the One is fractured in Two and from there, as Badiou has suggested, the (truly ethical) vistas of infinity open out: 'One, Two, infinity: such is the numericity of the amorous procedure'.[3] I will return to Badiou's loving count in a later chapter but we can already note, in anticipation of my discussion of Kierkegaard, how, as a result of this imbalance, one's first love must remain *qualitatively different* from the merely quantitative succession of all subsequent loves. This is witnessed by first love's remarkably labile ability to shift places within this numerical series as A, Kierkegaard's narrator in the chapter 'The First Love' from *Either/Or*, shortly discovers: 'I had not seen [my first love] for a long time, and I found her now, engaged, happy, and

---
1. See, for example, Rei Terada's brilliant instance of this trend, *Feeling in Theory: Emotion after the 'Death of the Subject'*, Cambridge, Harvard University Press, 2001.
2. Slavoj Žižek, 'A Plea for Ethical Violence', *Umbr(a)*, no. 1: War, 2004, pp. 75-89.
3. Badiou, Alain, 'What is Love?', trans. Justin Clemens, *Umbr(a)*, no. 1: Badiou, 1996, pp. 37-53, p. 45.

glad, and it was a pleasure for me to see her. She assured me that she had never loved me, but that her betrothed was her first love, and [...] that only the first love is the true love'.[4]

For this reason, too, one's first love can never become a partnership, with the reciprocity that this implies. Instead, our first love haunts us as the failure of what Lacan, in Seminar VIII, *Transference* (1960-61), calls love's 'signification'. In first love, there is no mysterious flower-turned-hand stretching back as one gropes toward it in the dark, as Lacan famously described the loving relationship in this seminar.[5] There is no transmogrifying loving 'miracle' that converts the loved object, *eromenos*, into the desiring subject, *erastes* willing, like Achilles with Patroclos, to take the place of the lover and assume his Symbolic 'debt'. What an entire literary tradition has dedicated itself to showing in not inconsiderable detail is the way first love offers nothing but the sublimity of a deep and lasting torment from which we never fully recover—even if, for some unknown reason, our 'first love' miraculously loves us back.[6] First love thus remains a deeply asymmetrical relation. It permanently defeats the closure of the ethical 'metaphor of love' that Lacan introduces in this seminar, which subjectifies the object and, in the work of love that is analysis, transforms the particularity of individual misery into the universality of common unhappiness. Even so, this initiation into heartache that is first love plays a fundamentally important role as we will see. For first love is ultimately what prevents love's 'metaphor' from fully crossing over into becoming a perverse circle with its accompanying escalating super-egoic demands.

A case in point right now is psychoanalysis itself. Psychoanalysis is increasingly beset on all sides by demands that it justify itself in relation to a host of competing discourses. 'The psychoanalytic

---

4. Søren Kierkegaard, *Either/Or*, vol. 1, trans. David F. Swenson and Lillian Marvin Swenson, rev. and foreword Howard A. Johnson, New York, Anchor, 1959, p. 242.

5. See Jacques Lacan, *Le Séminaire, Livre VIII, Le transfert*, texte établi par Jacques-Alain Miller, Paris, Seuil, 1991 (2001), p. 70.

6. In such a case, one must make a distinction between the 'first love' proper, and the moment of choice when one 'chooses' one's first choice again. It is only through such a repetition that one can properly marry one's first love. For a discussion of this paradox in Henry James, see my 'Portrait of an Act: Aesthetics and Ethics', in *The Portrait of a Lady, The Henry James* Review, vol. 25, no. 1, 2004, pp. 67-86. Stanley Cavell has also devoted some attention to this seeming paradox. See his *Pursuits of Happiness: The Hollywood Comedy of Remarriage*, Harvard University Press, 1981.

subject is the subject of science', goes one oft-repeated refrain. Opposing demands are heard from the recent religious recrudescence that has long tried to appropriate the psychoanalytic concept of the big Other for its own. Philosophy, too, has apparently claimed its own special place in the pantheon of psychoanalytic knowledge in the guise of the ethical turn. In a situation like this, psychoanalysis perhaps can be forgiven for returning to its own 'first love', literature.

\*\*\*

Set in early nineteenth-century Russia, Ivan Turgenev's short story 'First Love' describes the narrator's first summer of love when he meets the mercurial young princess Zinaida whose impecunious mother has taken rooms in the summer residence next door to his family.[7] As merely one of a band of six ardent suitors, the narrator despairs of being selected for Zinaida's special attentions, and he devotes himself to trying to discover which of the group is the favored one. One night, having received a hint that the successful suitor is to meet Zinaida for a midnight tryst by the fountain, he slips into the garden to confront his rival. Hearing footsteps, the narrator poises himself for the attack only to discover at the last minute, in a state of utter confusion and astonishment, the stranger is no one other than his own father. Shortly afterwards, upon receiving an anonymous letter detailing an affair between the princess and the narrator's father, the family leaves in haste for Moscow. Several weeks later, still nursing his emotional wound, the narrator and his father take a ride to the outskirts of town. The father leaves his horse with his son and disappears down a small alleyway. Eventually getting bored, the narrator follows the path his father had taken and finds him talking to Zinaida through a window. They appear to be arguing, with Zinaida 'saying words of only one syllable, without raising her eyes and simply smiling—smiling submissively and stubbornly'.[8] All of a sudden the unbelievable happens: 'my father suddenly raised his riding-crop, which he had been using to flick the dust of the folds of his coat, and I heard the sharp blow as it struck the arm bared to the elbow'. Instead of crying out, however, Zinaida merely shudders, gazes at her lover, and kisses the 'scarlet weal' that has appeared on her

---

7. Ivan Turgenev, *First Love and Other Stories*, trans. and intro. Richard Freeborn, Oxford, Oxford University Press, 1990.
8. Turgenev, *First Love and Other Stories*, p. 198.

arm. The father then flings the riding crop aside, dashes into the house, while the narrator himself flees from the scene back to the river. 'I stared senselessly at the river and didn't notice that there were tears pouring down my cheeks. "They're whipping her", I thought, "whipping her ... whipping her ..."'.[9] Later on that evening, the narrator muses on the scene he has witnessed. '"That's what love is" I told myself again, sitting at night in front of my desk on which books and notebooks had begun to appear. "That's real passion! Not to object, to bear a blow of any kind, even from someone you love very much—is that possible? It's possible, it seems, if you're in love..."'.[10]

Eight months later the father dies unexpectedly from a stroke following the receipt of another upsetting letter, and a large sum of money is mysteriously dispatched to Moscow. The son reads his father's final words in an unfinished letter addressed to him: 'My son, [...] beware a woman's love, beware that happiness, that poison ...'.[11] The narrator never sees Zinaida again, but four years later he hears that she had apparently become a Mrs. Dolsky who died recently in childbirth. 'So that's how it's all worked out!' the narrator reflects. 'It's to this that that young, ardent, brilliant life has come after all its haste and excitement!'[12] The story ends with the narrator attending the death of an old woman and marveling at the strength of the body's resistance to its approaching end. 'And I remember', he says, 'that as I stood there, beside the death-bed of that poor old woman, I began to feel terrified for Zinaida and I felt I wanted to pray for her, for my father—and for myself'.[13]

Let us begin with a simple question: who is the 'first love' of the tale? The first, and most obvious, answer is of course Zinaida, the object of the narrator's first youthful passion. The premise of the story itself—a group of friends sitting around after dinner agreeing to tell each other the story of their first love—urges this interpretation on us as we escort the narrator through the soaring ecstasies and piercing torments that issue from Zinaida's impulsive and capricious dealings with him. The second answer, no less patent, can be found in Zinaida's love for the narrator's father. In this older, elegant, sophisticated man—the narrator is unstinting in his admiration for his father who is invariably described as

---

9. Turgenev, *First Love and Other Stories*, p. 199.
10. Turgenev, *First Love and Other Stories*, pp. 199-200.
11. Turgenev, *First Love and Other Stories*, p. 200.
12. Turgenev, *First Love and Other Stories*, p. 201.
13. Turgenev, *First Love and Other Stories*, p. 202.

'intelligent, 'handsome', the 'ideal example of a man'—Zinaida finally discovers someone she cannot 'look down on', a man who can 'break [her] in two'.¹⁴ In contrast to the band of rivals, the father is evidently of an order apart and it is for his sake that she sacrifices her all, suffering torments which even the narrator, despite the abyssal soundings of his own wretchedness, can scarcely gauge:

> I knelt down at the edge of the path. She was so pale and such bitter sorrow, such profound exhaustion showed in every feature of her face that my heart sank and I muttered: 'What's wrong?' [...]. At that instant, I think, I would gladly have given up my life simply to make sure she stopped feeling so sad. I gazed at her, and though I didn't understand why she was so miserable I vividly imagined to myself how she had suddenly, in a fit of overwhelming grief, gone into the garden and fallen to the ground as though scythed down.¹⁵

The third, and perhaps less immediate, answer can be found in the father's own love for Zinaida, a love which similarly seems to be distinguished from the rest of his erotic adventures. This, perhaps his first, real passion is what ultimately seems to have killed him. The fourth answer is then easy to find in the competing band of rivals, each of whom strives to become 'first' in Zinaida's affections. Each rival thus appeals to a different part of Zinaida's nature and although each, as the narrator observes, 'was needed by her', none succeed in her eyes.¹⁶

> Belovzorov, whom she sometimes called 'my beast' [...] would gladly have flung himself into the flames for her. Placing no hopes on his intellectual resources and other attributes, he was always making her proposals of marriage, hinting that the others were so many talkers. Maidanov appealed to the poetic strings of her spirit: a man of fairly cold temperament, like almost all writers, he strove to assure her—and perhaps himself as well—that he adored her, wrote endless verses in her honour and declaimed them to her with a kind of unnatural and yet sincere enthusiasm. [...]. Lushin, the mocking, cynical doctor, knew her better than them all and loved her more than the others, though he scolded her to her eyes and behind her back. She respected him but didn't let him off scot-free and occasionally took a particularly malicious pleasure in making him feel that he was in her hands. [...]. I least understood

---

14. Turgenev, *First Love and Other Stories*, p. 164, p. 163, p. 167.
15. Turgenev, *First Love and Other Stories*, p. 169.
16. Turgenev, *First Love and Other Stories*, p. 166.

the relationship which existed between Zinaida and Count Malevsky. He was good-looking, capable and clever, but something dubious, something false was apparent in him even to me, a sixteen-year-old boy, and I was amazed that Zinaida didn't notice it. [...]. 'Why do you want to have Mr Malevsky about the place' I asked her once.
'He's got such beautiful little moustaches', she answered. 'Anyhow, it's none of your business'.[17]

There is a fifth answer, however, that I would like to venture here, namely, that the 'first love' of the tale is found in the psychoanalytic love of literature—literature, insofar as she proudly carries the scars of the signifier. Let me try to clarify this somewhat enigmatic statement.

During the course of their wild evenings in the summer residence, Zinaida invents two games. One is a game of forfeits where each suitor picks a ticket from a hat and the one who wins has the right to demand a forfeit from her. Zinaida determines the forfeits herself—a kiss, perhaps, or standing immobile as a statue using the 'ugly Nirmatsky' as a pedestal. One time, on winning the forfeit, the narrator relates how,

> I had to sit next to her, the two of us covered by a silk scarf, and I was ordered to tell her *my secret*. I remember how close our heads were in the stuffy, semi-transparent, perfumed shade, how closely and softly her eyes shone in this shade and how hot the breath was from her open lips and how I could see her teeth and felt the burning, tickling touch of the ends of her hair.[18]

The other game is called comparisons: some object is named, everyone has to try to compare it with something else and the best

---

17. Turgenev, *First Love and Other Stories*, p. 166. Interestingly, the fifth rival, the 'retired captain' Nirmatsky is left out from this litany of Zinaida's 'needs', but we know from elsewhere in the text that he is 'ugly', was made to dress as a bear and drink salt and water (Turgenev, p. 161). The other four, the Hussar, the Poet, the Doctor, and the Count each appeal respectively to the competing claims made on Zinaida by warring masculinity (and economic security), art, science and class status. Furthermore, these are all instances of what Freud called 'the narcissism of minor differences': while each rival is identified from the others by the possession of certain unique characteristics, they are all materially the same when it comes to the signifying difference of the signifier, as Zinaida's mocking reply to the narrator nicely conveys: i.e. to imagine that one is loved for one's particular phenomenal qualities is quite as absurd (and at the same ontic level) as imagining one is loved for one's mustache.
18. Turgenev, *First Love and Other Stories*, pp. 160-1.

comparison wins a prize.[19] The merry band play comparisons one day not long after the narrator has gleaned that Zinaida must be in love:

> 'What do those clouds look like?' Zinaida asked and, without waiting for one of us to answer, said 'I think they look like those purple sails on Cleopatra's golden ship when she sailed out to meet Antony. Do you remember, Maidanov, you recently told me about that?'
> We all agreed, like Polonius in Hamlet, that the clouds reminded us of those very sails and that not one of us would be able to find a better comparison.
> 'How old was Antony then?' asked Zinaida.
> 'He was probably a young man', Malevsky remarked.
> 'Yes, he was young', Maidanov confidently confirmed.
> 'Excuse me', exclaimed Lushin, 'but he was over forty'.
> 'Over forty', repeated Zinaida, shooting a quick glance at him.
> I soon went home. 'She's in love', my lips whispered despite themselves, 'but with whom?'[20]

It is not difficult to make out two of the three psychoanalytic psychic economies operative in these two games. The first game, forfeits, proceeds according to the logic of perversion: within the band of rivals, one person must assume the position of the exception, someone who is singled out from the pack and wins a special favor from the princess. What distinguishes this from the logic of neurosis, similarly founded upon an exception, is the way this game takes place within an entirely closed environment. In a forfeiture economy, there are only positives and negatives; one has either won or lost, and the entire game revolves around the princess as a regionally central Other who is forced to dispense favors and perform certain absurd acts on cue. The exception, or to put it into Hegelian terms, the negative, thus appears as a local event: one member of the band of rivals assumes a position that momentarily sets him apart from the rest before being jettisoned and re-absorbed once more into the general facelessness of the pack. There is no meaning to the structure aside from the chance event of winning the ticket: one cannot buy or sell one's location in the arrangement ('Sell me your ticket', Belovzorov suddenly bellowed in my ear. [...] I gave the hussar such a look of disapproval that Zinaida clapped her hands and Lushin exclaimed:

---

19. Turgenev, *First Love and Other Stories*, p. 174.
20. Turgenev, *First Love and Other Stories*, p. 174.

"Splendid!"[21]). And, despite Belovzorov's subsequent complaint, the game is in fact entirely 'fair' to the extent that it is played among true equals. Everyone has an equal chance of assuming the position of the exception.

Comparisons, on the other hand, entails something quite different, and its structure mirrors that of neurosis. In comparisons, a game which we note was invented *after* the princess has fallen in love with the narrator's father, the exception is located outside the circle of the rivals. One effect of this is to enable objects to stand in for one another without losing their original place in game. Clouds can become Cleopatra's sails, Cleopatra can stand in for Zinaida, and the entire comparison can become an oblique reference to the princess's desire to comparably 'sail out' to her lover, another Antony who, like the original, is 'over forty'. All of these substitutions can take place simply because the exception (the lover, the narrator's father) is in a position of perpetual exclusion outside the game. Such an expulsion frees up the earlier, binary logic of positives and negatives to allow objects or words to refer to two different things at the same time. The signifier has become detached from its signified and can now circulate in multiple, that is, non-binary relations and compositions. Furthermore, if the game of forfeits depended on the blind machinery of chance, comparisons relies on a relation of resemblance, introducing an element of necessity into the ludic equation.

Stated thus, the economic logic of the two games fails to tell us anything particularly new or psychoanalytically striking. What is interesting, however, is the way the figure of literature makes its appearance in the game of comparisons. The comparative economy is one that depends upon a body of literary knowledge in order for the comparison to work. The clouds cannot be just any sails, but must be *Cleopatra's* sails—and the rivals themselves must be ridiculously sycophantic not just in any ordinary way, but in a *Polonius in Hamlet* kind of way. What might this literary underpinning of the comparative or as we might as well now call it, the symbolic, economy tell us about the psychoanalytic psychic structures? Freud, of course, made no secret of the fact that many of his discoveries concerning the unconscious are sourced from the literary tradition—from Sophocles, Shakespeare, Jensen, Hoffmann, Dostoevsky, Goethe to name just some of the immediate ones, not to mention the well-documented presence of Greek myth, the biblical tradition

---

21. Turgenev, *First Love and Other Stories*, p. 160.

etc. in his thinking. Still, my intention is not to try to argue for some kind of literary 'primacy' for psychoanalysis—as if all the psychoanalytic insights discover their Ur-texts in literature and it is simply a matter of digging out their references. This would, to all intents and purposes, be a strictly perverse argument, one that inserts the psychoanalytic first love of literature into the circular, forfeiture economy of priority and belatedness. Although, as we saw, this is certainly one of the economies operative in Turgenev's text, it is not the only one and, in order to explore the others, we need to now go back in a little more detail to 'First Love'.

As far as the neurotic structure is concerned, for example, it is well known that Turgenev was profoundly fascinated by the complex relations between *Fathers and Sons*, to name only one of his better-known novels.[22] 'First Love' is thus far from unique within his oeuvre in its exploration of the theme of the 'superfluous man' (the title of the opening story in the *First Love* volume). The superfluous man is the man who never fully emerges from the long shadow cast by his father—the would-be lover collapsing back into impotent ridiculousness at the first appearance of the father's desire. Of the momentous scene by the fountain in 'First Love', for instance, the narrator recounts how he,

> The jealous Othello who had been ready to commit murder was suddenly turned into a schoolboy... I was so frightened by the unexpected appearance of my father that at first I didn't even notice where he had come from or where he had gone. [...]. From fear I dropped my penknife in the grass, but I didn't even start looking for it: I was very ashamed. I had come to my senses in a flash'.[23]

The Turgenev man is without question only a semi-Oedipalized man, unable fully to recover from the paternal cut of castration and inhabit the 'comparative' economy of Symbolic desire. He remains caught somewhere between the perverse band of dueling rivals and the neurotic realm of the exception. He is both inside *and* outside the circle at the same time, as the narrator's unusual position in relation to Zinaida makes clear. By turns encouraged and repelled by her capricious flirtations and inexplicable rebuffs, at first the narrator merely supplies one more member to the band of rivals. But after the princess falls in love with his father, the narrator becomes a unique favorite on the basis of father and son's

---

22. Ivan Turgenev, *Fathers and Sons*, intro and notes Ann Pasternak Slater, New York, Modern Library, 2001.
23. Turgenev, *First Love and Other Stories*, 190.

mutual resemblance: '"Yes. The very same eyes", she added, becoming thoughtful and covering her face with her hands', while later, in their final, unexpectedly passionate farewell, the narrator reflects, 'God knows who it was this prolonged farewell kiss sought to find, but I greedily savoured all its sweetness. I knew it would never be repeated'.[24] The name Zinaida bestows on this unique position is that of 'page-boy'.[25]

Despite its own potential for becoming ridiculous (the threat of which our Volodya, like other heroes of the Russian literary tradition, is acutely sensitive to), this title conveys something very important about the narrator's position. As Zinaida explains while presenting him a rose for his buttonhole as the 'sign' of his 'new position': 'pageboys must never be separated from their mistresses'.[26] In the game of forfeits, the favour was always contingent, momentary and elusive, but this time the narrator is decorated with a symbolic signifier that marks out his special relation (even if, like all tumescent flowers, it is soon destined to wither). While not quite King to her Queen like his father, he is nevertheless set apart from the eternal merry-go-round of unpredictable and nonsensical favors suffered by the rivals.

The question I wish now to introduce is which economy psychoanalysis itself presents, what is its own internal psychic structure? We know from Lacan that in the analytic discourse, the object $a$ occupies the position of agent, the split subject is in the position of the other, the product is the master signifier while its truth is unconscious knowledge. We know, too, that the analytic discourse, as Lacan puts it, is the 'sign of love' that emerges whenever a quarter-turn shift occurs in the three other discourses (the hysterical, university and master discourses).

Analytic Discourse
$$\frac{a}{S_2} \rightarrow \frac{\$}{S_1}$$

My question is why, their structural uniformity notwithstanding, the psychoanalytic discourse is not functionally perverse, even though this similarly positions the object $a$ in the place of the agent? $a \Diamond \$$. What prevents the desire of the analyst from becoming a perverse desire, despite its being articulated on the same subjective positional plane as perversion? In Seminar XII,

---

24. Turgenev, *First Love and Other Stories*, p. 169, p. 196.
25. Turgenev, *First Love and Other Stories*, p. 182.
26. Turgenev, *First Love and Other Stories*, p. 182.

*Crucial Problems for Psychoanalysis (1964-1965)*, during a session that has remarkable resonance for the present discussion, Lacan refers to the game the subject plays with its unconscious knowledge.[27] Like the children's game of paper, stone, scissors with which Lacan analogizes it, this is a game of 'rotating dominance' that pivots around the central stumbling block of sexual difference. Every time the subject believes it has beaten this stumbling point and finally become 'determined', that is, acquired a form of being through knowledge, this new certainty finds itself overturned so that Lacan can say the subject discovers his refuge in the 'pure default of sex'.[28] The game's ruling principle is to try to anticipate the unexpected but, as Lacan observes, the unexpected is thus not truly unexpected since it is precisely what one readies oneself for: 'one prepares oneself for the unexpected. [...] what is the unexpected if not what reveals itself as being already expected, but only when it arrives'.[29]

It is this circular game of the discordance between knowledge and being that engages the subject when it enters analysis. In fact, Lacan says that it 'grounds' the analytic operation which is, interestingly, similarly described as a game in this seminar. However, the two games operate in different ways. Lacan explains how the subject's game with its unconscious knowledge is reliant on a hidden sleight of hand that allows the subject, to the extent that he supposes the analyst to be the knowing subject, to secretly keep his 'hand in knowledge'. As Lacan puts it, 'the person holding the marbles knows whether their number is odd or even'. This then enables the subject to anticipate the unexpected and, consequently, to keep his distance from it. The analytic game, on the other hand, is characterized by an altogether different principle which Lacan describes in terms of waiting. The analytic 'game' is nothing but a waiting game in which the analyst waits for the patient to show him how to act: 'this is what the desire of the analyst is in its operation. To lead the patient to his original fantasy, is not to teach him anything, it is to learn from him how to act'. While the subject anticipates, and in anticipating defends himself against the unexpected, the analyst merely waits and consequently opens herself to surprise.

From here it is not difficult to see how the analyst's 'supreme complicity' with surprise, as Lacan calls it, is another way of

---

27. Jacques Lacan, *Seminar XII: Crucial Problems for Psychoanalysis (1964-1965)*, unpublished seminar (lesson of 19.5.65).

28. Lacan, *Seminar XII* (lesson of May 19, 1965).

29. Lacan, *Seminar XII* (lesson of May 19, 1965).

formulating the famous emptiness of the analytic position as the object *a*, which is thereby distinguished from that of the pervert. The pervert, as object *a*, is characterized by a supreme conviction that enables her to act on behalf of the Other's *jouissance* and become the instrument of its will. Perverse love is a love that circles around knowledge, as the perverse formula of disavowal expresses very clearly: 'I *know* very well [that the woman does not have the phallus], but all the same ...'. Analytic love, on the other hand, is not interested in knowledge and its games of deception but, rather, in truth.[30] Hence while the relationship of the pervert to the object *a* is one of identification—convinced it knows what the Other wants, the pervert identifies with the object *a* and becomes the instrument of the Other's will—the analyst, in the waiting game that is analysis, 'ends up with something other than an identification' to the extent that the analyst is able to recognize the object *a* as a 'semblance'. 'Love', Lacan explains in his twentieth seminar, 'is addressed to the semblance. And if it is true that the Other is only reached if it attaches itself [...] to a, the cause of desire, then love is also addressed to the semblance of being'.[31]

To unpack the implications of this, imagine the analytic situation. The analyst and analysand are engaged in the analytic work of love. Like Zinaida's suitors, the analysand tries desperately to establish his or her own priority in the analyst's affections, pondering the analyst's likes and dislikes, trying to comprehend the seemingly random acts of kindness and cruelty that the analyst capriciously doles out. What makes the analytic circle of rivals different from the game of forfeiture played by Zinaida? The difference is that, like Zinaida, the analyst is in love with another, with a figure who is beyond the immediate circle. Literature, as the *first love* of psychoanalysis, provides the conditions under which the game of (symbolic) comparisons can begin (whose other name is 'interpretation').

Let me explain. The crucial scene in the tale is when the narrator secretly follows his father down the alley and watches the older lover strike his beloved. Recall how the narrator then rushes from the scene back to the river and, with tears pouring down his

---

30. 'Indeed, the analyst [...] is the one who, by putting object *a* in the place of semblance, is in the best position to do what should rightfully (*juste*) be done, namely, to investigate the status of truth as knowledge'. *The Seminar of Jacques Lacan, Book XX: On Feminine Sexuality: The Limits of Love and Knowledge 1972-1973*, Jacques-Alain Miller (ed.), trans. and notes Bruce Fink, New York, Norton, 1998, p. 95.
31. Lacan, *Seminar XII*, p. 92.

cheeks, repeats to himself 'they're whipping her ... whipping her, whipping her'.[32] Yet despite displaying the hallmarks of a perverse scenario (including its ironic echo of an earlier scene in the garden when the princess lightly taps each suitor's forehead with a pale-mauve flower), this scene differs from perversion in one crucial respect: rather than positioning the narrator as the Other for whom the perverse scenario is being staged (and whose ultimate function, as is well known, is to deny or disavow feminine castration by the momentary singling out a winner (or fetish) who temporarily assumes and fills out the lack), this scene serves instead finally to extricate the narrator from the overpowering shadow of his father: by revealing that his father is castrated.

Two elements of this scene are important here. One is Zinaida's role in causing the violent eruption. Recall how Zinaida, 'saying words of only one syllable [...] and simply smiling—smiling submissively and stubbornly', finally forces the father to act. It is Zinaida's interminable, senseless *repetition of a single word*, along with her simultaneously stubborn and submissive smile that goads the father into striking her, and in that instant of acting he reveals his true impotence: 'My father flung the riding-crop aside and, hurriedly running up the porch steps, dashed into the house'.[33] Yet it is this very impotence that Zinaida ultimately provokes and loves—indeed, it is what every woman loves—and this is what distinguishes the narrator's father from the rest of the band of rivals, namely, *his castration*. Zinaida loves the father's castration precisely because it is evidence of the fact that there is someone or something *beyond him who is not castrated*. His castration is the guarantee of the presence of an other 'father', an exceptional, castrating but uncastrated father that Zinaida loves in and through her love for her impotent and castrated lover. One must point out here how markedly different this is from the perverse play of the game of forfeits. In forfeits the exceptional, that is, castrated, position always remains a temporary favor. Forfeits requires a black and white game of simple positives and negatives that always returns the (absent) phallus back into the unbroken circle. Any member of the band can momentarily assume the castrated position, but he will always fall back afterwards into the undifferentiated whole. The lack, in other words, is an imaginary lack and it circulates internally within a fetishistic economy. With the narrator's father, however, the lack is symbolic and therefore, and most vitally if we

---

32. Turgenev, *First Love and Other Stories*, p. 199.
33. Turgenev, *First Love and Other Stories*, p. 198.

remember the lesson of Little Hans, *detachable*, enabling it to be 'flung aside'.³⁴ As a symbolic lack, the phallus bears witness to a paternal impotence that is Real.

Second, although Zinaida desires a lover who will 'break [her] in two', it is the narrator who ultimately comes out of the story in two halves. The evidence of this lies in the other striking aspect of this scene, namely, the curious use of the plural form in the narrator's riverside wail: '*They're* whipping her ... whipping her, whipping her'. Why this sudden intrusion of the multiple into what is plainly an exchange between only two people? The first answer, which is clearly the narrator's own unconscious one, is that by this act the father has himself now entered the perverse circle of rivals, and become merely one of the 'many'. The dream the narrator has that night reveals just how incapable he really is of psychically assuming the new knowledge he has acquired:

> That very night I dreamed a strange and awful dream. I dreamed that I went into a dark low-ceilinged room. My father was standing there with a whip in his hand and stamping his feet. Zinaida was crouching in a corner and there was a bright red weal not on her arm but her forehead. And behind both there rose the figure of Belovzorov all covered in blood, and he opened his pale lips and angrily threatened my father.³⁵

Unable psychically to consent to what he has just seen, the narrator immediately resorts to the first game Zinaida has taught him and inserts the father into the band of rivals with its forfeiture economy.

But I would like to suggest another interpretation of the narrator's interesting slip.³⁶ When he cries out that 'they' are whipping Zinaida, it is hard not to think of the classic Freudian study, 'A Child is Being Beaten'. In his fifth seminar, the *Formations of the*

---

34. Recall Little Hans' delightful fantasy of a detachable penis that would screw into his belly. For Lacan, this *detachability* is the primary characteristic of the Symbolic phallus, enabling it to light upon any empirical object or signifier without losing its power of negation. See Lacan's discussion of this fantasy in Jacques Lacan, *Le Séminaire, Livre IV: La relation d'objet*, texte établi par Jacques-Alain Miller, Paris, Seuil, 1994, pp. 266-67.

35. Turgenev, *First Love and Other Stories*, p. 200.

36. Technically, in the Russian, this is not really a slip. The Russian reads '*Ee b'jut,- dumal ja,- b'jut... b'jut*' which Thomas Langerak explains can be translated in two ways (personal communication). The most literal is the one Richard Freeborn provides, i.e. '*they* are whipping her ...', where an impersonal action is expressed in Russian in the third person plural. The other translation possibility is 'she is being whipped'. Even with this second translation, however, we retain the sense of impersonality and objectivity that is typical of the third moment of the 'A Child is Being Beaten' fantasy and whose significance I discuss below.

*Unconscious*, Lacan reads this fantasy as a kind of allegory of subject formation which takes place in three logical rather than temporal stages: my father is beating a child whom I hate, I am being beaten by my father and, finally, the fantasy's title, a child is being beaten.[37] The second moment, however, is permanently omitted and must be reconstructed through a complicated, a-temporal chronology that goes from the third moment to the first and only then to the second.

In his reading, Lacan sees the first moment as articulating the primary intersubjective relation between a child and a rival whereupon I, seeing my father beating the other child (a sister or brother), take this to mean that the father does not love my rival who is thereby is negated, a statement which simultaneously contains its elated obverse, namely that I, in contrast, am loved—I exist.[38] The third moment which, as I said, occurs prior to the first and the second moments, presents an objectification of this primary relationship in the form of an external scene or an image—*a* child (i.e. an unnamed other rather than my brother or sister or myself) is being beaten and I am watching as a spectator. The second moment is the moment of cross-over between the first and third moments and is, for this reason, both 'necessary' and 'fugitive' as Lacan says elsewhere, and must be reconstructed, that is, it can never be represented in either memory or words.[39] Here the yet-to-be subject is itself being beaten and, judging by the pleasure with which the subject invests the other two moments, is also *enjoying* it. In Lacan's interpretation of 'A Child is Being Beaten', this second, occluded moment thus speaks of a fundamental masochistic enjoyment that accompanies the subject's entry into language. For the fantasy, as Dominiek Hoens has put it, 'is an imaginary representation of what happened to the child symbolically. The child brings into play and, one could say, fantasizes about what it means to be a subject of the Symbolic order: one is beaten away, rubbed out, by something from outside'.[40] Furthermore, and particularly of relevance to our purposes here, this primordial perverse enjoyment of the pounding by the paternal signifier

---

37. Jacques Lacan, *Le Séminaire, Livre V: Les formations de l'inconscient*, texte établi par Jacques-Alain Miller, Paris, Seuil, 1998.
38. Jacques Lacan, *Le Séminaire, Livre V*, p. 242.
39. Jacques Lacan, *Le Séminaire, Livre IV: La relation d'objet*, texte établi par Jacques-Alain Miller, Paris, Seuil, 1998, p. 116.
40. Dominiek Hoens, '*Hamlet* and the Letter a', *Umbr(a)*, vol. 2, no. 2, 2002, pp. 91-101, p. 94.

has the result, as Lacan points out, of permanently investing language with an element of eroticism.[41]

Hence I propose that, in the narrator's use of the plural form in his agonized wail that 'they' are 'whipping her', we find evidence of an occlusion or repression comparable to the second moment of the 'A Child is Being Beaten' fantasy. The narrator's peculiar use of 'they', that is, provides unconscious testimony of the fact that a moment of subjectification has occurred. Although, as in the fantasy, this second moment can never be represented or put into conscious form, we can glean from the presence of the third moment—whose element of spectatorship Turgenev quite deliberately highlights when he has Zinaida theatrically framed in the window-sill and half screened by a curtain—that subjectification must indeed have taken place.

Two consequences immediately follow. One is that we see now that it is not Zinaida, nor the father, nor any member of the band of rivals but language itself, in its primary form as the paternal signifier, that is the 'first (perverse) love' of the text—language, that is, to the extent that in it resides the fundamental masochistic erotic fantasy in which all subsequent fantasmatic desiring 'scenes' or loving representations participate. The other consequence is that it is this (per-)first love that succeeds in fracturing the One into a Two, as Badiou put it earlier. The subject having literally been broken in two, that is, irretrievably split between the first and third components of the fantasy, the 'numericity' of the amorous procedure may now commence as the quantitative count to infinity of all possible successive loves.

If my construction is correct, is analytic love a perverse love after all? Here we must recall Lacan's assertion that (analytic) love is always addressed to a *semblance*. A semblance is a counterfeit, a double, a wraithlike form that may possess either actual or apparent resemblance to something real. A semblance thus has no being in itself aside from that which it resembles—one could say that it is *nothing but* a relation (of similitude), which returns us to question of the emptiness of the analytic object *a*. To the extent that it is a semblance, the analyst as object *a* can be inhabited effectively by anyone. That is to say, any analyst can, in principle, be 'my' analyst. Analytic love does not depend upon any particular likeness (or difference) to the Real object in my life that is the support of my desire. As a semblance, the analyst as object *a* is, quite

---

41. Jacques Lacan, *Le Séminaire, Livre IV*, p. 117.

literally, 'nothing' aside from a relation, that is, it is a purely formal similitude, possessing no particular content. Despite the potential for confusion between the two terms, then, the analyst as the 'semblance of object $a$' embodies (the desire for) an 'absolute difference', as I cited Lacan saying in the previous chapter in his Seminar XI, *Identification*. By this I understand him to mean that, to the extent that the semblance has nothing grounding itself beyond its purely formal relation of similarity, it can never be the object of an identification. In the transference, there is nothing to identify with beyond the formal relation of likeness itself.[42]

But let us return to the third moment of subjectivity. When Freud discovered the deep structures of psychoanalysis in literature, he invented an Other scene for psychoanalysis in whose dim reddish light the singular shapes of his patients could emerge. The images that surfaced from this developing process are the classic psychoanalytic case histories whose doubles can be found hovering in the larger backdrop of literature. Every analysand thus enters analysis against this literary scene, but it is important to emphasize that analysis has nothing to do with mapping individual subjects onto a literary template—analysis does not take place inside the black and white economy of forfeits but rather in the semblances of comparisons; interpretations are not identity-seeking metaphors but likenesses, similes. Nevertheless, without the presence of this literary Other, analysis would be caught up in either an imaginary or a perverse game. The literary knowledge upon which comparisons is founded pries open what would otherwise be the closed analytic circle: either an imaginary round of hatred and rivalry, or a sado-masochistic scene of enjoyment. To change the metaphor a little, we might say that literature supplies a partially transparent, imaginary screen onto which the third moment of subjectivity can be projected, a screen that enables the generation of a plural 'they' whose principal feature is that it can refer simultaneously to the singular suffering individual of analysis *and* its exemplary double in the literary typology.

What prevents literature from becoming either just another fetish, that is, a temporary exception or forfeit whose sole function is to re-close the analytic circle,—or a religion, a founding exclusion that guarantees the comparison economy by ensuring that all signs, all signifieds, ultimately converge upon a single point,

---

42. 'The analyst's desire is not a pure desire. It is a desire to obtain absolute difference', Lacan, *The Four Fundamental Concepts of Psychoanalysis*, Jacques-Alain Miller (ed.), trans. Alan Sheridan, New York, Norton, 1981, p. 276.

whether we call that point God, the father, the master signifier, the phallus (or, as we will see in the following chapter, the lover)? The answer lies in literature itself which, in addition to being a discourse of love, is also the discourse of subjectivity par excellence. The two things are in fact the same: the discourse of love is nothing other than the discourse of the subject *as such*.[43] But for this reason, literature as psychoanalysis' Other, remains perpetually split and, as split, can never serve entirely on one or the other side of the circle. Like a pageboy, literature is always neither fully inside nor outside the analytic loop; it constitutes an Other but this is an Other that will be eternally incomplete and self-divided. It is this internal self-division of literature, whose scars of the signifying cut it proudly bears, that defends the analyst as object *a* against the acquisition of (perverse) content.

Could we not say, then, that literature is the 'pageboy' of psychoanalysis? Literature must never be separated from psychoanalysis, but nor may it ever become King to her Queen. It is marked out from all other rival discourses by a singular relation, precisely because they both possess the same first love for the signifier, for the primordial scarifying cut of language. Hence when Zinaida sees Cleopatra's sails in the purple clouds, or when an analyst discovers a 'veritable Hamlet' in one of her patients, or when a literary critic perhaps comes across an 'Antigone' in a Jamesian heroine, such comparisons are not straight-jackets of the imagination. Instead they are testimonies to the presence of analytic love, the love of letters in both of its senses, whose ethical function at the end of the day is to prevent the closure of the analyst and analysand's potentially perverse loving circle. We are narrative subjects, after all, and it is only our uniquely singular narratives, awkwardly traced out in relief against our uncanny doppelgängers in the backdrop of the literary Other, that slow down if not actually stop the inexorable closing of the blind, senseless machinery of contingency that makes up life's perverse cycle of birth and death.

Covered in rags, laid on hard boards, with a sack placed under her head [the old woman] was dying painfully and with

---

43. This is how I interpret Lacan's statement in *Encore* that love is a 'subject-to-subject relationship', whose formula Bruce Fink writes as S ◊ S. See Bruce Fink, 'Knowledge and Jouissance', in *Reading Seminar XX: Lacan's Major Work on Love, Knowledge, and Feminine Sexuality*, Suzanne Barnard and Bruce Fink (eds.), Albany, SUNY Press, 2002, pp. 21-45, p. 45. See also Lacan's statement, 'In love what is aimed at is the subject, the subject as such', which he qualifies as being 'nothing other than what slides in a chain of signifiers' as an 'effect' of the signifier. Lacan, *Seminar XX*, p. 50.

difficulty. [...]. She had seen no joy in her life, had never tasted the honey of happiness—why, then, I thought, shouldn't she be glad of death, of its freedom and its peace? And yet so long as her frail body still struggled, so long as her chest rose and fell agonizingly beneath the ice-cold hand resting on it, so long as her final strength remained the old woman went on crossing herself and whispering: 'Dear God, forgive me my sins', and it was only with the last spark of consciousness that there vanished from her eyes the look of fear and horror at her approaching end. And I remember that as I stood there, beside the death-bed of that poor old woman, I began to feel terrified for Zinaida and I felt I wanted to pray for her, for my father— and for myself.[44]

Given that the despair of prayer has ceased to be an option for many of us, how then ought one to respond ethically to the escalation of the Other's demands for more and more love? My earlier metaphor of the hostage might suggest an answer. One is a hostage, after all, only insofar as one desires to leave one's hostage-taker. Yet what would happen if one suddenly, unexpectedly assumed the hostage-taker's 'cause'?[45] What if one was to turn to one's guard and pronounce, in a preposterous and ridiculous evocation of the lover's solemn promise: 'I swear I will never, ever leave you. Even if you kill me, my love for you will only have been made stronger, because I will have become a martyr to your cause'? Yet isn't it something like such a radical shift in the parameters of discourse that love, to the extent that it is a *metaphor*, as Lacan tells us, succeeds in effecting? Like a metaphor, love's substitution of *erastes* for *eromenos* produces a decisive change in the ordinary logical distance between things.[46] From having been an object, one is transformed

---

44. Turgenev, *First Love and Other Stories*, p. 202.

45. Like, perhaps, the two French journalists, Christian Chesnot and Georges Malbrunot, who were taken hostage in Iraq in protest of the French ban on Muslim headscarves in French schools in 2004. Released in the meantime, there were rumours on the internet that they had been freed but had chosen to remain with their captors, the better to cover the Iraq war from the Iraqi perspective. It should be clear that the (impossible) gesture I am describing is conceptually different from what is known as the Stockholm syndrome. In the Stockholm syndrome, the hostage *identifies* with the hostage taker, in an ultimate form of self-defense. In 'love', the hostage gives up precisely all forms of identification. In the loving substitution, identity is radically suspended.

46. '[The] decisive problem that an interaction theory of metaphor has helped to delineate but not solve is the transition from literal incongruence to metaphorical congruence between two semantic fields. Here the metaphor of space is useful. It is as though a change of distance between meanings occurred within a

by the loving substitution into a subject that reaches back in desire. Not only does this give a new twist to the psychoanalytic imperative to become one's own cause, that is, one must become or adopt the particular cause that, as a hostage, one clearly already 'is' (and, in the process, 'give' what you don't 'have', another Lacanian definition of love). It also provides a succinct illustration of how loving someone is, strictly speaking, an intensely *political* (rather than purely ethical) act insofar as it radically transforms existing power relationships. As your lover-hostage, I meet your suspension of the law with an equally exceptional suspension; I subjectify, that is, '*politivize*' your objectifying appropriation of me through an equivalently political return embrace.

To close this discussion, let us turn back to another of the narrator's peculiar formulations. Recall how, after watching the strange scene between Zinaida and his father, the narrator reflects on the nature of love: '"That's what love is", I told myself again, sitting at night in front of my desk on which books and notebooks *had begun to appear.* "That's real passion!"'[47] It is surely no coincidence that, following the (reconstructed) moment of subjectification, books and notebooks begin as if spontaneously to propagate themselves on the narrator's desk. For while our narrator has yet to realize it, the truly loving partnership, it seems, lies in the mutual sharing of the 'real passion' for the signifier that first individually marked us as speaking subjects and whose scarlet welts we now lovingly caress in our beloved's tragic scars. Yet as it traces out the now faint ravages of the signifier, love's hand simultaneously discovers surprising new shapes, patterns and comparisons on the body's page. For that's what love is: the infinitely generative source for the stories we tell about ourselves and which ultimately compose us as narrative subjects.

---

logical space. The *new* pertinence or congruence proper to a meaningful metaphoric utterance proceeds from the kind of semantic proximity which suddenly obtains between terms in spite of their distance. Things or ideas which were remote now appear as close'. Paul Ricoeur, 'The Metaphorical Process as Cognition, Imagination, and Feeling', in *On Metaphor*, Sheldon Sacks (ed.), Chicago, Uiversity of Chicago Press, 1979, pp. 141-57, p. 145. What Ricoeur ultimately calls 'feeling' in this essay is thus not so far from what Lacan would call 'love'. Ricoeur writes, 'To *feel*, in the emotional sense of the word, is to make *ours* what has been put at a distance by thought in its objectifying phase. [...] Its function is to abolish the distance between knower and known without canceling the cognitive structure of thought and the intentional distance which it implies'. Ricoeur, p. 154.

47. Turgenev, *First Love and Other Stories*, pp. 199-200 (my emphasis).

## 3. IN THE SELF'S TEMPORARY LODGINGS: EUDORA WELTY

> With his huge hammer again Eros knocked me like a blacksmith
> And doused me in a wintry ditch
>
> —Anacreon

Compared to the other First Loves in this selection, Eudora Welty's short story 'First Love' is entirely unique, and this is not simply because it is written by the only woman in the group. Appearing originally in *The Wide Net*, Welty's 1943 collection of short stories set in and around the ancient Indian trail called the Natchez Trace in the southern United States, 'First Love' deals not with the archetypal story of the relation between a boy and a girl but with a young deaf child, Joel, and a man in early nineteenth-century America who is about to go on trial for treason.[1] Welty's tale concerns the historical figure, Aaron Burr, the third Vice President of the United States (1801-1805) whose fame in American history resides chiefly in having mortally wounded the former US Treasury Secretary and newspaper publisher, Alexander Hamilton, in a duel in 1804. Welty picks up the disgraced Vice President's story from the time after the murder when he fled west to the Louisiana Purchase area, where he was alleged to have led a plot to secede a number of southern states, including Mississippi, from the union.[2]

---

1. Eudora Welty, *The Collected Stories of Eudora Welty*, London, Marion Boyars, 1981.
2. For a full account of the so-called Burr conspiracy, see Alexander DeConde, *This Affair of Louisiana*, New York, Charles Scribners' Sons, 1976. Annette Trefzer speculates that given the presence of 'Old Man McCaleb' in the story, Welty probably obtained her information from Walter Flavius McCaleb's account of the affair in his *The Aaron Burr Conspiracy*, New York, Dodd, Mead & Co., 1903. See Annette

In her tale, Welty weaves a loose mixture of fact and fiction as she explores the last weeks leading up to Burr's trial in the town of Natchez as it is seen through the eyes of the young orphan Joel Mayes. A deaf and mute child, Joel is perceived as no threat to the men as Burr and his co-conspirator Harman Blennerhassett meet nightly in secret in the boy's room at the Inn to plot Burr's escape from the law. The central event around which the story revolves is an upward arm gesture Burr makes on the first night, with which Joel apparently falls in love:

> One of the two men lifted his right arm—a tense, yet gentle and easy motion—and made the dark wet cloak fall back. To Joel it was like the first movement he had ever seen, as if the world had been up to that night inanimate. It was like the signal to open some heavy gate or paddock [sic], and it did open to his complete astonishment upon a panorama in his own head, about which he knew first of all that he would never be able to speak—it was nothing but brightness, as full as the brightness on which he had opened his eyes.[3]

Clearly, Welty's 'First Love' is a strange, haunting little tale that is difficult to insert into the traditional narratives of first love. The handful of existing critical treatments tend to read the story as a narrative of redemption where Joel's love for Burr is advanced as the catalyst for the boy's subjective and, for one critic, a wider cultural reintegration. In a reading that is typical of this kind of approach, St. George Tucker Arnold, Jr. lays his emphasis on the cathartic closing scene where Joel, walking slowly along the frozen path 'into the wilderness' in pursuit of a disguised and fleeing Burr, comes across some dead birds that have frozen and fallen lifeless from the trees as a result of the extreme cold.[4] The pitiable

---

Trefzer, 'Tracing the Natchez Trace: Native Americans and National Anxieties in Eudora Welty's "First Love"', *Mississippi Quarterly*, vol. 55, no. 3, 2002, pp. 419-440, p. 436. See also Suzanne Marrs, *One Writer's Imagination: The Fiction of Eudora Welty*, Baton Rouge, Louisiana State Press, 2001, and especially her essay, 'The Conclusion of Eudora Welty's "First Love": Historical Backgrounds', *Notes on Mississippi Writers*, vol. 13, no. 2, 1981, pp. 73-8.

3. Welty, *The Collected Stories*, p. 157.
4. St. George Tucker Arnold, Jr., 'Eudora Welty's "First Love" and the Personalizing of Southern Regional History', *Journal of Regional Cultures*, vol. 1, no. 2, 1981, pp. 97-105, p. 105. See also John M. Warner, 'Eudora Welty: The Artist in "First Love"', *Notes on Mississippi Writers*, no. 9, 1976, pp. 77-87; Victor H. Thompson, 'Aaron Burr in Eudora Welty's "First Love"', *Notes on Mississippi Writers*, no. 8, 1976, pp. 75-81. For a useful discussion of cultural integration and memory, see Trefzer.

sight of these little corpses enables the boy to give way to the tears he has not yet been able to shed for his parents, whose death we have heard about in the tale's opening scene. Like a number of critics, Arnold thus regards first love as an emotionally empowering event, enabling Welty's little orphan to come to terms with his loss through a variety of visionary means such as memory, imagination, art, etc.

Everything we have learned about first love so far, however, should caution against such an interpretation. While it is undeniable that first love does have important things to say about reintegration, it will not be in the name of restoring any kind of whole or integrated self. If Welty's 'First Love' can tell us something substantially new about this emotional state, I suspect it will not be at the level of the story's *content* which, for all of its enigmatic, crystalline beauty, finally does seem to come down to the rather hackneyed tale of individual maturation that Arnold succeeds in retrieving from it.[5] It is for this reason I believe we must look elsewhere for Welty's insights into first love, understood this time as the first initial phase of love, when it is still tightly knotted with desire. My suggestion, in other words, is that we must look not to the tale's emplotment, but to the revolutionary way Welty makes literal the initial stages making up the discovery that one is in love so as to reveal these stages' original psychic source. Like in the two other tales of 'First Love' we have looked at, first love in Welty will be seen to be linked with the first signifying act, to the emergence of the signifier. What I find so bracing and instructive about Welty's version of 'First Love' is the disarmingly anti-sentimental way this author strips out the perennial 'boy meets girl' story that monopolizes, as a master narrative, the first love tales to enable us to view the skeletal structure of first love in its unadorned form: as a special kind of *linguistic condition*. To the extent that she transposes the affective stages of the first flush of love into a narrative revolving around a deaf-mute, a sign, a trial and an escape from the law, Welty formalizes the celebrated 'temporary madness' that makes up the experience of first (being in) love. In so doing, she awards us the tools to properly analyze first love's psychic structure for

---

5. 'Joel's recognizing the smallness of his hero-love, Burr, and feeling pity for the would-be great man, demonstrates the boy's maturing, through his crisis of first love, into a new comprehension of the intricacies and paradoxes of love, and of the harsh demands of personal courage'. Arnold, 'Eudora Welty's "First Love" and the Personalizing of Southern Regional History', p. 105.

the first time, namely, as a form of paranoid *delusion*, albeit one whose difference from psychotic delusion must be scrupulously delineated. What is more, by disentangling first love from literature's relentless obsession with the inner world of the individual subject, Welty redirects attention to a seminal aspect of first love that might otherwise be missed by this study, namely, the unique role first love plays in the creation of the social body. Although the two texts discussed so far have stressed the deeply personal nature of the experience of first love, Welty's critical insight will reveal it as having a profoundly trans-individual implication.

\*\*\*

As I mentioned, the plot of Welty's 'First Love' centers on the boy Joel whose parents were killed by Indians when they fell behind the settler party on the southward trek out from Virginia. Both deaf and mute, Joel was saved from his parents' fate by the leader of the party Old Man McCaleb who, Welty tells us, 'had herded them, the whole party alike, into the dense cane brake, deep down off the Trace'.[6] It was in that terrible moment, as the party hid from the Indians, that Joel became aware for the first time of what silence (and by extension, sound) means to others. From fear, Joel had made an involuntary cry upon which Old Man McCaleb rounded upon him in fury:

> He wept, and Old Man McCaleb first felled the excited dog with the blunt end of his axe, and then he turned a fierce face toward him and lifted the blade in the air, in a kind of ecstasy of protecting the silence they were keeping. Joel had made a sound.... . He gasped and put his mouth quicker than thought against the earth. He took the leaves in his mouth.... In that long time of lying motionless with the men and women in the cane brake he had learned what silence meant to other people.[7]

For a tale that literally turns around a gesture, this opening move is nothing if not intensely striking and, to readers primed with Lacanian ears, it cannot help but recall the threat of castration. Or at least it would, until one recalls how the priapic cut is supposed to open up a speech community, giving the subject entry to the symbolic world of language. In Joel's case, however, Old Man McCaleb's threat serves only to deepen the stubborn silence of his

---

6. Welty, *The Collected Stories*, p. 154.
7. Welty, *The Collected Stories*, p. 155.

world in its revelation of the miracle of sound. Joel's entry into a linguistic community comes to the boy in the form of a 'speechless embrace' the narrator tells us,[8] that bears none of the features we typically expect to accompany the cut of the phallic signifier: the address to the big Other, the receipt of one's message in inverted form, the constitution of a world of reality structured by signifiers, and so on. On the contrary, for Joel, the existence of 'another Other' lying beyond the little other of the imaginary, which is the 'necessary correlate of speech', as Lacan puts it in Seminar III, *The Psychoses* (1955-1956) is experienced as a debilitating closeness.[9] 'Through the danger', we read, Joel 'had felt acutely, even with horror, the nearness of his companions, a speechless embrace of which he had had no warning, a powerful crushing unity'.[10] This 'crushing unity' is surely the complete converse of the 'life-preserving' distance that we have always been taught the paternal interdiction institutes between the pre-Oedipal child and its mother's all-too-suffocating desire.

Nevertheless, as Lacan frequently cautioned his audience, it is at times worth trying to forget everything one thinks one knows about psychoanalysis and pay attention to what a text is actually saying. And in Welty's case, this is particularly good advice inasmuch as her tale will direct us to a critical facet of castration that might otherwise escape notice. Welty's 'First Love' draws our attention to the crucial role first love plays in enabling the subject to 'historicize' its castration, which turns out to be an essential factor in the creation of a neurotic, as opposed to a psychotic, subject. The significance of this 'historicization' is unprecedented for, as Lacan puts it in Seminar III, the signifier 'remains nothing as long as the subject doesn't cause it to enter into his history'.[11] This ability (or failure) to historicize one's castration will then also have far-reaching implications for the libidinal procedure by which subjects bind themselves to each other to form a social group or community.

What might it mean to 'historicize' one's castration? As we will see, for Welty, as for Lacan, it will have to do with a certain eroticization of the signifier.[12] We have already encountered one occasion

8. Welty, *The Collected Stories*, p. 155.
9. Lacan, *The Seminar of Jacques Lacan, Book III, The Psychoses (1955-1966)*, Jacques-Alain Miller (ed.), trans. Russell Grigg, New York, Norton, 1993, p. 146.
10. Welty, *The Collected Stories*, p. 155
11. Lacan, *Seminar III*, p. 156.
12. 'Sexual desire', as Lacan puts it, is 'effectively what man uses to historicize

of such eroticization, namely, in the masochistic fantasy or what Lacan also describes as the 'feminization' the subject undergoes when submitting to castration. In the previous chapter, I indicated how the occluded moment of enjoyment in the castration fantasy, 'A Child is Being Beaten', invests language with an unmistakable sexual element that will accompany the subject on its desiring trajectory, thereby shielding it from falling into perversion. In Welty's 'First Love', we obtain a more precise account of how and under what conditions this primordial 'turning', as Lacan puts it, 'in the relationship to language which may be called eroticization or pacification' occurs in the logical formation of a subject[13]. Welty tacitly reminds us how, insofar as it temporarily lifts the paternal law, first love paradoxically *completes* the act of castration. In one of the twists one has come to expect from psychoanalysis, it appears that a certain original madness, as André Green has theorized it, is a prerequisite against the psychosis proper into which the castrating act would otherwise fling the subject.[14]

Let us look more closely now at Welty's 'First Love'. In Joel, we find a subject whose castration is evidently incomplete in some way. Although Old Man McCaleb's axe stroke apparently instituted some form of radical intervention in the boy's discursive field ('he had learned what silence meant to other people'), this cut has failed to penetrate in any *meaningful* way in the child's psyche, for the simple reason that Joel is himself unable to hear. The distinction between silence and sound remains hypothetical rather than experienced or lived. One could say that Joel's castration remains a theoretical rather than an 'historical' cut. As a deaf-mute, Joel is unable to receive his message back from the big Other: he cannot hear his own speech. He thus cannot hear the uncanny voice that, as it enunciates the subject, simultaneously cuts that subject off from its enunciation in order to send it back to the subject in an inverted form. There is, therefore, something missing from Joel's symbolic network. The subjectifying cut has no correlative, no objective equivalent in the outside world, with the result that the signifier fails to fully transform itself into a Law. Mladen Dolar has expended considerable energy elaborating the necessity for this

---

himself'. Lacan, *Seminar III*, p. 156.

13. Lacan, *Seminar III*, p. 208.

14. See André Green, *On Private Madness*, London Hogarth Press, 1986. This original or 'maternal psychosis' has also many resonances with the ideas of Melanie Klein.

objectification. 'There is no law without the voice', he explains. 'The voice is what endows the letter with authority, making it not just a signifier, but an act'.[15]

Failing this aural dimension, Joel's entry into the symbolic register is only marginally successful, as is indicated by its effects: Joel's adhesion to the new speech community can only be felt as a 'powerful crushing unity'. Although Old Man McCaleb's threatening motion thrust the boy unceremoniously into a wider social group, this is evidently a sociality composed solely of what Lacan would call small others. And its effect, as we saw, is unbearable to the child. It calls to mind Lacan's description in Seminar III, of what a community of imaginary relations might conceivably look like. In the session of January 18, 1956 Lacan invites us to imagine a machine that, having no internal mechanism for coordinating its left and right legs, is reliant on seeing the image of another machine functioning in a coordinated way. Putting them into a closed environment, such as on the track of the dodg'em car ride of an amusement park, Lacan notes how, 'Each one being unified and regulated by the sight of another, it is not mathematically impossible to imagine that we would end up with all the little machines accumulated in the center of the track, blocked in a conglomeration the size of which would only be limited by the external resistance of the panelwork'. The result would be 'a collision, everything smashed to a pulp'.[16]

This comical vision of an imaginary community of smashed-up dodg'em cars is Lacan's image for the world of the psychotic subject who, as this illustration shows, is therefore not without access to some form of social grouping and therefore to some form of Other. As Lacan emphasizes in his third seminar, it not so much that the psychotic has failed to undergo castration, as one frequently hears, but rather that 'something hasn't functioned', something remains 'essentially incomplete, in the Oedipus complex.'[17] One might condense this by saying that the castrating cut has cut, as it were, in only one direction. While it has carved out a symbolic space for the subject in language, that is, it has separated the subject from the maternal body, it has failed in its obverse direction, *to cut the voice away from speech*. As a result, and counter to one's usual understanding perhaps, the psychotic is too profoundly—rather

---

15. Mladen Dolar, 'Vox', *Umbr(a)*, no. 1: Incurable, 2006, pp. 119-41, p. 128.
16. Lacan, *Seminar III*, p. 96.
17. Lacan, *Seminar III*, p. 201.

than insufficiently—in the symbolic. It is not so much that the psychotic is shut out from language. It is rather that he or she relates to language differently. Whereas the neurotic, as the 'subject of enunciation', inhabits language, the psychotic is 'inhabited, possessed by language', as Lacan puts it (Seminar III, p. 250).

Just in case one imagines that Joel is a special case, an atypical deaf-mute in a world of otherwise speaking and hearing others, we must remember that what Lacan is describing is in no way exceptional but is rather the potential condition of every speaking subject. That is to say, it is not self-evident that the castrating cut is automatically 'caused' to enter the subject's history, in Lacan's words, but requires something additional to occur if the subject is to step out of the 'conglomeration' that is the psychotic's imaginarily structured world and become a desiring (that is, neurotic) subject. The fundamental insight Welty brings to our attention in this opening episode is how it is very easy to form a 'cluster' of other individuals. It is less straightforward, however, to form a social group that is not felt by the subject to be simply an objective analogue of the suffocating maternal body. For this, for what Lacan calls a 'common discourse' or 'public discourse' to become established, a structuring principle is necessary that can 'regulate' the imaginary body beyond the mere imitation of the image that stands before it.[18] We will come back to this 'public discourse' later on but for the moment it suffices to observe how it is not sufficient for this structuring principle to be simply imposed from the outside, like Old Man McCaleb's axe-stroke. In order to operate effectively, it first needs to be subjectivized, given meaning by the subject or, as Welty thematizes it, it must be first eroticized—first *'loved'*.

## THE SIGN OF LOVE

Returning to Welty's tale, once the Indians had passed, 'one by one McCaleb's charges had to rise up and come out of the hiding place'.[19] Embarrassed that the others had witnessed their fear, there 'was little talking together, but a kind of shame and shuffling'.[20] This mutual shame, the affect that Jacques-Alain Miller identifies as holding a primary position in the subject's relation to the Other,

---

18. Lacan, *Seminar III*, p. 60.
19. Welty, *The Collected Stories*, p. 155.
20. Welty, *The Collected Stories*, p. 155

serves to temporarily bind the travelers together as a group.[21] However, once they arrive in Natchez the group disbands and Joel is deposited at the Inn. With nobody to care for him, he is allowed to remain there as a boot polisher. Joel's congenital silence will guarantee that the secret of the 'little cluster', the secret of their fear of death, will be kept safe. His responsibility for maintaining the integrity of the community, Joel's new-found sense of the utter precariousness of the hearing world, is something the boy now feels in the most profound way: 'It might seem to him that the whole world was sleeping in the lightest of trances, which the least movement would surely wake; but he only walked softly, stepping around and over, and got back to his room'.[22]

Into this silent and secretive world, however, a change miraculously occurs. Joel awakens in the early hours one morning to find 'the whole room shining brightly, like a brimming lake in the sun [...]. Joel was left in the shadow of the room, and there before him, in the center of the strange multiplied light, were two men in black capes sitting at his table'.[23] The men, as he discovers, are the co-conspirators Aaron Burr and Harman Blennerhassett: 'There was no one to inform him that the men were Aaron Burr and Harman Blennerhassett, but he knew', and he also knew, although 'No one had pointed out to him any way that he might know which was which, but he knew that: it was Burr who had made the gesture'.[24]

'A tense, yet gentle and easy motion'. This is how Welty describes Burr's action. It appears as a sudden revelation for the boy: 'It was like the first movement he had ever seen', a statement that increases in emotive force if one recalls how movement—*signing*—has been the sole means of communication available to the child until now.[25] Old Man McCaleb's downward axe-stroke thrust Joel into a speech community founded on the hitherto unperceived difference between sound and silence, but Aaron Burr's upward sweep now appears to reverse this movement. McCaleb's movement was a silencing gesture, but Burr's constitutes a 'signal' as Welty calls it, that opens up a 'panorama' in Joel's head:

---

21. Jacques-Alain Miller, 'On Shame' in Justin Clemens and Russell Grigg, (eds.), *Jacques Lacan and the Other Side of Psychoanalysis: Reflections on Seminar XVII*, Durham, Duke University Press, 2006, pp. 11-28, p. 13.
22. Welty, *The Collected Stories*, p. 156.
23. Welty, *The Collected Stories*, p. 156.
24. Welty, *The Collected Stories*, p. 158.
25. Welty, *The Collected Stories*, p. 157.

'it was nothing but brightness, as full as the brightness on which he had opened his eyes'.[26] The effect of this gesture on the boy is profound. Burr's gesture opens up a new interior space for Joel: 'Inside his room was still another interior, this meeting upon which all the light was turned, and within that was one more mystery, all that was being said'.[27] Welty employs the image of a key to describe the result. It was like unlocking 'some heavy gate or pad[l]ock' that evidently gives the boy access to something that had previously been tightly shut up in his mind. The effect of this change is that Joel begins to recover memories, although Welty is nevertheless emphatic that this will not lead to increased communicative abilities for the boy. We hear how, upon waking, Joel 'tried to remember everything of the night before, and he could, and then of the day before, and he rubbed belatedly at a boot in a long and deepening dream'.[28] Although 'it did open to his complete astonishment upon a panorama in his own head', Joel also knows that of this 'he would never be able to speak'.[29]

With this last statement, Welty debunks one of our most deeply held fantasies about love, one cherished in particular by lovers in the first flush of their discovery—the idea that love inaugurates a communication between two subjects. Although love's profound link with language is amply documented throughout the literary tradition, as this study will attest, contrary to the beliefs of lovers, the seemingly magical communication they share in the early phases of the amorous encounter is not a 'private language'. Indeed, Welty's description of what is taking place in Joel sounds a lot closer to the aymmetrical conversation of the 'delusional intuition' than to any discernibly intersubjective discourse. Like the first discovery of being in love, the initial stage of a psychotic episode, the delusional intuition, entails a similarly 'illuminating' experience for the subject, as Lacan goes on to elaborate in Seminar III. Lacan describes the intuition as 'a full phenomenon that has an overflowing, inundating character for the subject'. Like Joel's experience in the preceding episode, the delusion is also permeated with the revelation of 'a new perspective to [the psychotic], one whose stamp of originality, whose characteristic savor, he emphasizes'.[30]

---

26. Welty, *The Collected Stories*, p. 157.
27. Welty, *The Collected Stories*, p. 157.
28. Welty, *The Collected Stories*, p. 157.
29. Welty, *The Collected Stories*, p. 157.
30. Lacan, *Seminar III*, p. 33.

The chief point of intersection between the two states, however, may be located in the way both the delusional intuition and, a little counter-intuitively, first love jointly dispense with an object. Delusion, like the earliest phase of being in love, is traditionally regarded as a disturbance of the object relation (or, in the case of love, a sexual 'overvaluation' as Freud calls it, of the object). Lacan nevertheless admonishes repeatedly throughout Seminar III that it is primarily in reference to the *signifier* that delusion must best be understood. This Lacanian insight Welty implicitly confirms when she specifies how Joel fall in love with Burr's *gesture* (rather than simply with the man himself).[31] For both the paranoid subject and Welty's loving little deaf-mute, it is not an object but rather a signifier that classically becomes charged with an overwhelming meaning.

The curious aspect about this sudden infusion of meaning is the way, in both first love and psychotic delusion, the signifier ceases to conform to its usual activity of pointing towards another signifier in an interminable metonymy. Instead, in the delusional state, one seemingly randomly chosen signifier comes to point primarily to *itself*, to its own meaning-producing capacities. This generates a sort of discordance in language comparable, Lacan says, to that found in the neologism. About the psychotic's delusional speech in its intuitional phase Lacan writes, 'The meaning of these words that pull you up has the property of referring essentially to meaning as such. It's a meaning that essentially refers to nothing but itself, that remains irreducible'.[32] Hence the effect of this self-referential language is to suspend the infinite march of the chain of signifiers. In both delusion and first love, it is a question of an opening in language or, as Lacan puts it, of a 'hole, a fault, a point of rupture, in the structure of the external world'.[33]

We can take a moment now to quickly clear up a common mistake about psychosis. A frequent explanation for the 'hole' in the structure of the external world Lacan refers to is that it results

---

31. 'Delusion may be regarded as a disturbance of the object relation and therefore linked to a transference mechanism. But I wanted to show you that all its phenomena, and I even think I can say its dynamics, would be clarified in reference to the functions and structure of speech'. Lacan, *Seminar III*, p. 310. See also Sigmund Freud, 'Three Essays on the Theory of Sexuality', *The Standard Edition of the Complete Psychological Works of Sigmund Freud*, vol. VII (1901-1905), trans. James Strachey, London, Hogarth, 1953, pp. 130-243.
32. Lacan, *Seminar III*, p. 33.
33. Lacan, *Seminar III*, p. 45.

from the psychotic's 'foreclosure' of the paternal signifier which, as is well known, comprises the psychotic subject's psychic response to the lack represented by the phallus. By this logic, it is the paternal signifier that is consequently absent from the psychotic's world; the hole is left by the missing signifier which becomes subsequently patched over by the excesses of the psychotic delusion. But this is to read Lacan too quickly when he says in Seminar III that 'psychosis consists of a hole, a lack, at the level of the signifier'.[34] As we saw earlier, for Lacan it is not that the paternal signifier is entirely absent from the psychotic's world but rather that it has failed to function properly. What is lacking in the psychotic's universe is thus not the signifier per se.[35] As any clinical picture can show, the psychotic's discourse is nothing if not freighted with the gigantic weight of the signifier that imbues the psychotic subject's world with such immense and recondite meaning. The lack, in fact, lies *in* the signifier itself; the signifier is missing something that gives it its authority and transforms it into a Law. It is this missing something 'at the level of the signifier' that constitutes the famous 'hole' in the psychotic's universe. Instructively for us, Welty's tale demonstrates how a comparable 'hole' yawns in the structure of the world of every 'deaf-mute' subject prior to its historicization of the signifier.[36]

With this in mind, let us explore the young lover's elation in the first moments of his discovery that he is in love, an elation that again bears notable similarities to the psychotic delusion. Shortly after Burr's and Blennerhassett's first appearance in his room, Joel is requested to tack a notice to the saloon mirror announcing that 'the trial of Aaron Burr for treason would be held at Washington, capital of Mississippi Territory, on the campus of Jefferson College, where the crowds might be amply accommodated'.[37] In advance of the coming trial, the townsfolk hold a number of festivities for Burr. For Joel, of course, there is only one figure to watch, and from the lover's single-minded perspective, it seems that everyone

---

34. Lacan, *Seminar III*, p. 201.

35. Joel Dor has elaborated this point in *Structure and Perversions*, trans. Susan Fairfield, New York, Other Press, 2001, pp. 151-59. Again, for Dor it is a question of the paternal signifier acquiring the status of a law for the child by becoming 'associated with the signified of the mother's desire'. Dor, p. 153.

36. Roberto Harari calls this hole the 'psychotic kernel' present in every individual. Roberto Harari, *How James Joyce Made His Name: A Reading of the Final Lacan*, trans. Luke Thurston, New York, Other Press, 2002, p. 145.

37. Welty, *The Collected Stories*, p. 160.

else is watching Burr too: 'People now lighted their houses in entertainments [...] with Burr in the center of them always, dancing with the women, talking with the men'.[38] The object of the whole town's attention, Burr's presence starts to transform the townsfolk, casting a new lustrous radiance on people's faces who become in Joel's mind 'as gracious and as grand as Burr'.[39] As with earlier, Welty associates Burr with light, this time a phosphorescent lambency cast from the full winter moon. We hear how, 'Late at night the whole sky was lunar, like the surface of the moon brought as close as a cheek. The luminous ranges of all the clouds stretched one beyond the other in heavenly order. They seemed to be the streets where Joel was walking through the town'.[40]

One of the truths of first love that Welty appears to be driving at with these images is the 'treasonous' way the beloved effectively usurps the Name-of-the-Father in that first stage of falling in love. The beloved is discovered as an alternative 'light' source that competes with and, at least for a time, vanquishes the 'solar' realm of the paternal signifier. The effect is what, in the context of psychosis, one would call paranoia, and Welty makes it clear that there is an element of paranoia in the loving delusion as well. For Joel, all signs point inexorably back to the beloved, triggering everything with his meaning: 'the candlestick now stood on the table covered with the wonder of having been touched by unknown hands in his absence and see in his sleep'.[41] Joel's world suddenly blossoms into a text in which the name of the beloved is inscribed everywhere: coincidences take on deeper significance, certain places associated with him become holy sites, objects Burr has touched take on talismanic properties. Joel's entire world has become mysteriously riddled with signs, 'copied after the sky' and requiring decoding, charged as they have become with the lover's 'private omens'.[42]

Welty's choice of the historical figure of Aaron Burr suddenly starts to make sense for we are beginning to see how, like Burr, first love plots a secession from the Other's Law. In the rapture of their secret communication, the first lovers imagine it is they who dictate the laws founding their 'nation of two'. Welty signals something of this outlaw mentality characteristic of first

---

38. Welty, *The Collected Stories*, p. 161.
39. Welty, *The Collected Stories*, p. 161.
40. Welty, *The Collected Stories*, p. 161.
41. Welty, *The Collected Stories*, p. 158.
42. Welty, *The Collected Stories*, p. 158, p. 161.

love by dressing Burr in love's traditional image of a conqueror. 'Everything in the room was conquest', the narrator relates, 'all was a dream of delights and powers beyond its walls'.[43] Indeed, 'There was a kind of dominion promised in his gentlest glance'.[44] Burr is a conquistador who quite literally 'lights up' Joel's world, comprising the ubiquitous source—a new 'master' or 'primordial signifier'—from which all life and meaning springs.[45] With Burr's presence in the room, 'the fire would flame up and the reflections of the snowy world grew bright [...]. Lights shone in his eyes like travelers' fires seen far out on the river'.[46] Burr's invincible radiance is transmitted to anyone and anything that comes into contact with it: 'even the clumsy table seemed to change its substance and to become a part of a ceremony'.[47]

Once the beloved has been installed in the center of the lover's universe in this way, the center of gravity markedly shifts. Welty describes the way the people of Natchez, as if similarly drawn to Burr, 'followed and formed cotillion figures about the one who threatened or lured them, and their minuets skimmed across the nights like a pebble expertly skipped across water'.[48] People even unwittingly imitate his gesture, as if the sign of love inexorably spawns other signs, all of which refer back to the beloved: 'they pointed out the moon to him, to end the evening'.[49] The fullest reach of the lover's 'paranoia' however is reserved for the beloved himself, as a persecutory figure whose appearances are legion. Like the legendary hyper-alertness of the psychotic, the lover in this early phase sees (or thinks he sees) the beloved everywhere. The effect is reminiscent of how, once one becomes alert to something, the name of a book, for example, it suddenly seems to be on everyone's lips. Or again, how with the pain of a broken limb, it seems that everyone else suddenly has one too. One never realized how many broken bones there are in the world until one has one oneself. It is as if the 'hole' that first love punches in the symbolic is impossibly *larger* than its frame—there are *more* books, *more* broken bones, *more* loving signs within the subset of love than there are in the set that is the world.

---

43. Welty, *The Collected Stories*, p. 158.
44. Welty, *The Collected Stories*, p. 159.
45. Lacan, *Seminar III*, p. 151.
46. Welty, *The Collected Stories*, p. 159.
47. Welty, *The Collected Stories*, p. 159.
48. Welty, *The Collected Stories*, p. 161.
49. Welty, *The Collected Stories*, p. 161.

The result is that, in this elevated state of awareness that comprises the experience of first being in love, everyone else seems to be in love with the beloved too, his incandescence irradiating and transforming everyone he encounters. (Welty's special insight into this feature of first love might have been inspired by the historical tradition around Burr who, by various accounts, was a deeply loved figure in the popular imagination and whose celebrity, Jonathan Daniels observes, 'mounted with what seemed to be persecution of him').[50] Still, despite this adulation, the beloved keeps himself apart from these others, even as he draws them to him: 'But all the time, Joel believed, when he saw Burr go dancing by, that did not touch him at all. Joel knew his eyes saw nothing there and went always beyond the room, although usually the most beautiful woman there was somehow in his arms when the set was over'.[51] Since he is himself the magnetic pole towards which everyone and everything else is unwittingly pulled, the beloved can never fully become a part of love's adoring 'satellite' group.

Yet this is by no means to say that first love is a remotely joyous event, despite the lover's renowned elation. As Welty emphasizes when she sets her tale in 'the bitterest winter of all', these first stages of love are typically felt as a tremendous blight, introducing the lover to an anguish that is unlike anything he has ever felt, no matter how many times he has fallen in love before.[52] In recognition of this, the narrator speaks of Joel's 'suffering', the new and searing pain that comes from Burr's absence:

> Sometimes in the nights Joel would feel himself surely under their eyes, and think they must have come; but that would be a dream, and when he sat up on his bench he often saw nothing more than the dormant firelight stretched on the empty floor, and he would have a strange feeling of having been deserted and lost, not quite like anything he had ever felt in his life.[53]

It is only with Burr's appearance in the early dawn that Joel recovers, albeit with the self-effacing humility that the lover, in the early stages of an affair, is so famous for: 'When they were there, he sat restored, though they paid no more attention to him than they paid the presence of the firelight'.[54]

50. Jonathan Daniels, *The Devil's Backbone: The Story of the Natchez Trace*, Louisiana, Pelican, 1992, p. 164, cited in Trefzer, 'Tracing the Natchez Trace', p. 426.
51. Welty, *The Collected Stories*, p. 161.
52. Welty, *The Collected Stories*, p. 153.
53. Welty, *The Collected Stories*, p. 159-60.
54. Welty, *The Collected Stories*, p. 160.

## LOVE'S TRIAL

Neither the passional nor the psychotic delusion can last, however, and there finally comes a day when the subject is driven to act. After nearly a month of keeping silent vigil, of watching and waiting and reading and interpreting love's signs as best he can, Joel is one day 'driven to know everything'.[55] He sets out to see for himself the evidence of Burr's treachery, the flotilla of boats that is to form the core of the government's case against the renegade. We hear how Joel 'walked through the dark trodden snow all the way up the Trace to the Bayou Pierre'.[56] Once there, he sees what he thinks is the flotilla but all it is is a 'procession' of fallen trees that have broken in half beneath the weight of the snow:

> at first he thought he saw the fulfillment of all the rumor and promise—the flotilla coming around the bend, and he did not know whether he felt terror or pride. But then he saw that what covered the river over was a chain of great perfect trees floating down, lying on their sides in postures like slain giants and heroes of battle, black cedars and stone-white sycamores, magnolias with their heavy leaves shining as if they were in bloom, a long procession.[57]

At that point, Welty tells us, 'it was terror that he felt'. Joel continues on and, joining a group of townsfolk who have come out with the same intention, looks down with them from a snowy bluff to view the real flotilla. Instead of the expected galley, they see only nine small, unarmed flatboats, scarcely representing a threat to the Union: 'They seemed so small and delicate that he was shocked and distressed, and looked around at the faces of the others, who looked coolly back at him'.[58]

In this episode, Welty contrives an extraordinarily economical way of illustrating how, subjected to the ordinary calculus of the rational (that is, non-loving) mind, one's beloved will of course always come up short. The existential threat to the self the beloved represents—the threat to the One or ego, the 'union of states' that makes up a subject's identity—will never be matched by any phenomenal evidence to support it, at least when viewed from a

---

55. Welty, *The Collected Stories*, p. 161.
56. Welty, *The Collected Stories*, p. 161.
57. Welty, *The Collected Stories*, p. 162.
58. Welty, *The Collected Stories*, p. 162.

rational, bird's-eye perspective above. Joel's attempt to find out 'everything' must fail, if it is external proof he seeks for his love:

> Joel returned on the frozen path to the Inn, and stumbled into his room, and waited for Burr and Blennerhassett to come and talk together. His head ached.... All his walking about was no use. Where did people learn things? Where did they go to find them? How far.[59]

What Joel has failed to realize is that the threat the beloved represents to the self is perfectly real (and he is therefore quite justified in being terrified). However, this threat can only be accessed through imaginative means, as the 'slain giants and heroes of battle' Joel sees in the majestic procession of tree trunks. One could say that these fallen trees are the true 'flotilla' of love's plot of secession. Inaccessible to empirical knowledge, love's treasonous act is thus all the more terrifying for that reason and this makes Joel simultaneously proud and afraid of Burr. Although Joel went out to discover 'everything', all he encounters is the impossibility of matching objective data with an emotional fact. The beloved's true worthiness can never be proved, he or she will always fail any such test or trial if one attempts to put one's love into rational terms. The true trial, devised by the 'litigious' tendency that Lacan singles out as one of the chief characteristics of a 'passional psychosis', along with its milder sister, first love, must be sought elsewhere.[60]

On the final night before the trial, Burr and Blennerhassett return to Joel's room to continue their secret talks. Joel already has a profound sense that such talk can have no end. By the second night, the narrator told us previously, Joel could see 'that the secret was endlessly complex, for in two nights it was apparent that it could never all be told. All that they said never finished their conversation. They would always have to meet again'.[61] Nevertheless, Burr's and Blennerhassett's talk—reminiscent of nothing so much as the talk of first lovers whose conversation seems to inhabit an infinity because there is always *one more* thing to say—comes up against a definite limit. Time which, along with other natural (and narrative) laws appeared suspended in the lovers' new 'state', finally triumphs over the lovers' mutinous discourse. The lovers are at risk of being driven apart. It is at this point in the story that a new

---

59. Welty, *The Collected Stories*, p. 163.
60. See Lacan, *Seminar III*, p. 22.
61. Welty, *The Collected Stories*, p. 158.

entity is unexpectedly introduced into the group of conspirators, Blennerhassett's wife who, with a fiddle in her hand, had 'come to fetch [her husband] home'.[62] Mrs. Blennerhassett plays for them:

> Joel gazed at the girl, not much older than himself. She leaned her cheek against the fiddle. He had never examined a fiddle at all, and when she began to play it she frightened and dismayed him by her almost insect-like motions, the pensive antennae of her arms, her mask of a countenance. [...] The songs she played seemed to him to have no beginnings and no endings, but to be about many hills and valleys, and chains of lakes. She, like the men, knew of a place.... All of them spoke of a country. [...] There was no compassion in what this woman was doing, he knew that—there was only a frightening thing, a stern allurement. Try as he might, he could not comprehend it, though it was so calculated. He had instead a sensation of pain, the ends of his fingers were stinging. At first he did not realize that he had heard the sounds of her song, the only thing he had ever heard. Then all at once as she held the lifted bow still for a moment he gasped for breath at the interruption, and he did not care to learn her purpose or to wonder any longer, but bent his head and listened for the note that she would fling down upon them. And it was so gentle then, it touched him with surprise; it made him think of animals sleeping on their cushioned paws.[63]

As others have noted, this is without any doubt a transformational moment for Joel. John Warner is mostly right to regard it in his essay, 'Eudora Welty: The Artist in "First Love"', as evidence of a 'visionary' imaginary power that is capable, like love, of transcending time and the trauma that is separation and death. Its absorbing effect, he concludes, is to continue the de-alienating process that Joel's love for Burr has begun, allowing the boy to begin to come to terms with his occulted past.[64] Drawing an analogy between Mrs Blennerhassett and Keats's 'Belle Dame Sans Merci', Warner

---

62. Welty, *The Collected Stories*, p. 163.
63. Welty, *The Collected Stories*, p. 163-4.
64. In his discussion of this moment in 'First Love', John Warner suggests that Blennerhassett's wife's music embodies the visionary power of imagination, writing that, 'Her songs suggest the power of dream to lift men above mere historical necessity', Welty, *The Collected Stories*, p.82. While Joel is sympathetic to such visionary power, Warner claims, its ultimate function is to carry him not to a world beyond reality but back to his past, thus furthering the young orphan's psychic process of coming to terms with his traumatic history that the critic regards as the principal theme of 'First Love'.

proposes that the girl's melodies 'suggest the power of dream to lift men above mere historical necessity'.[65] For now, through the agency of the music, Joel finds himself jubilantly transported to an early childhood memory of his mother pointing at a mimosa tree in full bloom:

> It was in the little back field at his home in Virginia and his mother was leading him by the hand. Fragile, delicate, cloud-like it rose on its pale trunk and spread its long level arms. His mother pointed to it. Among the trembling leaves the feathery puffs of sweet bloom filled the tree like thousands of paradisical birds all alighted at an instant. He had known then the story of the Princess Labam, for his mother had told it to him, how she was so radiant that she sat on the roof-top at night and lighted the city. It seemed to be the mimosa tree that lighted the garden, for its brightness and fragrance overlaid all the rest. Out of its graciousness this tree suffered their presence and shed its splendor upon him and his mother. His mother pointed again, and its scent swayed like the Asiatic princess moving up and down the pink steps of its branches. Then the vision was gone.[66]

The question is how did this 'power of dream' become available to Joel? The answer, I believe, must be sought in Joel's curious sensation of pain during Mrs. Blennerhassett's performance: 'the ends of his fingers were stinging'.[67] This sensation Joel interprets as 'hearing': 'At first he did not realize that he had heard the sounds of her song, the only thing he had ever heard'.[68] The only way I can make sense of this peculiar statement is to regard it as evidence that something has altered in Joel's relation to the signifier. We have seen how, up till this point, the signifying cut was only partially etched into Joel's psyche for the simple reason that, as a deaf-mute, he was unable to receive—'hear'—his own message back from the Other. For although the castrating cut makes him theoretically aware that sound exists, this aural knowledge was unable to penetrate him to the extent of being 'lived' by him, as Lacan puts it in the *Psychoses* seminar. In contrast, Welty suggests that here the signifier has now come alive for him in some indeterminate manner, producing a painful sensation in his *signifying organ* (his hands).

---

65. Warner, 'Eudora Welty: The Artist in "First Love"', p. 83.
66. Welty, *The Collected Stories*, p. 163-4.
67. Welty, *The Collected Stories*, p. 164.
68. Welty, *The Collected Stories*, p. 164.

If I am right, the implication of this sensation of pain that suffuses Joel's visionary ordeal is that the 'hole at the level of the signifier' has finally succeeded in becoming rounded out into positive form, as forbidden and permanently off-limits to the subject as the Princess Labam of the Indian fairy-tale is to the Prince. This newly phenomenalized 'hole' that constitutes the imaginary fantasy (as we might as well now call Joel's visionary experience) bears the implicit promise that should the subject (like the fairy-tale prince in the mother's story) successfully overcome a series of impossible tasks (with the assistance perhaps of a few magical animals), the enthralling object of desire may eventually be won. The 'hole' in the signifier that previously had been flooded with first love's 'delusion' has become replaced by a cavalcade of phantasmagorical beings, headed by that famous and most fantastical creature of all, the elusive object $a$.

The question is, what could have caused this mysterious ontological conversion? One's first impulse is to say it resulted from the intrusion of the woman into what had until then been a thoroughly masculine universe—the appearance of Warner's 'Belle Dame Sans Merci' whose siren song leads the young boy back to the world of the mother and maternal love. The implication is that the feminine lack fills the 'hole' in the signifier with a positive object in the representational 'staging' Lacan calls the fantasy. This reading is correct—up to a point. The introduction of the feminine, or discovery of an Other sex, is indeed a crucial element in the sequence or logical 'history' of the subject's castration. Insofar as it gives a Real body to the paternal cut, the feminine lack crystallizes the threat of castration into a Law. However, it must be stated clearly that this solidification of threat into adamantine Law does not occur through the discovered presence of any actual woman. Welty's description of Mrs Blennerhassett as a woman who is psychically present to the boy only as another *masculine* figure confirms this, as it also does, incidentally, the Lacanian dictum that psychosis—and, I am proposing, the loving delusion—is a 'homosexual' discourse (that is, composed only of One sex[69]):

> There in the doorway with a fiddle in her hand stood Blennerhassett's wife, wearing breeches, come to fetch him home. The fiddle she had simply picked up in the Inn parlor as she came through, and Joel did not think she bothered now to speak at all. But she waited there before the fire, still a child

---

69. See Lacan, *Seminar III*, esp. pp. 193, 204.

and so clearly related to her husband that their sudden movements at the encounter were alike and made at the same time. They stood looking at each other there in the firelight like creatures balancing together on a raft, and then she lifted the bow and began to play.⁷⁰

If it is not the entry of the biologically female sex that causes the boy's emergence from the immobile loving delusion into the temporal *dispositif* that is the desiring fantasy, what then? My speculation is that Mrs Blennerhassett's music has given Joel access to some form of hitherto unexperienced enjoyment, albeit experienced as 'pain', that is specific to the signifying organ. Signification has become *eroticized* for him in some way through the music, according Joel a new kind of receptivity to his own message as it is returned back to him from the Other. Unlike for hearing people, this return of one's own message of desire is effected not in the form of the voice for the boy, but in the hands through which Joel communicates. We thus only go part-way if we say that the woman (as the conventional object of masculine desire) introduces the object *a* into Joel's psychic structure. This takes the imaginary fantasy, with its promise of the existence of the sexual relation, merely at its word. As before, one must look rather to Joel's own 'feminization' for the deeper cause of this change. By this I mean a new willingness to assume a 'feminine position' in relation to the signifier and identify with the lack that castration introduced into his world.⁷¹ Such a readiness or, even better, 'choice' to assume a 'feminine' position—the position of lack—towards the signifier becomes possible for the first time as a result of this new experience of *jouissance*, as a *jouissance* contained in the signifier.

Could we not say, then, that it is this susceptibility to submit to the signifier from a 'feminine position' (that is, a position identified with lack) that is the true 'trial' the first lover must undergo? The subject's feminization represents a further psychic 'secession', this time from the 'psychosis' induced by the original castrating cut.

---

70. Welty, *The Collected Stories*, p. 163.

71. Notably, for Schreber, too, the moment he starts to imagine he is transforming into a woman marks the beginning of his attempt at a 'cure' in response to 'God's' withdrawal of direct communications from him in the fundamental language. See Lacan's discussion of this moment in *Seminar III*, pp. 85-6. Both neurotics and psychotics, it would seem, are destined to face the same subjective trial, but where the psychotic responds at the level of the Real (his or her Real body), the neurotic's 'feminization' occurs in the symbolic register, in his or her psychic identification with the 'hole' in the signifier.

Tellingly, this binds Joel for the first time with a *community* rather than the previous psychotic 'cluster' of Imaginary figures: 'For a moment his love went like sound into a myriad life and was divided among all the people in his room. [...] There was one thing that shone in all their faces and that was how far they were from home, how far from everywhere that they knew'.[72] To the extent that we are speaking beings, each one of us is equally 'orphaned' by the signifier, as Joel discovers, covering his face to hide his 'pity' from the others at this new-found knowledge. However, as he also discovers, it is this same mutual dispossession that begets a community. Our mutually shared exile from the maternal body is the origin of our ability to form relations with others beyond the zero-sum game of mimetic rivalry that defines the Imaginary 'clustering'.

We can say that, in the final analysis, the subject's willingness to be 'pacified', as Lacan put it earlier, by some form of enjoyment specific to the signifier, complements and completes the castrating act. Welty, uniquely in 'First Love', demonstrates how the priapic cut not only slices downwards to sever the subject from the maternal dyad. As it raises itself back up, the phallus reciprocally carves an object *a* out of the newly created subject's world. Famously falling out of the neurotic subject's symbolic alphabet, the *a* thus lends itself to a formalization through which the subject creatively maps 'every possible relation' (as Lacan instructs us to read the lozenge in his formula for fantasy $ ◊ a) to the lost object in the fantasy. In the event of the absence of this *a*—a lack of this lack—we witness only the deadening effect Lacan describes in his third seminar: with the inevitable bursting of the psychotic delusion, the psychotic is left not with the endless narrative possibilities presented by desire's formalization but with an empty '*formula*' which, being the opposite pole of the delusional intuition, Lacan explains, can only be autistically 'repeated, reiterated, drummed in with a stereotypical insistence'.[73]

By way of conclusion, let us return to the stinging sensation Joel experienced during Mrs Blennerhassett's impromptu performance. Curiously, a similar tingling feeling returns in the final episode of the story when Joel, following the disguised and fleeing Burr, secretly witnesses the older man paying farewell to the girl with whom he had 'often danced with under the rings of tapers'.[74]

---

72. Welty, *The Collected Stories*, p. 164.
73. Lacan, *Seminar III*, p. 33.
74. Welty, *The Collected Stories*, p. 167.

The narrator tells how Joel experiences an odd 'pain like a sting' when the girl embraces Burr.[75] The repetition of this word, this time in the clear context of sexual jealousy, may give us a clue to its previous occurrence. If my reading has been correct, although this stinging sensation is felt and understood as 'pain', this is only because Joel presumably does not have a proper word for it, although this is not because he is mute and cannot speak. The sensation Joel feels in fact is most likely *pudeur*, a word that has no exact equivalent in English, describing a certain type of *erotic* shame— a red-hot, burning mortification that arises only in the context of desire. This feeling of shame, of *pudeur*, I take as proof that the bar of castration has descended once more. The first lovers have rejoined the realm of the paternal signifier and its Law. But different from its previous instantiation, the Law this time is a singular Law addressed uniquely to the Joel. It bears his own message back to him in a way he is now able to 'hear'. Joel's sensation of shame is our indication that he has heard and recognized his inverted message of desire for, inescapably accompanying such recognition, is always an acute burning of one's ears that testifies to a subject's having been overtaken by the uncanny alterity of its own voice or, in Joel's case, his signing hands. Such burning or tingling is the affective giveaway that the subject has become interpellated by the Law, which addresses him now in his utmost singularity, in his new capacity as a desiring (that is, fully castrated) being.

The result is that the Law has been subjectivized by the subject. Or, in Lacan's phrase, it has been 'historicized' by its momentary suspension in the temporary madness we call first love. We can thus with justification assert that castration literally *hinges* on first love—the castrating axe must be temporarily lifted if only so as to descend again, the second time as a fully-fledged subjective Law. It is this 'double time' of castration that is expressed in the Möbius strip that Lacan uses to theorize the relation of the subject, Other and *a* in the dialectic of demand and desire. The strip must be cut not once but *twice* down the middle in order to generate the looping intertwined S-shapes of the subject/Other and the extra little o-shape that, as a remainder, dangles off one of the loops of the 8.[76]

---

75. Welty, *The Collected Stories*, p. 167.
76. Lacan frequently comes back to the Möbius strip and other topological figures throughout his writings. See, for example, the discussion in *Seminar XIII, The Object of Psychoanalysis* (1965-1966), lesson of 15.12.65. He explains how 'the

One would be wrong, however, to imagine that the success of the Law's second, consolidating cut derives from the lovers giving up their crazy 'dream' in a gesture of a new 'realism' and voluntarily acceding fully to the paternal function. In Welty's tale, following the collapse of their loving delusion, the lovers do not voluntarily return to the community, shame-faced and ready to submit to its judgment. On the contrary, the lover and beloved continue to flee, Burr on horseback and Joel, far behind, on foot. Pursuing Burr, Joel walks on 'in the frozen path into the wilderness, on and on. He did not see how he could ever go back and still be the boot-boy at the Inn'.[77] Yet all the same, the Law catches up with him: 'He did not know how far he had gone on the Liberty Road when the posse came riding up behind and passed him. He walked on'.[78] With her usual efficiency, Welty describes here something of the inexorable way the symbolic reassimilates the lawless space that the loving delusion has opened up. If first love tears a hole in the Law, the Law, sliding like quicksilver, will always fill it in. However, through this repeated cycle of escape and arrest, love's westward expansion serves to populate the Law with new symbolic forms: the songs and poems, the loving names lovers gift one another in the early stages of love. The Law will always overtake the lovers and haul them back into its realm for the reason that, unlike psychotics, lovers are sexed subjects, bound to the community through a *pudeur* that betrays the presence of the *a*.

We are thus in a position to clarify what Miller means when he says shame is the 'primary affect' in the relation to the Other. This is not the shame that comes from the realization that others have witnessed your fear (of death)—the shame that formed the temporary community of the 'little cluster' on their way on to Natchez. The temporary nature of that social grouping in fact reveals this form of shame's inutility as an effective binding agent for a group, requiring as it does a scapegoat (Joel) who is entrusted with the secret of one's fear. From a psychoanalytic perspective, a social dynamic founded in this way cannot be anything but a kind

---

[castrating] cut itself has the structure of the surface called Möbius strip. Here you see it pictured by a double stroke of the scissors that you can also do, in which you would effectively cut the total figure of the projective plane, or of the cross-cap as I called it, in two parts: one Möbius strip on the one hand, here it is supposed to be cut, all on its own, and on the other hand a remainder which is what plays the same function of hole in its primitive shape'.

77. Welty, *The Collected Stories*, p. 168.
78. Welty, *The Collected Stories*, p. 168.

of social 'psychosis' that must (often violently) 'foreclose' one element in order to keep the consistency of the Imaginary social body intact. The shame named by the French word *pudeur*, on the other hand, represents not a defensive shunning of the knowledge one wants at all costs to keep secret but is rather, as Joan Copjec has beautifully put it, a 'flight into being'.[79] Both forms of shame are veils for a certain *jouissance*, but where the first projects our secret *jouissance* onto an other (who must then be policed and, if necessary jailed or killed in the group version of the psychotic's life-or-death struggle with a small other), in the second, the subject itself embodies—*lives*—the secret *jouissance* of its being as its unconscious desiring 'history', albeit not as anything he or she can ever know or reveal to others. The result, as Copjec says, is that 'instead of inhibiting us, this opacity now gives us that distance from ourselves and our world that allows us creatively to alter both; it gives us, in other words, a privacy, an interiority unbreachable even by ourselves'.[80]

As a result, although, as Welty indicates, the symbolic Law will always hunt down and overtake first lovers, it does not have an overarching reach. In fact, if love does one thing, as Welty reminds us, it recalls us to those 'places of the heart' for which there are no names, places forged in the privacy of that specifically *sexual* shame, *pudeur*. These dark forgotten spaces—glimpsed in the first moments of an affair as love temporarily lifts castration's catastrophic stroke, and occupied by what is most lost, silent and orphaned within us—will always be sought out by first lovers on the run from the law. Following in their wake as it hunts them down, the symbolic Law can be said to extend its reach—or, perhaps better, to acquire new depth, for these places are not solely the frontiers of westward expansion, the country of new conquests of which Blennerhassett's wife's music sang so rhapsodically. They are just as much to be found in what is closest and most familiar to us, in the 'dark little room [...] on the ground floor behind the saloon' of the self's temporary lodgings.[81] Since it is in these

---

79. Joan Copjec, 'May '68: The Emotional Month', in Slavoj Zizek ed., *Lacan: the Silent Partners*, London, Verso, 2006, pp. 90-114, p. 111. In an unpublished talk delivered in Paris, June 19-20, 1999, Dominiek Hoens explained the difference between the French words for shame, *honte* and *pudeur*. *Honte*, he says, is linked to a secret knowledge, while *pudeur* emerges at the moment the phallus is unveiled.

80. Copjec, 'May '68: The Emotional Month', p. 111.

81. Welty, *The Collected Stories*, p. 155.

unnamed places that first love continues to live 'behind' the public Law, one can never definitively say that anything 'happened' in those early days of love: 'Whatever happened, it happened in extraordinary times, in a season of dreams'.[82] For something to 'happen' there must be 'names for the places of the heart and the times for its shadowy and tragic events'.[83] It is from lack of such names, Welty can justifiably claim, that *'nothing had been told'*.[84]

---

82. Welty, *The Collected Stories*, p. 153.
83. Welty, *The Collected Stories*, p. 165.
84. Welty, *The Collected Stories*, p. 165 (my emphasis).

## 4. I MARY YOU: JOHN CLARE

'I look upon myself as a widow or bachelor I dont know which'
—John Clare: *Selected Letters*

'And how the One of Time, of Space the Three, Might in the Chain of Symbols girdled be'
—Sir William Rowan Hamilton

As we now turn to John Clare, the nineteenth-century 'peasant poet' from Helpston, England, we will be struck by just how securely in possession, this writer is, of a name for the event making up the loving encounter. Clare leaves us in no doubt that this event's name is 'Mary', named after Mary Joyce, the local girl the poet knew in his childhood who became immortalized in his poetry as Clare's 'first love' and eternal muse. The fundamental problem we will see Clare confronting here is not so much the question broached earlier concerning the origin of the resources of nomination. Clare's 'trouble' is not with the signifier, as it was for Beckett, Turgenev and Welty in different ways, but with what Badiou, to return to the philosopher for a moment, designates 'fidelity'. Can Clare (a self-confessedly uxorious man) remain faithful to the event whose name is 'Mary'? In this chapter, I propose to examine the two poems of Clare's that have been handed editorially down to us with the titles 'First Love'.[1] The fact that there

---

1. John Clare, 'First Love', in *John Clare: Major Works*, Eric Robinson, David Powell and Tom Paulin (eds.), Oxford, Oxford University Press, 2004, pp. 398-99 and 'First Love', in *Selected Poems of John Clare*, James Reeves (ed.), London, Heinemann, 1968, pp. 103-04. In Robinson and Summerfield's *The Later Poems of John Clare*, this second poem, (from MS. 6, p. 13 and MS. 57) is titled simply 'Song' and possesses an additional 18 lines to the Reeves edition. *The Later*

are two poems of first love should alert the reader to my immediate concerns. What is the relation between the uncounted One of love, spoken of seemingly infinitely in the amatory literary tradition, and the Two, which inaugurates the 'time' of the event in the Badiouian setup?

To set the scene for Clare's loving 'investigations', it helps to have Badiou's somewhat idiosyncratic conception of the Two, as developed in his papers on love, more firmly in mind. To begin with, unlike with art (and poetry), in his famous short essay, 'What is Love?' Badiou evidently does not have the same difficulty in identifying the loving encounter as an event in the strictest sense of the term.[2] In that essay, Badiou clearly states how love is to be understood as the 'ad-vent' [*l'avènement*] of the Two, and that this 'to-come' [*ad-venue*] that is the supposition of the Two is 'originally evental'.[3] Like all events, the event of love 'occurs only in its disappearance', and again like all other forms of events, the loving event is classically 'fixed' by a name. Notably for Badiou, however, this name is not a proper name such as 'Mary', but a *declaration*. The event-encounter, he writes, 'is fixed only by a nomination, and this nomination is a declaration, the declaration of love'.[4]

In keeping with Badiou's descriptions of events emerging under the other three truth 'conditions' (science, art and politics), the name that makes up love's world-shattering declaration—'I love you'—convokes the void. Given the fact that it is drawn from the void, this declaration/name solicits and 'puts into circulation' something uncountable and unaccountable, 'an unpresented element of the presented one of the site'.[5] In 'What is Love?' Badiou calls this unpresented element 'a vocable' that materializes from 'the null interval that disjoins man and woman'.[6] Yet rather than uniting and forming a couple of 'man' and 'woman' in the declaration of love, this 'vocable' serves to keep the two positions disjunct.

Badiou goes on to specify how the Two of which love is the 'operator' is not a two that derives from any count or count-as One.

---

*Poems of John Clare*, Eric Robinson and Geoffrey Summerfield (eds.), Manchester, Manchester University Press, 1964, pp. 51-52.

2. Alain Badiou, 'What is Love?', trans. Justin Clemens, *Umbr(a)*, no. 1: Badiou, 1996, pp. 37-53.

3. Badiou, 'What is Love?', pp. 44-5.

4. Badiou, 'What is Love?', p. 45.

5. Alain Badiou, *Being and Event*, trans. Oliver Feltham, London, Continuum, 2005, p. 204.

6. Badiou, 'What is Love?', p. 45.

The Two of love, Badiou claims, is 'subtracted from all calculation'.[7] It is, as he puts it in the essay 'The Scene of Two', a two counted in an immanent way, an 'originary Two', which he also, elsewhere, calls an 'interval of suspense'.[8] To be faithful to love's event is to organize, within the situation, what Badiou calls 'a new legitimacy of inclusions' founded on 'the supernumerary point which is the name of the event'.[9] Such fidelity, the work through which a 'counter-state' is constructed that diagonally crosses existing knowledge, conducts 'enquiries' or 'investigations' that have, as Badiou explains, only one aim: to determine whether or not any given multiple 'is within the field of effects entailed by the introduction into circulation of a supernumerary name'.[10] The militant loving subject's question toward any phenomenon it encounters must always be, 'this (thing, object, place, poem, film, love-song, late-blooming flower, but also riot in Myanmar, bowl of green tea, roar of airplane traffic over Brussels...), is it or is it not connected to the name of the event?'

I realize the way I am describing it risks implying that the work of fidelity represents merely the first lover's single-minded approach to the world we explored in the previous chapter. For Joel Mayes, all signs led paranoiacally back to the beloved—or at least, putting it back into Badiou's conceptualization, to the declaration of love that circulated as a new One or master signifier in the situation, comprising the founding law of a new structuration of a presented multiplicity. To the uncautious eye, fidelity might imply an imperative to remain at all costs in what I was calling the 'proto-psychotic' phase that makes up the first few days, weeks or months of 'first' falling in love. But to believe this would be to forget Badiou's principal admonishment: to be faithful to the event, the Two may neither be counted-as-One, nor may it ever serve as the basis for what Badiou theorizes as the 'second' count, that is, the meta-counting operation that forms (or 'counts') the count-as-One *into a One* that is capable of installing itself as the bedrock of a new situation in the form of that situation's founding Law. Insofar as it separates out what is connected or not connected to the event, fidelity simultaneously ensures the maintenance of a

---

7. Badiou, 'What is Love?', p. 44.

8. Badiou, Alain, 'The Scene of Two', trans. Barbara P. Fulks, *Lacanian Ink*, no. 21, 2003, pp. 42-55 <http://www.lacan.com/frameXXI3.htm> [accessed 20 February, 2008]. See also Badiou, *Being and Event*, p. 207.

9. Badiou, *Being and Event*, p. 327.

10. Badiou, *Being and Event*, p. 238, p. 330.

*distance* between the void and its name (that is, the loving declaration). The nominal intervention, which Badiou defines as 'any procedure by which a multiple is recognized as an event' is thus 'assigned to a double border effect'.[11] As it straddles 'the border of the void' and the 'border of the name', the intervention guarantees what Badiou insists is the 'undecidability' of the event's belonging to a situation.[12] He explains, 'if the event does not belong to the situation, then, given that the terms of its event-site are not presented, nothing will have taken place; if it does belong, then it will interpose itself between itself and the void, and thus be determined as ultra-one'.[13]

It is important to note that Badiou's crucial point here is not simply that naming, and the decision to conduct an operation of fidelity toward that name, will always in a sense be extra to a situation—'undecidable' because it is based on no ground or evidence that could be supplied by the situation itself. The Two Badiou has in mind is not an either/or, 'Two' possible situational outcomes to the question of whether or not an event has occurred. Such a conception of twoness he designates an 'imaginary Two'.[14] In contrast, Badiou's point is rather more subtle: the Two or, better, 'Twoness' arises as a certain *doubling of the evental name itself* insofar as this name 'interposes itself between itself and the void'.[15] This is more than even simply saying the name is perpetually Janus-faced, that is, turned on the one hand toward the situation of which it is a part (whose paradox lies in how, if the event truly did 'belong to the situation', it will not have been a genuine event), while being simultaneously turned toward the void. In Badiou's formulation, by contrast, the name interposes itself not between the void and the situation but, curiously, between the void that it names and *the name itself.*

No writer I am aware of is more sensitive to the mental gymnastics Badiou's notion of the Two demands than the English poet John Clare. Sometimes called *the* poet of first love, Clare's poetry displays a sophisticated awareness of the snares lying in wait for what Badiou calls 'speculative leftism', that is, for 'any thought of being which bases itself upon the theme of an absolute commencement'.[16] What will be of interest here is not simply how

11. Badiou, *Being and Event*, p. 207.
12. Badiou, *Being and Event*, p. 207.
13. Badiou, *Being and Event*, p. 201.
14. Badiou, *Being and Event*, p. 210.
15. Badiou, *Being and Event*, p. 201.
16. Badiou, *Being and Event*, p. 210.

Clare comes to 'solve' the problem of commencement—of where to begin to count from. My justification for including Clare's poems of 'First Love' in this investigation is the way he focuses our attention on a non-trivial fact that Badiou mentions only in passing but which contains vital ramifications for his philosophy, namely, that fidelity to an event also necessitates a certain betrayal of it. Clare is acutely and painfully aware of how it is only by giving in to what Badiou admits is always a 'necessary tendency' to betray the event, that the lover can remain faithful to it.[17] In what follows, I would like to explore this line of thought that makes only a brief appearance in Badiou's account of fidelity in *Being and Event*.

First a few words about John Clare himself who, as one of the 'forgotten' Romantic poets, is not as generally well known as his poetry deserves. Born in 1793 into the agricultural laboring class in Helpston, England, Clare came to public notice with the appearance of his first volume, *Poems Descriptive of Rural Life and Scenery*, published by John Taylor in 1820. The title page described him as a 'Northamptonshire Peasant', correcting, in what was to be the beginning of a lifelong struggle for editorial and orthographical control, Clare's original self-description as a 'Northamptonshire Pheasant'. In part as a result of the contemporary vogue for 'rustic' poetry, the book met with phenomenal literary and commercial success, selling over 3000 copies in the first year and going into four editions by the following year.[18] *Poems Descriptive* was quickly followed by a second volume, *The Village Minstrel and Other Poems* (1821), but its sales were hugely disappointing to Clare. Although the poet's literary reputation continued to grow, decreasing financial returns meant Clare could no longer hope his poetry would be the means for extricating himself and his family from their acute poverty. Yet despite this, he continued composing in moments snatched from his various laboring and gardening jobs—at least if we are to believe Taylor's 'Romantic' presentation of the 'peasant poet' in the introduction to *Poems Descriptive*—and seven years after his first publication he released, once again through Taylor, *The Shepherd's Calendar: with Village Stories and Other Poems*. In 1835, the last volume published during Clare's lifetime appeared, *The Rural Muse*. During this period Clare also made the acquaintance

---

17. Badiou, *Being and Event*, p. 238.
18. Hugh Haughton and Adam Phillips, 'Introduction: Relocating John Clare', in *John Clare in Context*, Hugh Haughton, Adam Phillips and Geoffrey Summerfield (eds.), Cambridge, Cambridge University Press, 1994, pp. 1-27, p. 4.

of numerous literary figures in several visits to London, including Keats, Lamb, Hazlitt, De Quincey, Reynolds and Cary.

The extent of Clare's disappointment in his literary ambitions and his increasingly desperate struggles to support himself and his family are well documented in his letters and autobiographical writings. Four years after marrying his wife Martha ('Patty') Turner in 1820, Clare descended into a cycle of ill-health and despair such that by 1830 he was explaining to Taylor how,

> I can scarcely manage even now to muster courage sufficient to feel myself able to [make out] write a letter but you will excuse all—I have been bled blistered & cupped and have now a seaton in my neck and tho much better I have many fears as to recovery but I keep my mind as quiet as I can & and am able to read a Newspaper.[19]

In a desperate letter written somewhere between 1834-1835, Clare describes his symptoms to his London physician, George Darling:

> sound affects me very much & things evil as well [as] good thoughts are continually rising in my mind I cannot sleep for I am asleep as it were with my eyes open & feel chills come over me & a sort of nightmare awake & I got no rest last night [...] I cannot keep my mind right as it were for I wish to read and cannot—there is a sort of numbing through my private parts with I cannot describe & when I was so indisposed last winter I felt as if I had circulation in the blood & at times as if it went round me & and at other time such a sinking as if I was going to sink through the bed.[20]

A series of nights such as these inevitably took a toll on Clare's mental state, and by 1837 Clare's London friends felt they must take matters into their own hands. 'Having set him up as a peasant poet, they would save him as a mad genius', Roy Porter explains, describing how Clare was taken into Matthew Allen's care at High Beech Asylum.[21] Although Allen's was by many accounts a comparatively benign institution by nineteenth-century standards, run along the new principles of 'moral therapy' that emphasized kindness and compassion along with a fair degree of freedom of movement, Clare could not help but experience his confinement at High Beech as an intolerable breach of his liberty. In a letter to

---

19. John Clare, *John Clare: Selected Letters*, Mark Storey (ed.), Oxford, Oxford University Press, 1990, p. 164 (Storey's square brackets).
20. Clare, *Selected Letters*, pp. 195-96.
21. Haughton and Phillips, 'Introduction: Relocating John Clare', p. 261.

his wife Patty from March, 1841, Clare declares indignantly that he would rather 'Be Packed In A Slave Ship For Affrica'.[22] A few months later, he complains to Eliza Philips, 'Having been cooped up in this Hell of a Madhouse till I seem to be disowned by my friends and even forgot by my enemies for there is none to accept my challanges which I have from time to time given to the public I am almost mad in waiting for a better place and better company and all to no purpose'.[23]

It was in his four years at High Beech that Clare began to amass a number of convictions that he would carry with him throughout the rest of his life.[24] One of these was his belief he had been a 'prize fighter', and another, most famously, that he was Lord George Gordon Byron (even rewriting two of the older poet's best known poems, 'Child Harold' [sic] and a hilariously scabrous version of 'Don Juan'). In addition, Clare became convinced that he had two wives: his actual, legal wife 'Patty', and his childhood sweetheart and 'first love' Mary Joyce. In fact, it was for this supposed bigamy that Clare believed he had been imprisoned in Matthew Allen's 'English Bastile', writing to Mary Joyce in 1841 that 'No one knows how sick I am of this confinement possessing two wives that ought to be my own & cannot see either'.[25] In another letter from the same year, he writes to both Mary and Patty: 'My dear wife Mary, I might have said my first wife first love & first everything—but I shall never forget my second wife & second love for I loved her once as dearly as yourself & and almost do so now so I determined to keep you both for ever'.[26] Clare's celebrated escape from High Beech, recounted in the heart-rending text 'The Journey from Essex', was intended to reunite him with his Mary and upon being told that she had died six years ago, Clare records his reaction: 'I took no notice of the blarney having seen her myself about a twelvemonth ago alive & well & young as ever', concluding that 'so here I am homeless at home & half gratified to feel I can be happy anywhere'.[27]

---

22. Clare, *Selected Letters*, p. 200.

23. Clare, *Selected Letters*, p. 202.

24. See Porter's thoughtful consideration of whether or not Clare really 'believed' in these fictional identities. 'John Clare and the Asylum' in *John Clare in Context*, Cambridge, Cambridge University Press, 1994, pp. 1-27, p. 4.

25. Haughton and Phillips, 'Introduction: Relocating John Clare', p. 8.

26. Cited in Mark Storey, *The Poetry of John Clare: A Critical Introduction*, London, Macmillan, 1974, p. 153.

27. John Clare, *The Prose of John Clare*, J. W. Tibble and Anne Tibble (eds.)

It is to Mary that the vast majority of Clare's most poignant expressions of love, joy, and loss in the asylum poems, in 'Child Harold' in particular, are directed. In the *Sketches in the Life of John Clare Written By Himself* (1821), Clare's autobiography written at the ripe old age of twenty-eight, Clare relates how Mary's family (and in time Mary herself) discouraged John's advances, and it is strange in retrospect how remarkably blithe Clare sounds about the whole affair in these early autobiographical writings, especially given the way the idea of Mary would come to haunt him throughout his later life and poetry. In his Sketches, Clare describes himself as,

> a lover very early in life my first attachment being a schoolboy affection was for Mary who cost me more ballads than sighs & was beloved with a romantic or Platonic sort of feeling if I could but haze on her face or fancy a smile on her countenance it was sufficient I went away satisfied.[28]

However, this idyll lasted only until Mary 'grew to womanhood' and, confronted with parental objections and Mary's own 'pretentions to something', Clare dispassionately explains how his 'passion coold with my reason & contented itself with another', although not without the proviso that '[I] felt a hopeful tenderness that I might one day renew the acquaintance & disclose the smotherd passion she was a beautiful girl & and as the dream never awoke into reality her beauty was always fresh in my memory'.[29] Two paragraphs later we find Clare claiming that 'my first love really was with a girl of Ashton whose name was Elizabeth Newbon She was no beauty but I fancyd she was everything'.[30]

By the 1840s, however, and with Clare's growing distress at his incarceration, the cooler head of his rational self appears to have fled and his passion for Mary Joyce returned. In various ways, which we will now begin to analyze, Mary comes to function as a strategic anchoring point for Clare's increasingly inchoate sense of identity.

## FIRST LOVE: (ONE)

'[T]here are two impossibillitys that can never happen—I shall never be in three places at once nor ever change to a woman and that ought to be some comfort amid this moral or immoral

---

London, Routledge and Kegan Paul, 1951, p. 250.
28. Clare, *The Prose of John Clare*, p. 44.
29. Clare, *The Prose of John Clare*, p. 44.
30. Clare, *The Prose of John Clare*, p. 44.

"changing" in life'.³¹ Clare penned these words in 1841, probably at the Northamptonshire General Lunatic Asylum where he had been incarcerated at Patty's request. This was the second—and final—time Clare was institutionalized, and it took place only five months after his escape from Dr. Matthew Allen's High Beech Asylum and his 'moral' therapy (to which Clare is perhaps alluding with his reference to this '"changing" in life'). The text in which these words appear is titled 'Self-Identity', a short, poignant meditation on remembering and forgetting in which Clare reflects on his apparent abandonment by his family and the world. Their sentiment is seemingly designed to serve as a sort of axiomatic stop-gap against the idea of his nonexistence brought on by the world's neglect. Clare describes how, 'I am often troubled at times to know that should the world have the impudence not to know me but willingly forgetting me wether any single individual would be honest enough to know me—such people would be usefull as the knocker to a door or the Bell to a cryer to own the dead alive or the lost found'.³² It is at this point Clare introduces the two intractable 'impossibillitys' that are presumably intended to comfort him in the absence of such an 'honest' individual. If nothing else, Clare reassures himself, he can at least count on the certitude of inhabiting one sole place in space and time, and on his sexual identity as a man. As it transpires, however, the comfort from these maxims will only be fleeting. The way Clare formulates the first of his 'impossibillitys' surreptitiously poses the involuntary question whether one can nevertheless be in *two* places at the same time, while the second prompts one to inquire whether the impossibility of his ever 'changing to a woman' results from the fact that he may already *be* one.

In Clare's poems of 'First Love', we encounter a speaker capable of considerably more theoretical acumen and sexual sophistication in his answer to these questions than the unhappy author of 'Self-Identity', whose attempts at a defiant Kantianism—'surely every man has the liberty to know himself'—cannot help but sound a little quavery coming on the epistemological heels of that other Kantian discovery, that 'truth has a bad herald when she is obliged to take lies for her trumpeters'³³ To investigate now the uniquely 'poetic' compass of these answers, let us turn to the first poem.

---

31. Clare, *The Prose of John Clare*, p. 239.
32. Clare, *The Prose of John Clare*, p. 239.
33. Clare, *The Prose of John Clare*, p. 329.

'First Love'

I ne'er was struck before that hour
With love so sudden and so sweet,
Her face it bloomed like a sweet flower
And stole my heart away complete.
My face turned pale as deadly pale.
My legs refused to walk away,
And when she looked, what could I ail?
My life and all seemed turned to clay.

And then my blood rushed to my face
And took my eyesight quite away,
The trees and bushes round the place
Seemed midnight at noonday.
I could not see a single thing,
Words from my eyes did start—
They spoke as chords do from the string,
And blood burnt round my heart.

Are flowers the winter's choice?
Is love's bed always snow?
She seemed to hear my silent voice,
Not love's appeals to know.
I never saw so sweet a face
As that I stood before.
My heart has left its dwelling-place
And can return no more.

On one point at least, Clare and Badiou are in complete agreement, namely, on the pure and utter randomness of the loving encounter. In Clare's poem, first love descends upon the speaker as a *coup de foudre*, a complete bolt out of the blue. Love's strike literally smites Clare's 'I' into existence—'I ne'er was struck before that hour'—tolling the speaker's first hour as a temporal being. The 'strike' of first love activates the subject's 'clock', starting the hands of time turning. One might say that, for Clare, as for Jean-Luc Nancy, Being is essentially metronomymic. 'Being *beats*', Nancy reminds us, 'it essentially is in the beating, indeed, in the e-motion of its own heart'.[34]

As it inaugurates the first 'turn' of the subject's clock, first love is also and implicitly for Clare the first rhetorical and organizational

---

34. Jean-Luc Nancy, *The Inoperative Community*, ed. and trans. Peter Connor, et. al., Minneapolis, University of Minnesota Press, 1991, p. 88.

trope governing his newly created subject's psyche. The radical beginning instituted by 'first love' determines how all subsequent experiences will be ordered in the speaker's future history; first love establishes the primordial set of differences and distinctions (including those governing one's succeeding love life) that any post-first love organizational system is based on. It is evidently time, not space, that is the privileged category of dialectics for Clare. For Clare, there 'is' no time before the event of first love. First love is the original cause of the temporal organization that brings the inconsistent multiplicity to its first presentation, subsequently forming what will come to appear as a natural ('statist', in Badiou's terminology) series of binary oppositions. Included among these are the poem's allusions to light and dark, day and night, movement and stasis, vision and blindness, summer and winter and, finally, home and exile, all of which cluster and more or less effortlessly unfold around the central image of the beloved's face, troped quite traditionally as a flower that doubles metaphorically as a sun—the beloved is a sun-flower, giver of life and of Clare's speaker's newly born self-identity. The most important opposition that 'first love' initiates, however, is the very one we saw haunting Clare in his prose piece 'Self-Identity', namely, being and nonbeing. First love, it transpires, supplies the speaker with the consciousness of self necessary to be able to say 'I AM' (as Clare does most famously in his best known poem, which bears that title). Like all statements of existence, however, this declarative also simultaneously hauls along with it the dispiriting threat of the I's negation. The first hour, '1am', must inexorably pass to 2 and 3, cycling the clock until the speaker's eventual demise.

    Up to this point in the poem, Clare appears to have little argument with the well-established tradition that aligns love with both the birth and death of the self. His claims chime well with the age-old paradox of love that Julia Kristeva adroitly sums up as 'a death sentence that causes me to be'.[35] The point where Clare departs from the philosophical tradition that posits love as the archaic principle of things, and which Aristotle, in the first book of his *Metaphysics*, credits Hesiod with inaugurating, is Clare's insistence on numbering his love for Mary *first*. For in doing so, Clare quite deliberately introduces a flaw into the smooth running of the dialectical program that love's 'strike' inaugurated. Presenting a sort of poetic, subjective version of the cosmological or 'first cause'

---

35. Julia Kristeva, *Tales of Love*, trans. Leon S. Roudiez, New York, Columbia, 1987, p. 36.

argument that troubled so many of the early fathers of Christianity, Clare's poem poses the philosophically troubling question, how can we 'count' our first love, if it is first love that opens up the very possibility of counting?

A self-taught mathematician, Clare would by no means have been oblivious to this mathematical dilemma he introduces at the outset of the poem. Marilyn Gaull, who has documented the creeping professionalism of the sciences over the course of the nineteenth century, explains that before 1830, 'it would not have been unusual for a self-educated farm labourer to puzzle over mathematics in his leisure time, or astronomy, botany or geology as well'. She goes on to explain that 'it was from among these people that the most original ideas and most of the instrumentation of science were generated'.[36] Although Clare, by his own admission, 'never came off with victories' in these fields of study, his fondness for 'puzzling over every thing in my hours of leisure [...] with a restless curiosity' would have meant that he was certainly aware of the sweeping transformation that the new developments in all of the sciences were effecting on traditional conceptions of the universe, and especially on those concerning number, time, space and life itself.[37] Separately but simultaneously, the new discoveries by William Herschel, James Hutton, Joseph Priestley, William Hunter and Erasmus Darwin were rapidly displacing the traditional, theologically defined universe and replacing it with a radically different vision of a secular, infinite and asymmetrical universe from which traditional certainties of space, time and spiritual meaning were increasingly being evacuated. Not surprisingly, the part played in this by the 'new mathematics' was substantial. It would be hard to overestimate both the mathematical and philosophical significance attached to the nineteenth century's 'legitimization' of imaginary and complex numbers; to the sweeping trend to algebraicize geometry begun by Descartes and continued, in England, by Sir William Rowan Hamilton and his 'science of pure time',[38] the 'arithmetization' of mathematics that became possible with the founding of infinitesmal calculus, and the spatial 'impossibilitys' introduced by non-Euclidean geometry, and its

---

36. Marilyn Gaull, 'Clare and "the Dark System"', in *John Clare in Context*, p. 280.
37. Gaull, 'Clare and "the Dark System"', pp. 279-80.
38. Sir William Rowan Hamilton, 'Theory of Conjugate Functions, or Algebraic Couples; with a Preliminary and Elementary Essay on Algebra as the Science of Pure Time' (1837).

revolutionary conceptualization of spaces of more than three dimensions by Riemann, Lobachevsky and Bolyai, to mention only the most well known.

Most critical to this changing vision of the universe, as many have noted, was the place the new sciences allotted to the human subject. Where previously mankind conceived itself as the chief actor on a stage 'perfectly suited [...] for human life',[39] this new world was 'indifferent at best, even inhospitable to human life' as Gaull puts it.[40] No longer firmly ensconced at the center of the cosmos, humankind had to adapt itself to the idea that it was merely an onlooker, a miniscule footnote in the history of the earth. The contemporary passion for fossil collecting, in which Clare was an eager participant, only confirmed this sense of the continual 'moral and immoral "changing" in life', as Clare described it in 'Self-Identity'. Thus Clare's concerns in that text may justifiably be regarded as having a wider application beyond simply the particular circumstances in which the poet found himself, locked away in the mid-part of the nineteenth century and doubting as to his continuing existence in the absence of friends, family and above all familiar places.

Clare's solution, as we saw, was to return to the instant when everything 'began', to his first love Mary, the one thing of which he could be absolutely certain. In the words of Eric Robinson and Geoffrey Summerfield, Clare's twentieth-century editors whose largely 'Romantic' presentation of the poet has had substantial influence on Clare's critical reception, Mary 'remained for the rest of [Clare's] days the symbol of innocence, the Eve of his Eden, the First Love which was to be the touchstone for all later experience'.[41] Mary would supply Clare with an anchoring point in a continuously 'changing' universe. The only difficulty, as noted already, is that this presents Clare with a chicken and egg dilemma: how can one count the first love, if it is only through first love that counting as such—including the counting out of one's hours to death—becomes possible? How can an ontic entity, that is, something that is already 'in' time, serve simultaneously as an ontological principle, as something that inaugurates time?

One answer to this problem is to say that the first is always only retroactively determined. From this perspective, one counts

---

39. Haughton and Phillips, 'Introduction: Relocating John Clare', p. 280.
40. Gaull, 'Clare and "the Dark System"', p. 280.
41. John Clare, *Selected Poems and Prose of John Clare*, Eric Robinson and Geoffrey Summerfield (eds.), Oxford, Oxford University Press, 1978, p. xix.

backwards, as it were, from an existing set of lovers and in this way arrives at the 'first'. However this manifestly only delays rather than solves the problem, for it fails to account for the original way our set of lovers was constructed. Subsequent lovers can belong to the set and possess a shared identity of being one of Clare's loves only because they come logically 'after' the first love who inaugurated the series. In his essay 'On Narcissism', Freud encountered an identical theoretical problem nearly a hundred years later in his own theory of first love. In answer, Freud was led to postulate two varieties of narcissistic love. His solution to this logical problem of commencement, that is, was to split 'first love' in two. The first form, primary narcissism, was thought to serve as the libidinal source for the subsequent object-directed, 'anaclitic' love. This latter, anaclitic love, Freud conceived as fluid, capable of converting back into its primary form under certain circumstances.[42] The 'development of the ego', Freud writes, 'consists in a departure from primary narcissism [...] brought about by means of the displacement of libido onto an ego ideal imposed from without'.[43]

As numerous post-Freudian psychoanalytic theorists have pointed out in the meantime, however, as a narrative of the I's prehistory, Freud's theory of self-love was powerless to explain where that primordial first love, primary narcissism, derived from—what is the mysterious 'new psychical action' as Freud adumbrates it in that essay, that jump-starts the autoerotic infant's loving history by inducing it to begin to love itself?[44] In the end, Freud opted for the aforementioned retroactive explanation, concluding that given its impenetrable origins, primary narcissism can only ever be inferred from the existence of (secondary) object love. '[N]ot until there is object-cathexis', Freud surmises, 'is it possible to discriminate a sexual energy—the libido—from an energy of the ego-instincts'.[45] Yet as demonstrated by the considerable amount of work that has been devoted to the elliptical question of narcissism ever since, Freud's solution to the problem has not been deemed entirely satisfactory. John Clare, by contrast, will take a different and

---

42. Freud's example is of cases of injury, where anaclitic love is turned inward onto the ego. He also notes how it is only once the body's organic needs have been satisfied that object love can assume predominance again. 'On Narcissism: An Introduction', *Standard Edition of the Complete Psychological Works of Sigmund Freud*, trans. James Strachey, vol. XIV (1914-1915), London, Hogarth, 1968, pp. 73-102.

43. Freud, 'On Narcissism', p. 100.

44. Freud, 'On Narcissism', p. 77.

45. Freud, 'On Narcissism', p. 76.

theoretically (if admittedly not emotionally) more rewarding tack. Rather than splitting first love chronologically, between a first 'first' and a second 'first' as Freud does, Clare will divide it spatially as we will now see.

The poem's second stanza witnesses Clare's speaker itemizing the physiological effects of love's first 'strike'. Of these, the most significant is the destitution love wreaks on the lover's eyesight. In consequence of this, time apparently stops again. Even as love's hammer blow pounded the subject's I into a temporal existence, its immediate, counter-intuitive result is to make it unexpectedly impossible to tell the time, to distinguish night from day. The speaker's sight, which should allow the poetic subject to descry (roughly) what hour it is by the sun's position in the sky, is reportedly taken 'quite away', while 'the trees and bushes round the place/ Seemed midnight at noonday'. What could have caused this sudden blinding? An initial hypothesis might posit that the vision of the beloved's face occasions an effect comparable to looking at the sun. In this case, first love would be conceived as a blinding force that entirely erases the subject's newly constituted Self-Identity. Analogous to the soul's vision of 'truth' in Plato's *Phaedrus*, the sight of the beloved's face would obliterate all distance from himself and the beloved, wiping out the very sense of self and separateness that first love originally brought into being. In such a case, Clare's first love would represent simply another poetic instance of the fusional tradition of love referenced by the poet's editors. Although it ostensibly divides and separates, love's 'true' work, this reading holds, lies in a seamless, 'Romantic' unification of the I with an All—an absolute One that pre-dates the loving subject.

There is another reading of this stanza, however, that presents a rather different explanation of the speaker's sudden loss of sight—and consequently, a different conception of Clare's first love. Up until now the sun has served as the gravitational draw around which the poem's heliotropic economy orbits, organizing the poetic economy's internal structure and consistency. But all of a sudden the solar body, giver of life and marker of time, has been abolished; it ceases its rotation in the sky, with the result that it becomes impossible to distinguish night from day. The sun has been blacked out, rubbed out by something. The question is, what blocks the sight of the sun? The sequence of events the poem has recounted so far might seem to suggest the paradoxical answer that it is the metaphorical 'sun' (that is, the beloved's face) that intervenes between the speaker and the sight of the (real) sun—resulting in what would be the logically impossible but not poetically unthinkable eclipse of the sun *by itself*—a 'sun' split between two registers (real sun and poetic 'sun-flower'), while still succeeding at its traditional role as the gravitational and rhetorical anchor for the poem. Plato's image of the cave would be the irresistible comparison here. In the Platonic fable, the cave dwellers are captivated by the shadowy images cast on the walls by the light. This light is supplied by a fire high up behind their heads, but behind this fire is the sun, the 'real' source of the light by which they see. Although the fire intervenes between the cave dwellers and the sun, blocking their sight of it, theirs nevertheless remains securely (if unwittingly) a solar economy. Lacan has described this system of overlapping layers as the topology of a sphere: a pattern of successively enveloping envelopes whose terminal point, the sun, he calls 'the identity of the being of the real and of the being of knowledge'.[46]

Nevertheless, I would want to draw attention to the speaker's association of himself with 'clay' in the previous stanza ('My life and all seemed turned to clay'), with clay recalling not only the stuff of Adamic life, of God's original creativity, but also, and especially for a figure like John Clare the peasant poet, the simple fundament of place, of earth, of the pre-mortal stuff out of which fleeting flowers (and their subjects) are made.[47] Such an association extends, then, a rather more discomforting suggestion. As the putative 'ground' or original source of the flower/sun, the speaker *himself* seems to be the cause of the sun's sudden disappearance, presenting us with the paradoxical image of a sun eclipsed not by one of its 'satellites' (such as the beloved 'sun-flower' or the fire of Plato's allegory). This time, the sun has been eclipsed by the earth. In a swift rotation, the earth blocks the sight of the sun *to itself*. It is the earth's own self-eclipse: I can no longer see the sun because I am myself standing in its way, I am in my own shadow.

---

46. Jacques Lacan, *Seminar XIII, The Object of Psychoanalysis (1965-1966)*, unpublished seminar, (lesson of 20.4.66).

47. Richard Cronin and Tom Paulin have each drawn attention to Clare as a poet of 'place'. See Cronin, 'In Place and Out of Place: Clare in *The Midsummer Cushion*', in *John Clare: New Approaches*, John Goodridge and Simon Kövesi (eds.), Helpston, John Clare Society, 2000, pp. 133-48; Tom Paulin, 'John Clare: A Bicentennial Celebration', in *John Clare: A Bicentenary Celebration*, Richard Foulkes (ed.), Northampton, University of Leicester Press, 1994, pp. 69-78.

This is typical Clare. At the height of the anticipated self-transparency promised by love, when full self-realization seems about to be possible, Clare splits in two, passing into a strange, otherworldly 'midnight at noonday'. His I, born in and as time, suffers an internal fracture that finds him inhabiting two logically incompatible places at once, simultaneously 'in' the solar economy, founded on first love—and 'outside' it, languishing in the shadow his own 'I' has cast. Consistent with this, here at the 'navel' of the poem, we detect a decisive shift in Clare's rhetorical architecture that reflects at a formal level what has just occurred at the thematic level. Dominated up till now by Keatsian similes (whose 'La Belle Dame sans Merci' loiters irresistibly in the background of Clare's sonnet), the poem moves inexorably into a more monumental, Wordsworthian mode:

> Words from my eyes did start—
> They spoke as chords do from the string,
> And blood burnt round my heart.

Could we not say that, with this strange image, Clare's use of metaphor comes to the 'rescue' of the speaker in a certain sense at his moment of crisis? Clare's figurative 'words' transform the speaker's physical blindness into a different form of sight: eyes that could not see suddenly and miraculously 'speak' (and, in one version of the poem at least, are understood[48]). Initially this seems like a fairly orthodox Wordsworthian move: confronted with a representational failure ('I could not see a single thing'), the speaker performs an inward identification that raises sight to the level of in-sight and enables the speaker to express himself in silent communication with his beloved. The only problem, however, is that the internalization or *Aufhebung* of sight into the insight constituting silent speech is one that requires that the 'speech' does in fact remain silent, that is, metaphorical, that is, by implication,

---

48. Note that the version of 'First Love' in James Reeves' edited volume diverges radically at this point from the version of the poem in the Tibbles' edited collection, *The Poems of John Clare* I have chosen here. In the Reeves edition, the line reads, 'She seemed to hear my silent voice/ And love's appeals to know'. In both versions, the implication is of a communication that has been 'heard' but understood differently. In one, the communication succeeds in conveying love's appeal and, hence, provides a negative answer to the rhetorical question, while the other (which strikes me as much more poetically plausible) is the conveyance of a communication about the eternal failure of love's promised communication. *Selected Poems of John Clare*, ed. and intro. James Reeves, London, Heineman, 1954 (reprinted. 1968), p. 129.

wordless, whereas what we find in Clare's account are quite precisely and unmistakably 'Words'. In a bizarre twist, words have become expected to carry the metaphorical burden of communication. That is, they must double up and become *metaphors of themselves* if the wider metaphorical economy of insight and silent speech is to succeed and inaugurate the process of the speaker's recovery. The pattern Clare effects is thus not the smooth dialectical movement from outside to inside and back again that one imagines the speaker was hoping for with this image, but something more like an interior 8: a single element has to do double duty as both the literal and figural pole in the metaphorical exchange.

In short, an 'eclipse' has taken place at the rhetorical level comparable to the one we saw occurring thematically. Both the thematic and the rhetorical systems successfully install a center around which a metaphorical galaxy can orbit, in the first case, an 'I' or a self that has been installed as the center of a loving, temporal universe divided between Platonic distinctions of light and dark, movement and stasis, being and non-being. In the second, the center discloses itself as a perceptual 'eye' that stabilizes a figurative system, enabling sight and in-sight to seamlessly exchange themselves for one another. However, in both cases this installation of a center, of a One, is achieved at the cost of that same center itself. The center, in each case, is doubled or, rather, split. The self around which the loving, temporal economy revolves is one that is radically and impossibly divorced from the 'light' (the sun/flower/beloved) of that same economy, trapped as it is behind its own 'shadow'. Similarly, the rhetorical cosmology of metaphorical insight and exchange is founded on the *dédoublement* of its axial point, 'words', which, in doubling up for themselves, block access to precisely the 'insight' (the wordless communication) they were intended to secure.

In this way, Clare 'solves' his mathematical dilemma of how to count the first love although, as I said, from the point of view of the author of 'Self-Identity', this solution is scarcely reassuring. Far from inhabiting a transcendental space outside of time, Clare's 'first love' according to this other, rather less 'Romantic' poet than that handed down to us by the editorial tradition, is only ever a product of time's 'count' and is, therefore, irremediably *in* time. But first love's time is mysteriously shorted; the subject occupies, if not the impossible 'three places at once' from Clare's prose text, then certainly *two* places at the same time. The desired One of love, the ideal fusion Clare's speaker seeks with his beloved, can only be achieved from *inside* the set of all loves as the 'first' of the series but, as we have seen, the very creation of that set required that Clare remain caught behind, *outside* the very representational system that 'he' constructed. From Clare's simultaneously internal and external position, flowers must indeed appear to be always the 'winter's choice', and love's bed 'always snow', for the very thing that brought the loving self into existence—time—ensures that the beloved Other remains permanently out of reach, blooming in a bower of bliss in an eternal summer where the sun never sets.

## 'FIRST LOVE' (TWO)

'There will always be in the field of arithmetic something that can be stated in the proper terms that it involves, which will not be within the grasp of what posits itself as a means to be held acceptable in the proof'—this is how Lacan, in Seminar XIX, paraphrases Gödel's theorem of incompletion, Clare's poetic version of which, it may already have struck the reader, has just been outlined.[49] Gödel's would be the equivalent mathematical justification for Clare's, and of course Badiou's, positions: in the field of representation there will always be an excess that cannot be grasped from inside the representational system that created it (or, as Gödel actually put it, 'there is no need for a logical system to be closed in upon itself in order to function as a consistent system for producing knowledge').

As we saw, Clare's response to this excess was to marshal the linear representational system ('time') into a topological space in which the certain 'impossibillitys' of standard (Euclidean) geometry no longer hold true. One can after all occupy if not three, then at least two places at the same time when time is doubled or, better, *folded* at that undecidable moment of noon/midnight which logically precedes but chronologically post-dates the strike of the One. To the extent that it is thus neither a transcendent principle, nor already a part of an existing situation, the Clarean subject offers a convincing poetic depiction of Badiou's fundamental axiom that the One (whether conceived as the Self, or as the Other) *is not*. Clare can be (with Mary) only for as long as he does not

---

49. Lacan, *The Seminar of Jacques Lacan, Book XIX: ...ou pire (1971-1972)*, unpublished seminar (lesson of 12 January, 1971).

exist. But the moment he enters existence, 'Mary' (that is, Mary and Clare) must be negated or at least cast into the nothingness that is the mathematical 'fate' of anything that is obliged to act as a first cause'.[50]

As I remarked, while this offers a solution to Clare's mathematical dilemma, it scarcely provides the author of 'Self-Identity' with much in the way of ontological comfort for, in this curved topological space, Clare can only watch from a place that can never coincide with the place of his beloved. Mary will always be on the 'other' side of the Möbius strip of Clare's loving circuit, no matter how far he manages to travel along it. All the signs are pointing to the inevitable conclusion that Clare's subject is 'nothing but the gap' separating these two irreparably divided realms, to use one of Slavoj Žižek's favoured phrases. Or, in Giorgio Agamben's words, 'the human is precisely this fracture of presence, which opens a world and over which language holds itself'.[51] Both thinkers are doubtless correct but with this proviso. As we will see when we turn shortly to Clare's second poem of 'First Love', a subject born from first love's incompletion theorem always inhabits this fold or gap in not one but *two* ways.

The two poems under consideration were written during Clare's final and permanent incarceration in the Northampton General Asylum where, as mentioned earlier, Clare was already deep into his delusion that he had married both Patty and Mary, for which act he believed he had been arrested and incarcerated. Remarkably, in addition to writing some of his most beautiful and haunting poetry in this period, Clare began to fill his notebooks with long lists of female names—in many cases, of women he had once known and apparently loved. Presumably a component of his Byron delusion, this story of Clare's list-making cannot help but recall Sganarelle's famous book in the Molière play in which the names and numerical score of Don Juan's conquests were recorded. In her discussion of the origins of the myth of Don Juan in *The Ethics of the Real*, Alenka Zupančič pointedly reminds us how the story we commonly know as Don Juan is in fact a conflation

---

50. 'Existence is analogous to number. Affirmation of existence is in nothing but denial of the number nought', Gottlob Frege, *Die Grundlagen der Arithmetik* (1884), translated as *The Foundations of Arithmetic*, trans. J. L. Austin, Evanston, Northwestern University Press, 1980, §51.

51. Giorgio Agamben, 'The Proper and the Improper', *Stanzas: Word and Phantasm in Western Culture*, trans. Ronald L. Martinez, Minneapolis, University of Minnesota Press, 1993, p. 148.

of two distinct legends—the first, the familiar story of the prodigious seducer of women into which the narrative of Don Juan has meanwhile precipitated. But an earlier version of the Don Juan tale features the hero as a man who invites Death to dinner. For Zupančič, the supercession of the dinner story by the seducer myth in our popular memory of the Don Juan legend can best be understood as a defense against the disturbing idea contained in the forgotten earlier myth. She recommends that we understand the serial solution of women 'as a solution to a certain impasse—a solution which, precisely because of its continual failure to provide a real solution, only reveals the true scandal: the fact that one half of the human race is actually composed of the "living dead": that is, beings with no signifier of their own that would adequately represent them in the symbolic'.[52]

If Zupančič uncharacteristically misses the crucial point that Clare's 'First Love' enjoins us to see, it is because the situation is actually inverted. It is not women—the 'one half' Zupančič is referring to—who embody the living dead, but rather *men*, or, more universally, every speaking subject insofar as all of us are only half alive, cut off from our 'true life' (of Being) and compelled to wander in exile in our own bodies. The serial seduction of women, the fusional fantasy that the sexual relation really exists, is not the solution, therefore, but the very problem itself. We are 'half alive' *only if we think there is a missing part of ourselves from which we have been divorced*. The incontrovertible fact Clare alerts us to in his remarkably precise and vivid way is that, although it presents itself as an answer to an originary division, the fantasy of fusion with a beloved is itself the *cause* of the idea that we are lost to Being, not the other way around.

This point can be better clarified by returning to the navel of the poem, to the critical moment of sightlessness when the speaker recounts how he 'could not see a single thing'. Evidently this statement can be read in several ways. On a first reading, it implies the speaker is blind, incapable of seeing anything. On the other hand, the speaker may simply be ruminating on a certain failure of definition. In this case, we could read the line as implying the speaker sees not *one* thing, but many indeterminate things. Or again, the statement might convey the experience of seeing nothing: if I 'could not see a single thing', that is perhaps because there was *nothing to see* which, as Freud never failed to remind us,

---

52. Alenka Zupančič, *Ethics of the Real*, London, Verso, 2000, p.130.

is potentially a profoundly traumatic event, at least in some very young boys' lives. Of these three possible readings, however, only the first is ultimately given credence for, when the 'words' suddenly 'start' from the speaker's eyes, they secure a reading of the sentence that *retroactively* decides it as the first possibility, that is, as a statement about blindness. One could say that the 'words' quite literally block the speaker's view—they 'start' or begin the rotation of the subject's representational system in a specific direction, which might otherwise, potentially, have gone another way. Clare's 'words' confirm that the speaker cannot see by *literally standing in his way*, in effect causing a representational crisis where there was not (necessarily) one before. They transform a potential ontological crisis—the crisis of being that is raised by the presence of a nothing where one expects there to be something—into a crisis of vision: it was not that there was 'nothing' to see. I could see nothing because I was (safely) blind.

Here we have a remarkably cogent depiction of the subject's logic when confronted with the unnameable Badiou calls the void. And how it chooses to see or 'read' this unnameable has profound consequences for the subject's subsequent (sexual) identity. In our speaker's case, faced with the (potentially) traumatic sight of nothingness, the (masculine) subject opts for the first reading, electing to see the void as a lack. The speaker, that is, veils the nothing or void with a signifier that can designate either presence or absence. In this way, the signifier converts the nothing-to-see into a problem of sight: I can either see (something), or I am blind (and cannot see anything).

As is well-known, psychoanalysis calls this signifier that designates presence or absence the phallus. Yet despite this corporeal inflection, the logic of the psychoanalytic move is strictly mathematical, as Jacques-Alain Miller has indicated in his celebrated essay 'Suture'.[53] In that essay, Miller pinpoints a fundamental *error in counting* that a subject inevitably makes when it assumes an identity with a signifier. The classic example of this computational error, to which Lacan repeatedly comes back, is the Cartesian equation, 'I think therefore I am' (or in Clare's poetic counterpart, 'I love therefore I am'). It is scarcely an exaggeration to say that an entire philosophical history is contained in this

---

53. Jacques-Alain Miller, 'Suture (Elements of the Logic of the Signifier)', *The Symptom*, no. 8, 2007, <http://www.lacan.com/symptom8_articles/miller8.html> [accessed October 28, 2008].

'therefore', in the problems raised in and by the Parmenidean uniting of thinking and being in the One.[54] Miller and, implicitly, Badiou will follow Lacan's Fregean lead in declaring that any One or 'I' that is produced through such a conflation is the result of a miscount: the mathematical 'error' that first allows a signifier to represent a subject for another signifier in the identificatory statement 'I AM I'.

The beauty of this primordial error, this 'suturing' of the subject to the signifier, however, lies in how it allows the subject to deal with the case of a signifier representing absence. Brooking no indeterminacy, the signifier designates merely presence or absence, but the unexpected gain the subject obtains from this narrowing of the 'unpresented multiplicity' down to a series of binary choices is a new-found ability to manage absence as postponement, as the promise of future presence. Funneling the unpresented multiplicity through a sort of litmus test that delivers only present or absent signifiers, the original erroneous signifier is *itself* responsible for the fiction of the lost object that must one day be re-found. Absence is *retroactively posited by the phallic signifier as loss*. The phallus is, then, in a very real sense the problem it purports to solve: there is, strictly speaking, nothing missing prior to the invention of the phallic signifier. It is the signifier that retroactively 'reads' the unrepresentable as something absent (and which might therefore be regained).

In Seminar XIII, *The Object of Psychoanalysis (1965-1966)*, Lacan ironically refers to philosophy as a sort of nursemaid to this original miscount through which A was made to equal A, that lies, primally repressed, at the origin of modern science and modern mathematics. As Lacan puts it in his lesson of 20.4.66, philosophy has historically acted as a 'bandage' (Lacan is punning on the homonym *'pansement/pensement'*) for the wound of this original suturing.[55] But despite his stated fondness for book learning Clare, however, was not a philosopher or at least not a very good one, for his attempt at 'bandaging' this original suture by way of a phallic or symbolic solution clearly begins to unravel in his second poem of 'First Love'. Turning to this poem now will also enable us to revisit some of the issues raised at the beginning concerning what

---

54. An excellent introduction to these problems, especially as they relate to Badiou, is Peter Hallward's *Badiou: A Subject to Truth*, Minneapolis, University of Minnesota Press, 2003, pp. 49-78.
55. Lacan, *Seminar XII*, lesson of 20.4.66.

I was calling, following Badiou, a certain 'necessity tendency' by which the lover is inevitably caused to 'betray' an event.

To first quickly sketch out Badiou's concerns surrounding fidelity in *Being and Event*, in meditation 23, 'Fidelity, Connection', Badiou contends that every event confronts what he calls a 'necessary tendency' toward betrayal. Betrayal occurs when the event's faithful subjects are driven to 'ontologize' the event. Commenting on the way the faithful subject or subjects construct a 'counter-state' inside the situation, Badiou observes how it is always tempting for a fidelity to consider this '*other* situation' (his emphasis) that is comprised of the multiples 'marked by the event' 'as its own body, as the acting effectiveness of the event, as the true situation, or flock of the Faithful'.[56] This Badiou describes as an 'ecclesiastical version of fidelity' because these eventally-marked multiples effectively form a 'Church of the event'. Ecclesiastical fidelity thus represents a mistaken 'ontologization', an instance of the 'spontaneist thesis' that claims 'the only ones who can take part in an event are those who made it such'.[57]

Lovers appear particularly at risk of falling into this spontaneist thesis and forming a 'Church' of their love, composed of the exclusive two, the 'body' of the couple. And as a number of commentators have pointed out, it is in fact quite difficult to understand in what way a love affair between two individuals is capable of the universalization that is required of a truth procedure other than through such a mistaken 'ontologization' of the event. This has led some to suggest that Badiou remains deeply cathected onto a Christian conception of love as *agape*.[58] While a closer look at Badiou's conception of love ought to mitigate the bulk of these fears, I agree that something remains unsatisfying about Badiou's account of the universalization performed in love, and my belief is that this can be traced back to how the philosopher decides to name the event of love. For Badiou, as we recall, the event-encounter is fixed by a nomination and this nomination is the declaration of love, 'I love you'. For Clare, on the other hand, the name of love's event is and will always remain 'Mary'.

---

56. Badiou, *Being and Event*, p. 238.
57. Badiou, *Being and Event*, p. 237.
58. See for example Marc de Kesel, 'Truth as Formal Catholicism: On Alain Badiou, Saint Paul, *La fondation de l'universalisme*', *Communication and Cognition*, vol. 37, no. 3-4, 2004, pp. 167-97. See also his 'Ontologie als katholicisme: Over Alain Badiou's Paulusinterpretatie', *Yang*, no. 1, 2004, pp. 17-32.

'First Love'

No single hour can pass for naught,
No moment-hand can move,
But calendars an aching thought
Of my first lonely love.

Where silence doth the loudest call
My secret to betray,
As moonlight holds the night in thrall,
As suns reveal the day,

I hide it in the silent shades,
Till silence finds a tongue;
I make its grave where time invades,
Till time becomes a song.

I bid my foolish heart be still,
But hopes will not be chid:
My heart will beat, and burn, and chill,
First love will not be hid.

When summer ceases to be green,
And winter bare and blea,
Death may forget what I have been
When I shall cease to be.

When words refuse before the crowd
My Mary's name to give,
The muse in silence sings aloud:
And there my love will live.

The striking thing about this second poem of 'First Love' is how Clare now expresses doubts about the validity of the arithmetic performed in the other poem. 'No single hour', he warns, can 'pass for naught'—there is no One, no I, no 'presented' signifier, that can adequately bestow the 'naught' with a form. The representational or 'phallic' solution of the previous poem, that saw 'words' stepping in to shield the subject from the 'sight' of nothing, proves unsuccessful in this case for, although the poet's 'words' clearly performed the duty Clare asked of them—that is, to present (and consequently veil) the void—they apparently fail to block the persistent refrain that is Mary's name: 'When words refuse before the crowd/My Mary's name to give,/The muse in silence sings aloud'. Silence, time, the poet's body, even his death itself, it seems, is terminally infected by a song that exceeds the poet's own songs and which will resonate long after the poet, his first love, and his poems of first love cease to exist. Something in (or 'about') the word 'Mary' remains perpetually unaccounted for in the 'situation' that she herself, in the previous poem, brought into existence.

Readers of Lacan's twentieth seminar, *Encore*, will find it hard to resist identifying this elusive yet resonant element as Clare's version of what Lacan calls in that seminar the *jouissance* of the Other, an excess or 'Joycesseance' that escapes and therefore supplements the phallic 'count'. 'There is a *jouissance*' states Lacan in the lesson of February 20, 1973, 'that is hers (*à elle*), that belongs to that 'she' (*elle*) that doesn't exist and doesn't signify anything'.[59] Such '*jouissance* beyond the phallus' doesn't signify or count for anything because it is literally uncounted, unsubjected to the suturing operation that (mis)counted the void as the first (phallic) signifier or One. Many of the features of this *'lalangue'*, as it is also called in Seminar XX, are recognizable from Lacan's earlier discussions of the letter, particularly in Seminar IX, *Identification (1961-1962)*. As we saw in an earlier chapter, in that seminar, Lacan reflects on the nature of the proper name as something that partakes in the 'order of the letter'. He contends, 'there cannot be a definition of the proper name except in the measure that we are aware of the relationship which in its radical nature is of the order of the letter'.[60] Names possess an 'idiotic character' that marks them uniquely as proper names, he goes on to explain. They carry a 'certain sonant difference' which, although ignored and mostly forgotten in everyday discourse, articulates 'something which is perhaps indeed the function of the subject, but of the subject defined completely differently than by anything whatsoever which is of the order of concrete psychology, of the subject in so far as we could, as we must, as we will define it properly speaking by its reference to the signifier'. Lacan concludes:

> there is a subject which is not confused with the signifier as such, but which is unfolded in this reference to the signifier with traits, characters which are perfectly articulatable and

---

59. Lacan, *The Seminar of Jacques Lacan, Book XX: Encore, On Feminine Sexuality: The Limits of Love and Knowledge (1972-1973)*, Jacques-Alain Miller (ed.), trans. Bruce Fink, New York, Norton, 1998, p. 74.
60. Lacan, *Seminar IX* (lesson of 20.12.61).

formalisable and which ought to permit us to grasp, to discern as such the idiotic character [...] as such of the proper name.[61]

Pointedly, Badiou dispenses almost entirely with this 'idiotic' dimension when he turns to his most extensive discussion of the Two in his celebrated essay, 'The Scene of Two'. This magisterial piece occupies a remarkable place in Badiou's *oeuvre* inasmuch as it provides the most detailed account not only of his conception of love, but also because, as the implicit underlying structure governing every nomination of the event in any of the truth domains (art, politics, science, and love), it offers a sort of meta-account of the 'double border effect' enacted in any evental intervention (leading Zupančič, for one, to suggest love actually represents a 'fifth' condition if Badiou's philosophy, that is, both part of and a reflexive account of the Badiouian system[62]). In 'The Scene of Two', Badiou develops the concept of the 'vocable' proposed in 'What is Love?' which appears to be his philosophical version of the Lacanian object *a*: the non-nul term or 'atomic element' $u$ which, being shared in common by the two incompatible positions of the sexes, ensures that, while not absolutely disjunct, they nevertheless do not compose a whole.

However, in addition to this disjunction, the $u$ sustains another function, Badiou explains, which is that of a 'point' from which a Two can be counted immanently, that is, not on the basis of any One. An 'immanent' count occurs when the $u$, the shared object of 'misunderstanding' between the irreparably non-related sexes, is subtracted, giving rise to what Badiou calls the 'scene of Two': the shared investigation of the world insofar as it forms the site for the effects entailed by the introduction of the evental name. Between the first and second 'readings', as Badiou calls these two functions of the $u$, lies the 'double border effect' Badiou assigns to any intervention: a doubling of the evental name between the void and itself.

Badiou explains that love or the 'amorous event' is 'no more than the hazardous authorization given to the double reading [...] to the double function of $u$'. Love is where or how the $u$ is thought together in both its functions. In the first 'reading', the $u$ is the site of a misunderstanding about the other as object of desire. This misunderstanding, whose debt to the Lacanian conception of 'desire' is unmistakable, sustains the non-relation of the sexes,

---

61. Lacan, *Seminar IX* (lesson of 20.12.61).
62. Alenka Zupančič, 'The Fifth Condition', in Peter Hallward (ed.), *Think Again*, London, Continuum, 2004, pp. 191-201.

ensuring that every time the object seems about to be reached, it will slip from one's grasp. In this reading, Badiou explains, 'the $u$ is the One from which the Two slips away'—there is no Two in desire, just One sex and the Other sex that 'are' only in their misunderstanding of the cause of their common desire.

In the second reading, though, Badiou explains how once the $u$ has been constructed, it may be mutually 'internally excised' from the sexed positions. It is in this way that the $u$ supports a Two, Badiou says, insofar as the $u$ functions 'as the separated common One from which the Two is positioned in the universe'. Such a Two is thus not counted from a One, but is counted immanently by 'pairing the two external "halves" side by side through $u$, (W - $u$) and (M - $u$)'. In this way 'the atom $u$ supports the Two of the positions while being subtracted'.

In Badiou's formulation, love is to be found neither in the first reading, whereby the two sexes misunderstand the $u$, the common cause of their desire. Nor does it lie in the 'second' reading *per se*, that is, in the 'scene of Two' constructed from the subtraction of the $u$. Because of this mutual excision of the object, the scene of Two can only be sublime, or 'platonic love', as Badiou specifies, whereas love proper, that is, as a truth procedure, is found in the 'limping rhythm' through which the first and second readings are exercised together, in a 'double reading' that alternates between a contracting movement back toward the atomic object, with its mutual misunderstanding between the sexes, and the expansive movement outward through which the Two conduct their 'inquiries' about the world and its 'common practices'.

Briefly now, it is not difficult to see how Badiou's 'first reading' of love corresponds effectively to what was developed in Clare's first poem of 'First Love', where the (masculine) subject enters into existence only through a 'misunderstanding' of the object. Mary will always slip from the subject's grasp insofar as she 'is' nothing other than the subject's own being, the object Clare's speaker 'lost' when he assumed a representational identity, I (or One), founded on the phallic count. However, in his second poem of 'First Love', Clare will offer a different answer than Badiou's to the question whether we can ever escape this eternal round of 'misunderstanding' of the object Lacan calls desire—and, in the process, extend the beginnings of a different solution to the problem of how love's universalization is to be understood. For Badiou, as we saw, love's universalization takes effect through the alternating movement between the 'systolic', desiring 'reading' founded on a misunderstanding of the *u* and the diastolic, 'shared investigations of the world' by the Two insofar as this is supported by the subtraction of the object (or *u*). As Badiou's use of the term 'atomic' to describe the *u* implies, love can only ever be a matter of an 'all or nothing', a difficult and hazardous undertaking in which the indeterminate *u* will either be present or absent, but the task of love's fidelity is to try to read them together. For Badiou, love as a truth procedure presents a sort of duck/rabbit problem: an alternating, flickering between expansion and contraction in a 'limping movement' that tries, mostly unsuccessfully as he admits, to 'read' them together simultaneously. Nevertheless, despite the difficulty of holding these two 'readings' together, all is not entirely lost for, with each return from the diastolic expansion to the systolic reading 'which ineluctably leads a love toward centering on its sexual indeterminacy', Badiou suggests that something is retained from the scene of the Two. He explains, 'something of the scene constructed of the Two "sticks" to the M and W positions, in such a way that it is not exactly in the same configuration that the misunderstanding inscribes'. The result is 'that sexual non-rapport is topologically situated in another configuration than that in which it was originally deployed'. Desire has become 'saturated' with the scene of the Two, and it is in this saturation, as I understand Badiou to be saying, that love's 'universalization' takes place. Through 'tarrying' in the Two of the 'second reading', the singular, object-directed sexual misunderstanding becomes universalized to the extent that a 'double reading' of the declaration of love really does become possible. Love's nomination, the declaration 'I love you' can now refer simultaneously to the you of the individual lover *and* to the You of humanity at large. In this way, the unique individual lover becomes at the same time an impersonal subject of truth that bears the 'humanity function' (x): 'The some-one', says Badiou in his essay on *Ethics*, 'thus caught up in what attests that he belongs to the truth process as one of its foundation-points is simultaneously *himself*, nothing other than himself, a multiple singularity recognizable among all others, and *in excess of himself*, because the uncertain course [*tracé aléatoire*] of fidelity *passes through him*, transfixes his singular body and inscribes him, from within time, in an instant of eternity'.[63]

---

63. Badiou, *Ethics: An Essay on the Understanding of Evil*, trans. Peter Hallward, London, Verso, 2001, p. 45.

When Clare, on the other hand, names his love-event 'Mary', there is no question of a 'scene of Two' in Badiou's sense. Through his insistence on the absolute specificity of *Mary*, Clare and his first love will never undergo the 'mutual excision' of the *u* whose subtraction founds the Two. One could accuse Clare thereby of performing the ontologization, or betrayal of the event, we saw Badiou earlier cautioning against. By naming the event 'Mary' (rather than Badiou's generic 'I love you'), he quite clearly falls into the spontaneist thesis, saying that Mary and only Mary is capable of taking part in the event that is Clare's speaker's 'first love'. Together with Mary, Clare forms, in Badiou's words, a 'Church of the event', an exclusive couple separated off from the rest of humanity, and, as we saw in the first poem, irremediably *in* time, uninscribed in Badiou's universal 'instant of eternity'.

Nevertheless I wish to suggest that there is still a 'universal' dimension to Clare's first love(s), and it can be found precisely in what seems (in the Badiouian schema) to be the obstacle: Mary's name. As evinced by Clare's second poem of 'First Love', he did not need to wait for Lacan to point out how uncanny and otherworldly a beloved's name can begin to seem when one obsessively repeats it. Despite his different terminology, Clare is thus nothing if not acutely aware of how, in the doubling by which the name interposes itself between the void and its own circulation within the situation in Badiou's account, this *repetition* activates something in language that, as Lacan puts it, is not of the order of communication, not of the order of the signifier and not in the service of the word as he puts it in Seminar XIII.[64] This *lalangue* or 'sonant material' that is also carried implicitly in every word is nevertheless heard most acutely and disturbingly, most pressingly in the 'idiotic character' of the proper name, and never more so than when it is repeated. And under which conditions do we find ourselves repeating, idiotically, a proper name? Aside from in the games of childhood, it is, as Clare is our star witness, in the state we have learned to call 'love'.

The difference between Badiou's and Clare's (or as it becomes clear, Lacan's) positions come down to this: for Clare (and Lacan), the object is never 'subtracted' but remains present in both the first (or 'phallic') reading *and in the second reading*. Badiou's conception of a scene of Two, founded on the exclusion of the object, has no place in a Clarean or Lacanian universe. Once having been

---

64. Lacan, *Seminar XX*, p. 139. See also Lacan, Seminar XIII (lesson of 5.1.66).

constructed through the strike of first love, the object can never simply be taken away again, 'mutually internally excised', because the Lacanian object *a*—and, by extension Clare's Mary—is not a *term* that, like a signifier, can be posited or negated, added or subtracted but is, as Lacan continually emphasized, a *topological object*.[65] It is this topological identity of the object which ensures that, if it is present in its absence in the case of the 'first' reading (desire's metonymy), it will also always be present, as an all too pressing presence, in the second reading in the form of what Mladen Dolar judiciously calls 'the object within the signifier'.[66]

Hence one consequence of Badiou's 'flattening' of the Lacanian concept of object *a* into the (purely 'Symbolic') non-null term *u* is that he thus also, implicitly, reverts to the Euclidean conception of space and its certain logical 'impossibillitys' that poor Clare, in his prose work 'Self-Identity', found to be of little real consolation during his long incarceration. Unlike Badiou's 'atomic' term, a topological object is not subject to the principle of non-contradiction that informs the mathematical relations of inclusion and belonging, for in the topological 'plane' of projective geometry that constitutes the subject's relation to the Other, the object not only can be, but always inevitably is, in 'two places at once'—the *a* 'is' both the subject *and* its counterpart in the desired impossible object. It is, in other words, nothing less than the 'objective' form of the subject's original split and 'error in counting' that enabled Clare to count himself as One and, as such, is constitutively non-subtractable.

If Clare the prose writer remained caught fast by logical impossibility, Clare the poet, by contrast, apparently comes off with more mathematical 'victories', for in the repeated refrain of Mary's name, he discovers a *jouissance* that is apparently not under the jurisdiction of the phallus and its order of representation founded on the One. He discovers, that is, what Lacan calls the 'feminine' *jouissance* that resounds in any proper name, including of course his own. Could it be that by filling his notebooks with lists of girls' names, Clare was not adding up or 'counting' his real or imagined conquests like his Byronic hero Don Juan, but taking matters into his own hands, having waiting in vain to be released from his

65. In the seminars from the mid-sixties, when Lacan was developing his conception of the object *a*, he repeatedly claimed that for him, topology was not a metaphor, not a figure of speech but the Real support of his thinking. See for example his opening words in the lesson of 4 May, 1966, *Seminar XIII, The Object of Psychoanalysis*.

66. Mladen Dolar, *A Voice and Nothing More*, Cambridge, MIT Press, 2006, p. 149.

'English Bastile'? Could it be that by writing female name after female name Clare accessed something that in a sense 'freed' him from the confines of the Law (perhaps enabling him to better tolerate the actual constraints on his physical freedom)? A phrase from another of Clare's poems comes irresistibly to mind at this point:
>Say what is love? Is it to be
>In prison still and still be free—
>Or seem as free?

My next question is more speculative still: isn't the proper name always, therefore, like Clare's a *feminine* name, the privileged carrier in language of both a phallic *jouissance* and an Other *jouissance* that comes logically prior to the desiring fantasies? A name is, after all, the first and original 'face' of the object a, its first personification or *prosopopeia*. The name is the original hook that catches one, as it were, in the act of falling in love, a point of highly-charged linguistic enjoyment around which desire orbits. The beloved's name provides floating metonymic desire with its obsessive point of symbolic fixation, whose effect is to allow the desiring fantasy proper to settle in and populate itself with the empirical features and determinations of a specific beloved. Normally only the province of saints and madwomen, this Other *jouissance* can apparently be accessed, Clare discovered, in the repetitive poem lovers write of their loved one's name in the secret recesses of their hearts.

Clare's insistence on the absolute and uncompromising specificity of his first love, Mary, recalls Lacan's own similar insistence that love cannot be thought without a body. In Seminar IX, *Identification*, Lacan says, 'The fundamental element of *Liebesbedingung*, of the condition of love, the moral is: in a certain sense I only love [...] my body, even when I transfer this love onto the body of the other' (lesson of 21.5.62). The body, as the support of *jouissance*, requires us now to turn away from Badiou's notion of the objectless Two and back to the One, for the body is always, as Lacan says, a One. What we can take away with us from Badiou's conception of the Two, however, is its demonstration that a number can be obtained that is not the product of an addition. Precisely how we obtain the uncounted 'One' of love that we are now closing in on will be the topic of the final chapter. But to close the present discussion, let me end with the following observation: in the 'Scene of Two', Badiou puns on the close homonym between the French *Je t'aime* and *je te matheme* (I love you and I matheme you). Clare's pun is evidently even closer: I marry you and I Mary you.

Perhaps Clare's true delusion lay in mistaking his sinthome for his symptom, misreading his own pun. Clare did not marry two women, he 'Mary-ed' the entire world.

## 5. 'THE FIRST LOVE IS THE TRUE LOVE AND ONE ONLY LOVES ONCE': SØREN KIERKEGAARD WITH EUGENE SCRIBE

By now it seems clear that whatever makes love 'first' for each of our writers, it is not something that is given from the outset but instead needs to be constructed, in some sense, by the loving subject. As a result, the 'One' of first love emerges from our readings in disparate ways, enabling us to understand the uniform title, *First Love*, in a variety of fashions: as the source of regeneration for the first or 'unary' trait that brings the subject into being as a singular One; as the mark of priority in the Other's affections (the 'first' or *most* loved); as the inaugural (proto-psychotic) phase when one 'first' falls in love; or, in the previous chapter, as a phrase expressing something of the mathematical paradoxes inherent in the idea of love's 'first time'. To conclude this discussion, I suggest we look now in closer detail at the operation by which these different possible 'Ones' of 'First Love' are generated by turning to Kierkegaard's chapter, 'The First Love', in *Either/Or*.[1] One immediate consequence of this approach is the way Kierkegaard will oblige us to explicitly address the part that literature plays in the operation through which the One of 'First Love' is attained.

Aside from the fact that it appears in what is generally regarded as a masterpiece of 'philosophy', the other formal difference between Kierkegaard's 'The First Love' and the other texts discussed so far lies in the way it is not itself a novel, short story or poem titled 'First Love' but a 'review' (that is, a piece of literary criticism) of Eugene Scribe's play *Les premières amours*. The text appears as

---

1. Søren Kierkegaard, *Either/Or*, vol. 1, trans. David F. Swenson and Lillian Marvin Swenson, revised and foreword Howard A. Johnson, New York, Anchor Books, 1959.

the seventh chapter of *Either/Or* (1843) which, according to the work's premises, is composed of a group of texts that the Editor ('Victor Eremita') discovered in a hidden receptacle of an old secretary and published at his own expense. The chapter, 'The First Love', belongs to the first half of this collection, representing a selection of aesthetic essays written by an individual that Victor Eremita names A, while the second half is composed of letters to A from a magistrate, 'Judge William', whom the editor names B. A's review of Scribe's play forms part of what the editor describes as A's attempt 'to formulate an aesthetic philosophy of life', while the writings of B in *Or* supposedly represent arguments in favor of an ethical view of life.[2]

Because of this dual structure, *Either/Or* has frequently been read as a choice in philosophical ethics that asks the reader to decide between the aesthetic life or the ethical life. However, Roger Poole has recently made a strong case for regarding the entire work itself as 'aesthetic', arguing that both of the offers made within it are, in effect, 'aesthetic offers'.[3] The entire book, he asserts, is 'a literary work *first and foremost*', whose chief predecessor in its genre is Goethe's *Wilhelm Meister*, which established the set of literary conventions Kierkegaard deploys: 'the exchange of letters, the inset narratives that are read aloud, the diary form, a collection of aphorisms, and scattered observations taken from an archive'.[4] Other important influences Poole identifies include Friedrich Schlegel's *Lucinde* (1799), Ludwig Tieck's *Franz Sternbalds Wanderungen* (1798), Jean Paul's *Titan* (1800-1803) and Novalis with *Heinrich von Ofterdingen* (1802).

Poole's reminder is timely because it has become commonplace to regard Kierkegaard as a philosopher first and a writer second, and to privilege, in accordance with this distinction, Kierkegaard's supposed final emphasis on the religious discourse that occupied much of his writings in the later parts of his life. It has thus become typical of such 'philosophical' readings to regard the erotic love (*Elskov*) championed by both 'A' and 'B' (albeit in opposing ways) as subsumed beneath the more truly abiding, 'eternal' love (*Kjerlighed*) that connects 'the temporal and eternity' that

---

2. Kierkegaard, *Either/Or*, p. 13.

3. Roger Poole, 'Reading *Either/Or* for the Very First Time', in *The New Kierkegaard*, Elsebet Jegstrup (ed.), Bloomington, Indiana University Press, 2004, pp. 42-54, p. 47.

4. Poole, 'Reading *Either/Or* for the Very First Time', p. 46.

Kierkegaard, in *Works of Love,* names religious love or 'Christian love'.[5] Peculiarly unself-conscious in its implicit Hegelianism, especially given Kierkegaard's own fraught relation to Hegel, this philosophical narrative has come under increasing fire from more literarily-minded critics. Already in *The Deconstructive Turn,* Christopher Norris contested what was until the post-war period the widely accepted idea that the aesthetic works are merely stages on the way to an overarching religious perspective that sublates and transcends them.[6] Norris points out how Kierkegaard himself is at pains to convey how both kinds of production 'were carried on simultaneously at every stage of his authorship, rather than forming a linear progression which might be equated with the gradual maturing of Kierkegaard's soul'.[7] Accordingly, Norris refers to Kierkegaard's late article, 'The Crisis and A Crisis in the Life of an Actress', that reminds us how, 'The Religious is present from the beginning. Conversely, the aesthetic is present again at the last moment'.[8]

Louis Mackey, in a similar vein, critiques the philosophical tradition for its relative neglect of Kierkegaard's 'poetic' use of pseudonyms. Mackey sees this neglect as symptomatic of an attempt to draw Kierkegaard's diversity of viewpoints together under a single, dominating 'Point of view'.[9] Meanwhile, George Pattison has offered what is perhaps the most far-reaching literary revision of the Kierkegaadian philosophical 'stages' when he suggests these be understood not temporally, as different phases that are successively overcome, but rather as different representational *forms,* corresponding to the genres of the drama, the novel and the discourse.[10] Pattison's recommendation is long overdue, not least because of the way it enables us to by-pass the 'moral' (philosophical) reading of Kierkegaard, but there is one further step I feel we need to take: my claim is that the aesthetic, ethical and religious discourses are

---

5. Kierkegaard, *Works of Love,* ed. and trans. Howard V. Hong and Edna H. Hong, Princeton, Princeton University Press, 1995, p. 6.

6. Christopher Norris, *The Deconstructive Turn: Essays in the Rhetoric of Philosophy,* London, Routledge, 1989.

7. Norris, *The Deconstructive Turn,* p. 86.

8. Norris, *The Deconstructive Turn,* p. 86.

9. Louis Mackey, 'Philosophy and Poetry in Kierkegaard', *The Review of Metaphysics,* vol. 23, 1969, pp. 316-32. See also his *Kierkegaard: A Kind of Poet,* Philadelphia, University of Pennsylvania Press, 1971.

10. George Pattison, *Kierkegaard: the Aesthetic and the Religious: From the Magic Theatre to the Crucifixion of the Image,* London, SCM Press, 1999, p. xvi.

to be understood not so much as forms but *formalizations*, that is, different ways of 'writing' what Lacan calls the 'myth' of love.[11]

## THE FIRST LOVE ...

In Scribe's comedy, *Les premières amours*, A finds a superlative expression of the aesthetic theories he has been developing throughout the course of *Either*. Immensely popular in Kierkegaard's Copenhagen, *Les premières amours* was one of a number of Scribe's works that helped to definitively cement the Danish public's taste for French drama (and French comedy in particular) in the midpart of the nineteenth-century. Ronald Grimsley reports that *Les premières amours* received 131 performances over a span of nearly fifty years, the greatest number of which occurred during Kierkegaard's productive years, from the beginnings of his probable interest in the theatre as a young man in 1831 until his death in 1855.[12] As we learn in the preamble to the review, Kierkegaard's aesthete shares the general acclaim for the play, calling it 'a play without a fault', a play 'so perfect that it alone should make Scribe immortal'.[13] We soon learn that it occupies a unique place in A's own personal history as well, as a play he first watched in the presence of his own former sweetheart, his own 'first love'.

In the tradition of good French comedy, the plot is certainly stupid enough: Emmeline, the only daughter of a wealthy ironfounder, is about to be married off to the young man Rinville. Brought up on an unhealthy diet of romantic novels by her Aunt Judith, Emmeline refuses to meet him, claiming she is still in love with her childhood sweetheart, her cousin Charles whom she last saw when she was eight. Upon intercepting a letter that informs him where Emmeline's heart really lies, Rinville decides to increase his chance of success by passing himself off as the long absent Charles. When Charles unexpectedly arrives home, already secretly married and with debts he hopes his uncle will pay, he agrees to join in the masquerade. The comedic change of identity has its desired effect: Emmeline, on first meeting 'Charles' again (really Rinville), declares her undying love for him, but once she

---

11. Lacan, *Le Séminaire de Jacques Lacan, Livre VIII, Le transfert*, texte établi par Jacques-Alain Miller, Paris, Seuil, 2001, (lesson of 7.12.60).

12. Ronald Grimsley, *Søren Kierkegaard and French Literature*, Cardiff, University of Wales Press, 1966, pp. 112-13.

13. Kierkegaard, *Either/Or*, p. 246.

discovers he no longer has the ring she gave him, she falls rapidly out of love. Her love mysteriously returns as soon as 'Charles' is able to produce the token. After much hilarious confusion, their true identities are finally revealed, upon which Emmeline agrees to marry Rinville. 'It was a mistake', she tells him, 'I confused the past with the future'.[14]

The key to the aesthete's reading of the play—what makes it for him a 'masterpiece of dramatic perfection' and thus a worthy literary expression of his aesthetic philosophy—lies in this final statement of Emmeline's, which he emphatically does not take as an admission of a mistake, that is, as a sign of a change in Emmeline's outlook. Indeed, it is against this 'moralizing' (or 'philosophical') narrative of ethical progress that his entire reading of the play is pitted. For A, there is 'not the least thing discernible in the play to indicate that her choice of Rinville might be more reasonable than anything else she has done'.[15] For A, 'Emmeline's nature is infinite nonsense, she is quite as silly at the end as in the beginning'. In A's reading of the play, Emmeline does not marry Rinville because she suddenly realizes that she has loved him all along as the pseudo-Charles and, in so recognizing, discovers the error of her maxim, learned from their Aunt Judith in the course of their literary education, that 'the first love is the true love and one only loves once'. Quite the contrary, says A. If Emmeline discovers that the real Charles is not her Charles, she soon discovers that Rinville is not her Charles either, leaving open the possibility that 'a new figure will appear, who resembles Charles, and so forth'.[16] Thus, far from ending, the play continues in an 'infinite jest' about Emmeline, and her final speech must be understood in the following way: 'Previously', says A, 'her illusion lay behind her in the past, now she will seek it in the world and in the future, for she has not renounced the romantic Charles'.[17] Her closing speech thus indicates not a change of heart but 'a change of movement' but 'whether she travels forward or backward, her expedition in search of the first love is comparable to the journey one undertakes in search of health which, as someone has said, is always one station ahead'.[18]

---

14. Kierkegaard, *Either/Or*, p. 253.
15. Kierkegaard, *Either/Or*, p. 255.
16. Kierkegaard, *Either/Or*, p. 256.
17. Kierkegaard, *Either/Or*, p. 257.
18. Kierkegaard, *Either/Or*, p. 252.

The reader will not find it hard to recognize shades of the Freudian lost object in A's description of first love. The lost object, classically the mother for Freud, is permanently 'one station ahead', requiring not to be found but *re*-found—re-found, because as soon as we believe we have reached it, we immediately discover that 'that's not it!', obliging us to begin the search anew. In the dominant interpretation of this Freudian narrative as represented by a tradition of psychoanalytic literary criticism that arguably begins with Marie Bonaparte and extends into the present with critics such as John Robert Keller, the paths we trace in desire represent our attempts recover the original blissful union with this irretrievably lost first love, the mother. I scarcely need add that this attempt is notoriously hopeless, simply because no real object can ever match the mythical maternal ideal which, as psychoanalysis also reminds us, has no more real existence than Emmeline's Charles. The entire ensuing trajectory of the subject as a subject of desire revolves around this originally missing object that we can subsequently only approach piecemeal, through the exigency of what Lacan calls the object *a*—the little piece of the subject that was cut loose by castration and had to be given up in order to accede to a symbolic identity. Assuming objective form as the *Unheimlich* objects Lacan identifies as the voice, the gaze, the faeces and the breast, the principal feature of the object *a* lies in the way it continually slips from the subject's grasp.[19] The moment this infinitely desired object is reached, it immediately divests itself of its magical qualities which get passed over onto another now desired object ad infinitum in what Lacan calls the metonymy of desire. Psychoanalytically speaking, we are all Emmelines, 'spirits of the ring': held in thrall by some nonsensical little nullity, literally a nothing, a zero that we chase after, we obey—that is to say, fall in love with—anyone along the way who is regarded 'as hav[ing] the ring in his hand'.[20]

The only problem with this Freudian story of course is that it isn't true. Like Emmeline's enchanted vision of the love she and Charles shared as eight year olds, the experience of unity with the mother never happened; it is a myth. But like the other famous psychoanalytic 'myth' (the primal 'father of enjoyment' from

---

19. In his seminar devoted to the object *a*, for example, Lacan offers a working definition of the object *a* as what 'falls' (*chute*) from the field of the symbolic. See, for example, the lesson of 22.12.65, *Seminar XIII, The Object of Psychoanalysis (1965-1966)*, unpublished seminar.

20. Kierkegaard, *Either/Or*, p. 269.

*Totem and Taboo*[21]), the fact that it has no empirical reality does not mean that it has no 'truth'. For psychoanalysis, which famously distinguishes between truth and knowledge, the lack of a basis in physical reality has never stopped one from claiming that something—an hysterical symptom, say—possesses *truth*.[22]

## ... is the true love

Without question, Badiou is the contemporary philosopher who has put the most sustained effort into revitalizing the notion of truth in recent times. In the context of today's widespread relativism, Badiou's call for the reinvigoration of truth as a viable philosophical category sounds strangely out of touch with the contemporary scene, almost as if in the philosopher we find a sort of avuncular philosophical analogue of Emmeline's and Charles' Aunt Judith, keen reader of romance literature and pedagogical source of Emmeline's seemingly disastrous 'theory'. However, as we take a closer look now at Badiou's idea of truth as a procedure of the 'fidelity' we explored in the previous chapter, it will appear as anything but sentimental or 'psychological'. For starters, a 'subject' of a truth procedure is not the 'organisation' as Badiou puts it, 'of a sense experience'.[23] It is not a substance, let alone the interiorized self so beloved of a certain Romantic tradition but, rather, a decidedly gravelly-sounding 'local configuration of a generic procedure from which a truth is supported'.[24]

To gain a better understanding of what is at issue, it will help to refresh ourselves with a number of Badiou's basic concepts and their terminology. A 'generic procedure' refers to the way an event—the eruption of the void—is 'incorporated' into an existing system of representation or 'situation'. A 'situation', as we recall, is Badiou's term for the consistently presented multiplicity, that is, a presentation that has been structured by a founding Law.[25]

---

21. Sigmund Freud, 'Totem and Taboo', *The Standard Edition of the Complete Psychological Works of Sigmund Freud*, vol XIII (1913-1914), trans James Strachey, London, Hogarth, 1955, pp. 1-255.

22. As Lacan puts it in *Seminar XX, Encore*, 'Something true can still be said about what cannot be demonstrated'. *The Seminar of Jacques Lacan, Book XX, Encore: On Feminine Sexuality, The Limits of Love and Knowledge (1972-1973)*, Jacques-Alain Miller (ed.), trans. Bruce Fink (New York: Norton, 1998), p. 119.

23. Alain Badiou, *Being and Event*, trans. Oliver Feltham, London, Continuum, 2005, p. 391.

24. Badiou, *Being and Event*, p. 391.

25. See Badiou's entry in the glossary in *Being and Event*, p. 522.

Badiou's classic example of a generic procedure is the Christian Church. The Church responds to the 'event' of the 'death of God' by assembling all the terms of the situation (the previous state of affairs) that are positively connected to the event in what Badiou calls a generic procedure of fidelity, which he also calls a 'truth'.[26] As is well-known, generic procedures of fidelity can be initiated in different fields or 'domains'—love, art, science and politics—each of which produce truths specific to their domains. As an example of a political truth Badiou suggests Bolshevism (the generic procedure initiated by the event of revolution), for science, set theory (initiated by the event of infinite multiples), for art, serialism (initiated by the event of the destruction of the tonal system) and, finally, for love, the declaration (initiated by the encounter or 'meeting').[27]

As we will see, the question of truth is intimately linked to what Badiou calls subjectivization. Subjectivization describes what happens in the truth procedure when the name of the generic procedure is 'subsumed' beneath the proper name of an individual. It is, as Badiou puts it in his admittedly formidable prose, 'the interventional nomination from the standpoint of the situation, that is, the rule of the intra-situational effects of the supernumerary name's [that is, the name of the void] entrance into circulation'.[28] One might paraphrase this by saying subjectivization represents the process by which a local or immanent name comes to embody the law or structure governing the new situation following the event. Such proper names include—to continue working from the above list—Lenin for the Party, Cantor for ontology, Schoenberg for music but also, as Badiou explicitly says, 'Simon, Bernard or Claire, if they declare themselves to be in love'.[29] Each of these names, Badiou asserts, are the names of what he calls 'the subjectivizing split' that inheres between the name of an event (the general proper name bestowed in an illicit nominal intervention) and the initiation of its generic procedure (or 'truth'). They thus play a role similar to that which we saw 'Mary' performing for John Clare, namely, as embodying the unique and *particular* name through which a truth can nevertheless undergo 'universaliza-

---

26. Badiou writes, 'A truth is the infinite positive total—the gathering together of x(+)'s—of a procedure which, for each and every determinant of the encyclopedia, contains at least one enquiry which avoids it'. Badiou, *Being and Event*, p. 338.

27. Badiou, *Being and Event*, p. 393.
28. Badiou, *Being and Event*, p. 393.
29. Badiou, *Being and Event*, p. 393.

tion'. Accordingly, as a concept, subjectivization supplements and goes some way toward resolving the problem I located in Badiou's nomination of the loving encounter. For here, Badiou suggests, a proper name can apparently act in the place of the generic declaration 'I love you' without suffering a loss of its universal potential (that is, without being falsely or illegally 'ontologized').

We will come back to Badiou's concept of subjectivization later on but in the meantime it should be apparent even from this very cursory account that Badiou's concept of truth is a rigorous affair, and not undertaken lightly nor even very often. For Badiou, a subject and its truth are *rare* occurrences, sharing in this something of the exceptional or 'occasional' nature (to use the key term A opens with in his preamble to his discussion of Scribe) of Emmeline's notion of the first love as a once-in-a-lifetime occurrence.[30] And indeed, between these two theorists of love there is more than a passing resemblance. In what follows, I will suggest that Emmeline's romantic maxim—'the first love is the true love and one only loves once'—is not simply the girlish nonsense of an inexperienced girl brought up on romance novels, but has its own element of rigour as fully as 'mathematical' as Badiou's—and is perhaps just as singular if not entirely as rare.

So let us take Emmeline's motto as our starting point. On an initial reading, it appears both categorical and irrevocable: 'the first love is the true love and one only loves once'. You have only one chance in your life, it seems to say, to really love someone, and that person is the only one you will ever really love. Nevertheless, as we hear in the preamble in which A tells the story of his own 'first love', in practice the 'first' turns out to be a rather slippery category. In his lead-up to his review of Scribe, A relates the story of how on meeting his former sweetheart again—the same one with whom he had first attended a performance of *Les premières amours*—he discovered her telling exactly the same story as Emmeline: the first love is the true love and one only love's once. But in A's former lover's case, 'She assured me that she had never loved me, but that her betrothed was her first love, and that 'only the first love is the true love'.[31] For this young woman, the first love is evidently not a numerical but a qualitative category, and one that allows a certain (convenient) revisionism in one's personal history.

---

30. 'The subject is not an invariable of presentation. The subject is rare, in that the generic procedure is a diagonal of the situation'. Badiou, *Being and Event*, p. 392.
31. Kierkegaard, *Either/Or*, p. 242.

This, however, is assuredly not what Emmeline has in mind. Nor would it make *Les premières amours* in A's estimation, a play that is 'infinitely comic',[32] with Emmeline a character whose nature is 'infinite nonsense'.[33] From such a 'sophistical' approach to the question of first love, Emmeline would on the contrary recoil in horror. As A explains:

> When a widower and a widow join fortunes, and each one brings five children along, then they still assure each other on their wedding day that this love is their first love. Emmeline in her romantic orthodoxy would look upon such a connection with aversion; it would be to her a mendacious abomination, which would be as loathsome to her as a marriage between a monk and a nun was to the Middle Ages.[34]

Emmeline, by contrast, 'holds fast to her proposition numerically understood', which A qualifies a page later in this way: 'She loves [Charles] with an objective, *mathematical* love'.[35] The manner in which we understand this 'mathematical' love, as 'numerically understood', will decide whether the wit of Scribe's play stands or falls for, as A puts it, Emmeline 'must now acquire experience and the experience refutes her. It appears that she loves Rinville'.[36] To determine whether the play is 'infinitely comic, or finitely moralizing', the validity of Emmeline's maxim must be put to the test.[37]

The irony lies in the statement's patent falsity, for not only does Emmeline love more than once (first Charles and then Rinville), at another level she has never loved at all: to the extent that she refuses to give up her 'illusion' of Charles, Emmeline's first love is 'always one station ahead'.[38] How can she claim, then, to love only once? The only meaningful counter to this rebuff is that Emmeline's statement refers not to any actual or imagined loved object but to the manner, the *way* in which Emmeline loves. For psychoanalysis, it is perfectly reasonable to say that one 'only loves once', even if one can rattle off a reel of past lovers, each of whom enjoyed the genuine privilege of being the 'first' and 'true' love. However, the apparent relativism of this psychoanalytic approach to love differs markedly from A's former sweetheart's revisionist notion of first love, for this

---

32. Kierkegaard, *Either/Or*, p. 253.
33. Kierkegaard, *Either/Or*, p. 255.
34. Kierkegaard, *Either/Or*, p. 252.
35. Kierkegaard, *Either/Or*, p. 252, p. 253 (my emphasis).
36. Kierkegaard, *Either/Or*, p. 253.
37. Kierkegaard, *Either/Or*, p. 253.
38. Kierkegaard, *Either/Or*, p. 257.

formula holds just as true even if one has yet to find one's 'true love'. What the psychoanalytic formula refers to, in other words, is an original choice, expressed by the Freudian term *Neurosenwahl*. This is the choice we carry with us throughout all of our loving history that directs which 'stage' our subjective drama will be performed on, whether neurotic, perverse or psychotic. In this sense, to say 'one loves only once' is to say we are capable of only one desiring scenario, one fundamental fantasy that organizes the multiple encounters (real and imagined) of our love lives and which itself *never changes*. The fantasy is what guarantees that beyond all of their infinite variety or superficial or 'small' differences, each of our lovers is at some unconscious level the Same, a partner in a specific pattern of desire that, chosen once and once only, cannot be undone.[39]

As Freud's term *'choice'* suggests, there always remains a dimension of freedom in the way one 'chooses' to love. Nevertheless, one must add that this is not in any way a choice that can be consciously made but is, rather, something that can only be discovered in the past tense, as having already *been* made. It is only in and through its subsequent effects—that is, in the actual lived loves and choice of lovers, and the way we position or 'number' them within our personal histories—that this choice is testified to and given actuality. Recalling Badiou's terms above, one might say that our love lives are the 'truth operation' of this choice of fundamental fantasy. By remaining faithful to this 'first love' or pattern of desire, we give expression to the freedom implicitly contained in that original choice, even if our actual experience is that of being mastered—tugged away from what we consciously think we want by strange and inexplicable, repetitive 'mistakes' (as we typically interpret them) in our loving histories.

### ... and one only loves once

This should become clearer as we now look a little more closely at the ways Emmeline and Charles 'love only once'. Emmeline, as

---

39. Both Freud and Lacan have wavered on this point, with Freud ultimately opting for an original, non-negotiable choice which is 'independent of experience'. See Freud's discussion of a seeming conversion from anxiety hysteria to obsessional neurosis in 'The Disposition to Obsessional Neurosis'. Sigmund Freud, *Standard Edition* vol. XII, pp. 317-26. But even if the choice itself can never be undone, this is not to say that the *way* it was made cannot be revised as Paul Verhaeghe explains in his elaboration of psychoanalysis' various 'therapeutic effects'. See Paul Verhaeghe, *On Being Normal and Other Disorders*, trans. Sigi Jöttkandt, New York, Other Press, 2004.

we saw, is perpetually in search of the 'first love' as an event that is infinitely to come. No single lover comes up to her vision of the 'romantic Charles' which, the aesthete never stops reminding us, is an 'illusion'. Charles, too, is in the grip of an illusion, insofar as he had the same 'romantic training' as Emmeline, but unlike his cousin, who is 'hidden from [her]self' as A puts it, Charles believes he can hide from others. Charles's belief in his own powers of mystification, A tells us, 'is just as fantastic as Emmeline's illusion, and one recognizes Judith's schooling in both'.[40]

In these two eager readers of romantic novels, one finds a remarkable illustration of two different ways a lover can miss the 'true' love. Or, to put it into A's mathematical terminology, we could say that in Emmeline and Charles we discover two complementary but opposing strategies by which one can fail to 'count to One'. Eternally in search of the first, Emmeline must always begin her quest for Charles anew, for each time she finds him he will fail to be 'Charles'. More acquainted with the 'pinch of reality', Charles, on the other hand, has already expended his illusion and, having become 'a dissolute fellow', finds himself tricked into marriage by a woman more well-versed in mystification than he.[41] Not one to admit defeat, Charles will employ any number of disguises to obtain his goal—as A puts it, 'he knows that there are five or six ways whereby one can move an uncle's heart'—and if the first is unsuccessful, he will try on another, and then another in an infinite display of confidence in his ability 'not to be recognized'.[42]

Thus while both Emmeline's and Charles's different attempts to reach the One will inevitably fail, what is of interest is the way each of these failures generates its own unique form of infinity. It is not difficult to see how the infinity produced by Emmeline's failure to count to One corresponds to the infinity found in Zeno's paradox of Achilles and the tortoise. Racing each other, Achilles permits the tortoise a head-start only to find that he can never catch up with her since, in the time he is covering the distance the tortoise has already traveled, the tortoise will have 'run' farther ahead. To catch up, Achilles must then cover the new distance, by which time the tortoise will have advanced further still. Discussing this paradox in Seminar XX, Lacan explains that Achilles can only

---

40. Kierkegaard, *Either/Or*, p. 249.
41. Kierkegaard, *Either/Or*, p. 247.
42. Kierkegaard, *Either/Or*, p. 248.

pass or leap-frog the tortoise: 'He cannot catch up with it. He only catches up with it at infinity'.[43] In much the same way, Emmeline must always be either behind or ahead of 'Charles', constantly under- or over-shooting her mark and forced to begin again.

With Charles, on the other hand, we obtain another kind of infinity. Charles' infinity corresponds to that found in Zeno's other paradox—that of the arrow in motion. The paradox here is Zeno's proof of motion's 'impossibility': the arrow will never 'move' since it can eternally be divided into ever smaller units of measurement. While Emmeline's One lies forever in the future, Charles's One is already in the past—as a married man, he has already found his 'One' (Paméla). Yet Charles's difficulty lies in how, as a master of disguise himself, he can never really be sure which was the very 'first' One, that is, whether he is not still being taken in by Paméla or Rinville or indeed even by Emmeline. Like the arrow's 'endlessly interrupted flight that can only asymptotically approach its goal', as Joan Copjec puts it, Charles's 'count' is strictly speaking immobile—he can never get to Two because he can never agree on where the 'One' really began.[44]

In his chapter on Hegel in *Being and Event,* Badiou identifies the dialectical logic specific to the two kinds of infinity we have just described, noting how the first, corresponding to what Hegel calls the 'qualitative infinity', 'is infinite according to a dialectic of *identification*'. Here the one 'proceeds from the other'. The second type of infinity, 'quantity', 'is infinite according to a dialectic of *proliferation*'. In this case, the 'same proceeds from the One'.[45] What I find especially useful about Badiou's insight here is the way it prompts us to recognize the way Emmeline's and Charles's two forms of infinity correlate with the desiring neuroses. As is well-known, Lacan writes the formula for fantasy as $\$ \diamond a$. However in the seminar on the transference, Seminar VIII, what one might call this 'generic' formula of fantasy is given further specification in the formulas of the hysterical and obsessional fantasies which are written as follows:

Hysterical fantasy: $\frac{a}{-\varphi} \diamond A$

Obsessional fantasy: $\bcancel{A} \diamond \varphi \, (a' \, a'' \, a''' \, ...)$

---

43. Lacan, Seminar XX, p. 8.
44. Joan Copjec, *Read My Desire: Lacan Against the Historicists,* Cambridge, MIT Press, 1994, p. 52.
45. Badiou, *Being and Event,* p. 168.

The first formula, that of the hysterical fantasy, depicts a strategy for covering over one's own intrinsic lack (-φ) by way of an *identification* with what one believes the Other desires (a). When this identification fails, as of course it always will for the Emmelines of the world, this is not so much because 'Charles' does not match up to her illusion of him—although this is how we customarily explain the hysteric's constitutive disappointment in the Master. For as A continually reminds us, Emmeline fundamentally does not *know* Charles, thus how could she know what to match him against? Thus when Emmeline becomes convinced that 'Charles' is not 'Charles', we must conclude that this realization occurs not because of any change in Charles's real or imagined characteristics, but rather because at some level he has failed to recognize *her*. A explains how Emmeline 'does not seek the alteration in the fact that Charles has become a spendthrift or possibly something even worse, but in that he has not confided everything to her, as he was accustomed to do'.[46] It is this, rather than any failure to match up to any ideal, that convinces the hysteric that 'Charles' 'is not the same anymore'.[47] Kierkegaard thus gives an intriguing new slant to the hysteric's eternal question to the Master, 'what [or who] am I?'[48] For in this case we see that the hysteric knows very well who *she* is—her question concerns whether the Master also knows, and when it becomes apparent he does not, she reembarks on her quest for a new One, a Master who *truly* knows and recognizes who she is.

As can be seen from the second formula, a different objective drives the obsessional fantasy, which in this case is not propelled by the subject's lack. The obsessional, famously, does not feel he lacks anything. It is, on the contrary, precisely because he feels he satisfies the Other all too well that he is led in his fantasy to emphasize the lack in the Other ($\cancel{A}$). Accordingly, the obsessional's entire fantasmatic scenario is designed to keep the Other in a state of desire, of wanting more, which he employs as a defense against the threat of being entirely swallowed up by the (m)Other. Thus, like Charles, the obsessional becomes an expert in mystification. He generates, in Badiou's formulation, a *proliferating* series of substitutive objects—the traditional obsessional behaviours or 'disguises' that are to keep the Other (in Charles' case, his uncle

---

46. Kierkegaard, *Either/Or*, p. 268.
47. Kierkegaard, *Either/Or*, p. 267.
48. See Lacan's lesson of 19.4.61, *Seminar VIII, Transference*.

and Emmeline) occupied while preserving his real identity (that is, a married man) beyond the Other's reach. These 'disguises' are expressed in the obsessional's formula in the shape of the little *a*s, semblances of the semblance that he, as the Other's *a*, attempts to hide behind. Of course what the obsessional doesn't realize is that, like Charles, it is he who is the most taken in by his disguises. As A puts it, Charles 'believes it is he who contrives intrigues, he who mystifies, and yet the spectator sees that the mystification was in operation before Charles appears'.[49] Imagining that he is the puppet master generating illusion, the obsessional in fact 'give[s] the whole thing away'.[50]

As implied by these descriptions, the fundamental fantasies are in fact defense mechanisms that attempt to offer what Mladen Dolar describes as a 'provisional understanding of something which eludes understanding'.[51] Their psychic function, as is well-known, is to mitigate an original trauma Freud termed an 'internal' arousal, which Lacan renamed *jouissance*. The fantasies achieve this by providing this incomprehensible arousal or *jouissance* with some kind of interim representation. This provisional representation reduces and siphons off the anxiety the subject experiences in its confrontation with what it cannot comprehend—the Other's desire[52]—by supplying some kind of form to the nothing, the original 'object' of anxiety. One should accordingly regard the different fantasies—hysteric, obsessional and perverse—as different ways of 'dramatizing' this nothing.[53] Like comedy, with which they therefore share an intrinsic kinship, the fantasies put the nothing or 'void', as Badiou calls it, *on stage*.[54] The fantasies, 'the sexuo-erotic template that provides an answer to the desire of the Other', as Dany Nobus has described them, do the same thing.[55] They 'convoke' the void as some form of 'appearance'.

---

49. Kierkegaard, *Either/Or*, p. 259.
50. Kierkegaard, *Either/Or*, p. 260.
51. Mladen Dolar, *A Voice and Nothing More*, Cambridge, MIT Press, 2006, p. 137.
52. In Seminar IX, Lacan defines anxiety as 'the sensation of the desire of the Other'. *The Seminar of Jacques Lacan, Book IX, Identification (1961-1962)*, unpublished seminar (lesson of 4 April, 1962).
53. Recall that psychosis, as we saw in a previous chapter, has no fantasy but is instead described by Lacan as 'delusion'.
54. Alenka Zupančič observes of comedy that one its 'fundamental gestures [...] is to make an appearance out of what is behind the appearance. They make the truth (of the Real) not so much reveal itself, as appear. See her *The Shortest Shadow: Nietzsche's Philosophy of the Two*, Cambridge, MIT Press, 2003, p. 168.
55. Dany Nobus, 'Unpredictable Inevitability and the Boundaries of Psychic Life',

Like Scribe's play, although that which the fantasies turn on is therefore literally 'nothing', and 'that which comes out of [them] is [also] nothing', in A's words, the fantasies nevertheless create a remarkable effect.[56] By being channeled through this primary act of what Badiou would call 'presentation', the nothing of the void is transformed from an incomprehensible and thus anxiety-producing nothing into something that is far more manageable, namely, a subject-object relation. This 'something' is infinitely more manageable for the subject because, as a relation to an object that can be either present or absent, the hope is maintained that if we could only find the right object or 'true love'—or *successfully count to One*—the original psychic imbalance introduced by the intrusion of jouissance would be 'solved'.

My suggestion, then, is that we conceive of the 'first love', understood in this sense of the fundamental fantasies or original 'pattern' of desire, as various methods for literally working out a mathematical equation whose result is always ideally a return to a state of non-tension or 'inertia', as Freud calls it. One could say that the fantasies surround the void with subjective brackets, enabling this now-bracketed void to emerge as a counter or placeholder or 'empty set' that, lending itself to being 'counted as One', serves to re-balance the subjective economy that has been upset by the introduction of the absolute 'negativity' of unrepresentable *jouissance*.

The fantasy's 'equation' can accordingly be written in this way:

$$\emptyset \sim (\{\emptyset\} = 1) = 0$$

Here we see how the void or unpresentable point of being $\emptyset$ is made 'equivalent to' the empty set $\{\emptyset\}$ which can serve as the first placeholder for the count as One. The result of this 'equation' is zero, or 'inertia'—the ideal state of the subject prior to the eruption of *jouissance*. The empty set, counted as (positive) One, balances out the pure negative (or minus 'One') of the void. Expressing the equation in words, we read:

> Void, made equivalent to the empty set, which is 'counted as One', results in 'inertia' or zero

What we must now determine is the status of this 'making equivalent', the subject's first heretical act of equation that enables a

---

in *The Catastrophic Imperative: Time, Subjectivity, Memory in Contemporary Thought*, Dominiek Hoens, Sigi Jöttkandt, Gert Buelens (eds.), London, Palgrave, 2009.

56. Kierkegaard, *Either/Or*, p. 260.

nothing to be represented as something (the empty set) which can then serve as the basis for the count. As we see from the above, this empty set is the void that has been framed in some way, or to recall Badiou's terms, it is the void that has been 'named'. By saying this, Badiou cautions us against thinking that the void is now successfully contained in or 'belongs' to the set {∅} 'because the void belongs to no presented multiple [...]. What belongs to this set is the proper name which constitutes the suture-to-being of the axiomatic presentation of the pure multiple; that is, the presentation of presentation'.[57] As the 'existent mark of the unpresentable', the name sutures a new situation to its 'being'.[58]

Let us take one final step before we leave this part of the discussion. It should be clear by now that for psychoanalysis, the phallus is the name for the empty set: the phallus or 'castration' is the 'illegal' and heretical name that we, as 'subjects of psychoanalytic truth', give to the unrepresentable event or void, enabling it to be presented as a 'consistent multiplicity' and thus to serve as the basis for structuring the inconsistent multiplicity (the 'presentation' that Badiou calls the count-as-One). And, to put it unambiguously, the way the subject orchestrates its relation to the phallus—the precise way it chooses to 'stage' its counting of the empty set as One—is what Lacan calls the fundamental fantasies. Each fantasy thus relates to the empty set that is the phallic signifier in a different way: the neurotic fantasies (hysteric and obsessional) famously repress it, the perverse fantasy disavows it, while the psychotic, in foreclosing it, does not strictly speaking have a 'relation' to it (and therefore is not one of the fundamental 'fantasies' proper).

But while each of the fantasies employs the phallus as the beginning or basis for its 'count to One', because of the different ways the phallus can be 'made to appear', to recall Zupančič's phrase, each fantasmatic 'count' generates a different kind of what Badiou calls the 'One-as-effect'.[59] In *Being and Event*, Badiou describes the One-as-effect or One-result as the 'fictive beings' that are retroactively produced through the counting operation.[60] The One-as-effect results from submitting the count-as-One to the second count or count-of-the-count. The distinction is between Badiou's notions of counting-as-One and forming-into-

---

57. Badiou, *Being and Event*, p. 89.
58. Badiou, *Being and Event*, p. 88.
59. Badiou, *Being and Event*, p. 90.
60. Badiou, *Being and Event*, p. 90.

One. From the perspective of the fantasmatic equation, the count-as-One describes the equivalence operation that permits the void to be named as the empty set (or, in psychoanalysis, the 'phallic signifier'). However, Badiou specifies that this count is always doubled by a second operation, a second 'count' that Badiou calls forming-into-One. The purpose of this second count is to avert the 'danger of the void', the 'disaster of presentation' that would otherwise occur because of the 'errancy of the void':[61] the fact that in every presentation, something always escapes the count, namely, the count itself.[62]

Here is Badiou:

> Any operation of the count-as-one (of terms) is in some manner doubled by a count of the count, which guarantees, at every moment, that the gap between the consistent multiple (such that it results, composed of ones) and the inconsistent multiple (which is solely the presupposition of the void, and does not present anything) is veritably null. It thus ensures that there is no possibility of that disaster of presentation ever occurring which would be the presentational occurrence, in torsion, of the structure's own void.[63]

'Re-presenting' the first count's 'presentation', the second count guarantees the One as operation, as Badiou puts it (which is moreover, and as we know, the only form of One Badiou recognizes). Insofar as it structures the structure, forming-into-One thus guarantees that the presentation (the first count) does not encounter its own void and result in the ruin of the structure.[64]

We can perhaps make better sense of what is admittedly a fairly technical discussion once we understand the forming-as-One or 'second count' as the undertaking of the fundamental fantasies. I said earlier that the fantasies surround the void with subjective brackets, but we can now go a step further to say that, like

---

61. Badiou, *Being and Event*, p. 90.
62. Badiou, *Being and Event*, p. 93.
63. Badiou, *Being and Event*, p. 94.
64. Badiou writes, 'The fictive one-effect occurs when, via a shortcut whose danger has already been mentioned, I allow myself to say that the ø is "the void", thereby assigning the predicate of the one to the suture-to-being that is the name, and presenting the unpresentable *as such*. The mathematical theory itself is more rigorous in its paradox: speaking of the "void-set", it maintains that this name, which does not present anything, is nevertheless that of a multiple, once, as name, it is submitted to the axiomatic Ideas of the multiple'. Badiou, *Being and Event*, p. 90.

the forming-into-One, this subjective 'bracketing' entails a certain *imaginarization* of the count-as-One. The One-as-effect is the One aimed for in the fantasy, the ideal Ones that the counting operation attempts to reach but, as we saw in the discussion of the infinities above, never actually attains. The fantasies can thus be conceived as conferring a certain 'body' to the One of the count, which is why the individual features of this One-result will be as mercurial as the different fantasies themselves. Each One-result will have its own unique 'character' or 'look' as a result of the way it was constructed.

In order to render this more concrete, let us return to the neurotic fantasies to see what shape(s) this forming-into-One takes for the hysteric and the obsessional. The full 'mathematical' equation of the hysterical fantasy can now be filled in as follows:

$$\varnothing \sim (\{\tfrac{a}{-\varphi} \lozenge A\} = 1) = 0$$

Here the generic empty set $\{\varnothing\}$ of the earlier equation has been filled in with the specific values of how the hysteric 'stages' the appearance of the 'nothing' or void. The formula depicts how the hysterical subject positions herself in the fantasy as vertically split between her phallic castration (minus phi) and the object *a* which, as we saw, represents her identification with what she believes the Other (A) wants from her.[65] Although her fantasy aims for a successful count-to-One (whose ultimate result, as for all the fantasies, is a return to inertia: zero), the difficulty lies in the *a*, the semblance of the Other's desire with which the hysteric attempts to cover over her imaginary lack (-$\varphi$). This *a*, which Lacan in Seminar XV calls the 'source of the mirage of the all', is what ensures that her count will always, Achilles-like, either over- or undershoot its mark.

The reason for this permanent over- or under-shooting lies in the fact that the field of representation, the site where the fantasy is 'staged', is not flat but is topologically distorted by the *a* insofar as it belongs to another order than the symbolic 'count' and its imaginary staging. As a real object, the *a*, in Badiou's terms partakes of the 'errancy of the void'.[66] Created in the original nominal act

---

65. See Lacan's discussion of the hysteric's fantasy in *Seminar VIII, Transference*, lesson of 19.4.61. For a refreshingly lucid explanation of this formula, see Verhaeghe, *On Being Normal and Other Disorders*, pp. 373-81.

66. Lacan, *The Seminar of Jacques Lacan, Book XV, The Psychoanalytic Act*, (1967-1968), unpublished seminar (lesson of 13.3.68).

of 'making equivalence' that enabled the ∅ to be bracketed as the empty set/phallus and counted-as-One, the *a* is that part of the void that was never completely taken up by the provisional presentation psychoanalysis calls the phallic signifier. As a result, the *a* ensures that every fantasmatic equation's 'staging' of a subject-object relation will always be inflected with something of the original traumatic *jouissance* that the fantasies were intended to palliate. This little sliver of *jouissance* that somehow slipped into the symbolic through the back-stage door during the original catastrophic naming of the void ('castration') ensures that the imaginary fantasy of a complete or intact One (that is, an utterly seamless fusion of the subject and object in the One-as-effect) will never be attained. For it is this *a* that drives the subject's unconscious repetition. The *a* is the source of the continual failure that causes every count to One to always begin again. For this reason, any 'mathematical' equation that contains the *a* will always come up lacking in a very precise way in its final result.[67] The One-result of the hysterical fantasy will always necessarily be missing a little bit as the presence of the *a* ensures the Other (A) will never be completely satisfied with her. Despite all the 'narcissistic coatings' as Lacan puts it, that subsequently come to envelop and surround it, the *a* never fully succeeds in covering over the minus phi of the hysteric's castration, meaning that the One that the hysterical fantasy 'counts' to will always fall short.[68]

A similar but opposite thing happens with the obsessional. Although his desiring formula also counts to One, his One-result will always be a little bit in surfeit, again because it is produced by an object *a* that carries along with it something of the same void. In the obsessional's formula, this surplus is indicated as the little distinguishing supra symbols that mark the substitute *a* objects with which he showers the Other in the fantasy (*a' a'' a'''* etc.).

---

67. For a mathematical explanation of the derivation of the *a*, see Lacan's discussion in *Seminar XIV, Logic of Fantasy (1966-1967)*, lessons of 22 and 29 January, 1969. Briefly, the a is not 'equal' to 1, but holds the value of the relation of one term in a Fibonacci series to the next. Thus, if 1+1+2, 1+2+3, in the converging series (hysteria) or, in reverse, the diverging series (obsession) 1-a, 2a-1, 2-3a etc. the 'value' of *a* will always be the proportional difference between one term and the next in the Fibonacci series, a difference which is computed as 0.618. Lacan's use of the Fibonacci series here and elsewhere is designed to model the relationship of the speaking subject to the signifier which represents the subject for another signifier. As Lacan explains, 'here it is the relationship not of 1 to 1 but of 1 to 2 that is at stake'. See his discussion in lesson of 29.1.69.

68. Lacan, *Seminar XV* (lesson of 21 February, 1968).

'The First Love is the True Love and One Only Loves Once'   141

These marks give themselves away as the semblances of $a$ that they are:

$$\varnothing \sim (\{\text{\AA} \lozenge \varphi \, (a' \, a'' \, a''' \, ...)\} = 1) = 0$$

One might ask why, in one case, the $a$ carries with it a certain insufficiency, while in the other carries a certain surplus. Why will the obsessional's One-result always be a tiny bit more than One, while the hysteric's always a little less? The reason for this stems from the neurotic structures' original affective response to the traumatic arousal of *jouissance*. In his 1896 essay, 'Heredity and the Aetiology of the Neuroses', Freud locates at the basis of hysteria an original experience of unpleasure, 'an event of passive sexuality' that was 'submitted to with indifference or with a small degree of annoyance or fright'.[69] Accordingly, as a 'representative' (*Vorstellung*) of this original experience, the $a$ hauls something of this unpleasure along with it into the hysterical desiring fantasy, ensuring that her One-result will always be inflected with a tiny little lacking sign or 'minus'. For the obsessional, on the other hand, it concerns an event which originally, Freud says, 'has given pleasure'. The obsessional's $a$ will thus ensure that his One-result always suffers from a tiny little surfeit, expressing how the obsessional's 'disguises' are just that tiny bit too successful in deceiving the Other. The Other takes him too literally, thereby sabotaging his fantasy that he can endlessly keep substituting new objects for himself in the count's run-out to infinity.

Hence although they are invisible to naked eyes, these tiny little 'pluses' or 'minuses' that successfully manage to ruin each fantasy's One-result must be regarded in the following way: they are immanent expressions in the situation of the original freedom in which the subject made its primordial 'choice' of fundamental fantasy. As testaments to this freedom, the $a$ is what guarantees that there will always remain an excess in the second count's 'meta-structure', that something will remain 'uncounted'. One could justifiably say, then, that the object $a$ is that point in a represented situation that touches upon the void, enabling us to recognize it as the Lacanian equivalent of what Badiou calls an 'evental site': 'entirely abnormal multiples' that are 'admitted' into the count without having to result from 'previous counts'.[70] Tellingly, such

---

69. Sigmund Freud, 'Heredity and the Aetiology of the Neuroses', *Standard Edition*, vol. 3 (1893-1899), pp. 141-56.
70. Badiou, *Being and Event*, p. 175.

abnormal multiples 'block the infinite regression of combinations of multiples', halting what would otherwise be a count to a simple infinity. 'It is therefore correct to say that sites *found* the situation because they are the absolutely primary terms therein', claims Badiou in a formulation that helps us now to gain a greater intuitive understanding of a key tenet of Lacanian psychoanalysis.[71] For as Badiou's terms help us to see, to the extent that the analyst famously positions him- or herself as the object *a* in relation to the analysand, he or she occupies that point in the subject's psychic structure—the subject's 'Achilles' heel' as it were—that has the capacity to *ruin* the subject's fantasy of a successful sexual relation (or One), thereby supplying the potential conditions for the radical transformational change Lacan calls 'the pass'.

## 'HE NEED DO NOTHING'

Let us now step back a little from this discussion and return to Scribe's play for there remains a third figure we have yet to examine. Rinville's position in the desiring comedy will help to clarify the difference between the type of infinity generated by a simple count—that is, one that successfully counts the void as a One and enables us to move on to Two and Three (what Badiou called the 'infinite regression of combinations of multiples')—and the infinities produced by the hysterical and the obsessional.

Like Charles, Rinville is a man of the world, the aesthete tells us, but unlike Charles with his 'romantic training', Emmeline's appointed suitor 'is too well acquainted with the world to be sentimental'.[72] His reasons for wanting to marry Emmeline are four-fold: she is rich, their fathers are friends, he has joked to his friends that he will make a conquest of her and, finally, as 'an afterthought' says A, 'she is really a lovable girl'.[73] As we know, Rinville has initiated the deception and, to that extent, he is the true director of Charles's fantasmatic scene. But does also he direct Emmeline's? A is very clear on one point, which is that Emmeline 'practically forces Rinville to be Charles; to this extent he is blameless'.[74]

We know that Emmeline only 'recognizes' Rinville as Charles because he holds her ring. 'How negligible he is', says A, 'appears

---

71. Badiou, *Being and Event*, p. 175.
72. Kierkegaard, *Either/Or*, p. 251.
73. Kierkegaard, *Either/Or*, p. 251.
74. Kierkegaard, *Either/Or*, p. 264.

also from the fact that when he does not have the ring she does not love him; when he gets the ring she loves him again'.[75] Emmeline 'simply does not see Rinville at all'.[76] Rinville's position is therefore perfectly easy, A tells us. He 'need do nothing [and] can remain quite calm', for Emmeline 'has got her eyes open'.[77] Where, then, does Rinville go wrong? His fundamental mistake, which is always the mistake of the last desiring fantasy we will now look at, lies in his belief that 'there actually was a Charles'.[78] Thus although Rinville possesses none of the typical 'psychological' features one tends to associate with the pervert, we can still confidently describe him as such because of the way he positions himself in relation to Emmeline's fantasy.

The pervert's fantasy is written thus:

$$a \diamond \$$$

The glancing similarities between the obsessional and the perverse psychic structures come down to how they are both driven by an original excess of pleasure—the feeling of being exactly what the Other wants and desires—but unlike the obsessional, the pervert does not experience this as disturbing or traumatic in any way. On the contrary, the pervert wants nothing more than to remain the totally satisfying object of the Other's desire but he is nevertheless forced at some level to recognize the reality of castration, that is, that lack does exist. The perverse subject's response to this lack is the disavowal through which mechanism he is able to simultaneously recognize the phallic lack for the rest of the world (and for the father in particular) while denying it for himself (and for the mother). The result, as Paul Verhaeghe explains, 'is a clearcut split: the pervert lives in a divided world where lack and the regulating law are both recognized and denied at the same time'.[79]

In order to construct a One, the pervert thus must perform a 'counting' operation that is fundamentally different from that of the two neurotic fantasies. Through his strategy of disavowal, the pervert effectively splits the original void into *two* (more or less) *equal halves*—one inflected with a positive charge that denies the lack of the (maternal) phallus, and another that possesses a

---

75. Kierkegaard, *Either/Or*, p. 253.
76. Kierkegaard, *Either/Or*, p. 254.
77. Kierkegaard, *Either/Or*, p. 264.
78. Kierkegaard, *Either/Or*, p. 266.
79. Verhaeghe, *On Being Normal and Other Disorders*, p. 411.

negative charge, representing the world of the symbolic Law beyond the bedroom. One could describe the pervert's subjective division as horizontal rather than the vertical *Spaltung* of the hysteric's and obsessional's repression. Split between two different 'scenes', both of which occur at the same structural 'level', the pervert effectively 'sees' different things with each eye. *Either*, a private scenario in which there is no lack. *Or*, the public symbolic world that is suffused by lack.

To create a One, the pervert must therefore add the two 'halves' together as in the following equation:

$$\varnothing \sim (\{^+1/2 + {}^-1/2\} = 1) = 0$$

Populated with the formula of the perverse fantasy, we obtain:

$$\varnothing \sim (\{a \diamond \$ + \cancel{A}\} = 1) = 0$$

We can read this as follows: the void, made equivalent to, on the one hand, a scenario of total satisfaction inside the bedroom (+1/2), and a scenario of the Other's lack in the outside world (-1/2) which, added together, result in zero (the empty set) that can be counted as 1, thus balancing out the 'negative' 1 of the unrepresentable void.

In theory, the addition should work beautifully, but a closer look will reveal how the first or positive 'half' of the pervert's scenario is in fact the inverse of the hysterical fantasy, where the pervert positions himself in the position of the Master, the one who *really* knows what the desiring subject wants. It is this that introduces the pervert's fundamental problem: as a result of how her *a* was created, the hysteric's One-result will always fall a little short, with the consequence that, left to her own devices, she will eventually leave in search of a new Master (or One). To avoid this eventuality, the pervert must keep her against her will and repeat the original count-as-One, that is to say, he must re-name the void over and over again in his repeated attempts to fully satisfy her. Technically-speaking, it is in this *'doing* [the] *nothing'* that the true 'sadism' of the pervert really lies, namely, in the 'violence' with which the pervert continually convokes and re-convokes the void. With each new repetition of his count-as-One, the pervert thus aims 'to kill his victim twice'—to reach beyond the hysteric's constitutive dissatisfaction and truly satisfy her this time—and in this way bring their (positive) side of his fantasmatic equation up to the absolute One Half he requires in order to successfully perform the computational procedure of the disavowal. Because of this dependence upon the hysteric in his desiring fantasy—a dependence which Rinville shows us is born of his erroneous belief in the real existence of her One he is always trying to impersonate—the pervert is at a very deep, even 'tragic' level at the mercy of his victim. Although the pervert succeeds very well in occupying the position of object *a*, it is the hysteric and her unsatisfiable desire for the non-existent Charles that causes the perverse fantasy to fail.

This brings us now to the final psychic structure recognized by psychoanalysis: psychosis. Since we have already looked in some detail at the psychotic in a previous chapter, it is enough just to observe the following: having 'foreclosed' the phallic signifier, there is, strictly speaking, no psychotic 'count'. In her psychic tool-kit, the psychotic does not have the symbolic resource of the phallic 'empty set' to count-as-One, although this is not to say there was no original traumatic arousal. As any clinical picture can easily show, the psychotic is certainly familiar with the trauma of *jouissance*.[80] Moreover, the same clinical picture will additionally divulge how the psychotic clearly recognizes the existence of a One, who typically appears as the persecuting figure of the psychotic's paranoid delusion. However, it is necessary to point out that, because it is not constructed by a count (which requires the empty set), this One is fundamentally different from the Ones of the previous desiring structures. The psychotic's One is, if you will, the only genuinely numerical One, in the sense of an absolute First One (a One that pre-exists the subject). The psychotic's, in other words, is the mythical or axiomatic One of the philosophers, the One which, if it really existed, would mean the collapse of all desire and of the psychotic's continuing existence, which is precisely why she is driven in the course of her psychotic delusion to try to destroy it.

## ORDINAL AND CARDINAL INFINITIES

Returning now to the desiring fantasies proper, the above discussion enables us to appreciate how the infinity the Rinvilles of the world generate is of a radically different kind to those produced in the hysterical and obsessional desiring fantasies. The infinity the pervert generates is what mathematicians call the 'ordinal'

---

80. Verhaeghe observes how this traumatic *jouissance* frequently appears at the beginning of a psychotic episode in the form of a paroxysmic anxiety. See his description of the etiology of psychosis in his chapter, 'The Psychotic Structure of the Subject' in *On Being Normal and Other Disorders*, pp. 429-58.

infinity—an infinity one tries to reach by simple counting. Each time the pervert re-forms (or 'convokes' to use the Badiouian term) the void into the empty set, he counts it as another 1 that, being added to the last, generates the next number (or 'successor') in the series. In this way, he manages to count beyond 1 but only as an infinite repetition of the illegal act of nomination that first turned the nothing into something that can be counted:

$$0 = \emptyset$$
$$1 = \{\emptyset\} = \{0\}$$
$$2 = \{\emptyset, \{\emptyset\}\} = \{0, 1\}$$
$$3 = \{\emptyset, \{\emptyset\}, \{\emptyset\}\}\} = \{0, 1, 2\}$$

In contrast, as we saw, the hysteric and the obsessional never even successfully make it to One, let alone to Two or Three. Because of the way their $a$ inevitably ruins their One-result—which thus always remains what Lacan nicely calls a 'perforated One'[81]—they remain stuck at the first step, forced to begin their 'count' over and over again in the process psychoanalysis calls 'unconscious repetition'.

And yet, as we saw too, this failed count also enables one to enter into a realm of infinity—or rather, into two forms, named previously as the 'qualitative' and 'quantitative' infinities. Differing from the ordinal or what Badiou calls the 'natural' infinity (the infinity one tries to reach by perversely counting), these infinities were in each case produced by the introduction of a *limit*. The limit Emmeline encountered lies in what Badiou astutely locates as the '*introjection of alterity*'.[82] As expressed in her desiring equivalent of the paradox of Achilles and the tortoise, her limit becomes corporealized as a 'frontier'. Badiou explains that, 'the essential time of the qualitative something is the introjection of alterity (the limit thereby becoming frontier)',[83] in which description we can also clearly discern the hysteric's fundamental problem—the way she will always be 'other' to herself insofar as she identifies with the Other's desire. Charles, by contrast, discovered his limit in what Badiou calls 'the *externalization of identity*'.[84] As what brings about the 'quantitative infinity', Charles's limit lies in the way he never

---

81. Lacan, *The Seminar of Jacques Lacan, Book XIV, The Logic of Fantasy (1966-1967)*, unpublished seminar (lesson of 10 May, 1967).

82. Badiou, *Being and Event*, p. 168 (Badiou's emphasis).

83. Badiou, *Being and Event*, p. 168.

84. Badiou, *Being and Event*, p. 169 (Badiou's emphasis).

obtains the 'unity whose repose lies in spreading itself beyond itself' as a result of his propensity to divide himself into multiple-Ones (or a's).[85] The reason he will never attain this unity is because, inevitably, at some point or other, the Other will mistake one of the obsessional's semblances or 'gifts' for the real thing. This 'error' in the Other, which was born from the specific way the obsessional's *a* was formed, short-circuits the enigmatic little game of mirrors through whose mechanism the obsessional attempts to slip from the Other's lethal embrace.

To comprehend the mathematical basis for how this imposition of a limit still makes it possible to enter into the realm of infinity, we can turn to the distinction Georg Cantor makes between ordinal and cardinal numbers. As mentioned, in mathematics, ordinal numbers are those that are obtained by counting, that is, by the addition of quantities of empty sets. Cardinal numbers, by contrast, define the size or 'number of elements' of the set they describe. They represent the name of the unit amount once the computation, the ordinal count, has been completed. Within the realm of finite numbers, both ordinal and cardinal numbers are the same: $1 + 1 + 1 =$ (both ordinal and cardinal) 3. However, once we enter the realm of infinity this changes. There are both infinite ordinals and infinite cardinals. The infinite ordinal—the limit one would reach if one could count to infinity—is called omega, while the infinite cardinal is Aleph-zero. What is the difference between the two? The difference is that Aleph-zero enables us to count 'beyond' the ordinal infinity.

Rather than taxing ourselves with the mathematical explanation of this statement, we can turn to a more immediately intuitive—more 'literary'—way of clarifying this. My example is the one Lacan himself employs in Seminar XIV, *The Logic of Fantasy*, in his discussion of Russell's famous paradox regarding the catalogue of all catalogues that do not contain themselves. After first outlining the Russellian inside-outside paradox (that is, whether the catalogue of all catalogues that do not contain themselves ought itself be to contained in the catalogue), Lacan adverts to same Mallarméan dream we saw Badiou cautioning against in the first chapter, the dream of a 'metapoem' or an Absolute Book.[86] This Book, the 'poetic fantasy par excellence' as Lacan puts it, is the dream of a book encompassing 'the whole signifying chain'.

---

85. Badiou, *Being and Event*, p. 168.
86. Lacan, Seminar XIV (lesson of 23 November, 1966).

Telling 'everything', such a Book would be nothing less than the whole 'Universe of discourse'.

Clearly, as Russell's paradox convincingly shows, this is impossible for the simple reason that 'the signifier cannot signify itself' or, to recall Lacan's other famous formulation of this point, there is no Other of the Other: there is no metalanguage in which one could 'say it all'. Or again, to recall Badiou's clarion call, *'it is an essential property of being qua being that there cannot exist a whole of beings, once beings are thought solely on the basis of their beingness'*.[87] Although he has no quarrel with this fundamental axiom, Lacan will, in Seminar XIV, begin to veer in a different direction for here he introduces the idea of a catalogue of all the books referred to in a single book's bibliography. Unlike Russell's catalogue, there is no question of whether the book whose bibliography is being listed should be included (of course it should not). However, a second catalogue that lists all the books that a second book's bibliography contains, may well include the title of the first book (although, naturally, not that of the second). By effectively grouping the books into 'sets' in this way, Lacan demonstrates how a totality may be achieved without falling into Russell's paradox. For, as Lacan explains, although each bibliographic catalogue will not include the title of the book from which it has been derived, once we put these catalogues *together into a series*, it is not unthinkable that between them, they will succeed in listing *all* of the books in the world.[88]

It should be clear from this that the 'all' in the statement 'all the books in the world' is not a totality that has been illegitimately arrived at, imposed, say, from outside the world in the kind of meta-linguistic or meta-ontological gesture that both Lacan and Badiou in their different ways prohibit. But nor has this 'all' been obtained by *counting* to infinity, where every last number has finally been counted, including the 'count' itself—something that

---

87. Badiou, *Theoretical Writings*, ed. and trans. Ray Brassier and Alberto Toscano, London, Continuum, 2004, p. 169.

88. This can be expressed in the following diagram, where each letter outside each set represents the title of the 'book' whose bibliography is being catalogued:

A (B, C, D)
B (A, C, D)
C (A, B, D)
D (A, B, C)

Between them, every 'book' has thus been catalogued (represented), even though there is no single catalogue that contains them all.

is in any event impossible. Its mathematical justification derives from Cantor's Power Set Axiom which states that 'the power set of x is bigger than x'. Translated into less technical terms, this means that if there is an infinite set that cannot be matched on a one-to-one basis to the proper subsets of itself, it must possess a larger cardinality (than the sum total or 'ordinality' of *all* of its subsets). This is an infinity that has been created through the imposition of a limit (the limit ordinal, omega, which is also sometimes called the 'completed' infinity).[89]

By the same logic, insofar as they, too, are produced by the imposition of a limit, the infinities of Emmeline's and Charles's counts—the infinities of the neurotic desiring structures—must be greater than the infinity generated by the perverse subject, Rinville. Obeying what A, in his essay 'The Rotation Method' that follows the Scribe review, calls 'the principle of limitation', the neurotic or, as I now propose to begin calling them for reasons that should soon be apparent, the 'aesthetic' psychic structures seem to understand how 'the more you limit yourself, the more fertile you become in invention'.[90] Although limited in advance by a structural failure that ensures that none of their attempts to count to One will succeed, if each of these unsuccessful attempts are placed together into a series, an 'all' is created that is more than the sum of its individual parts. In Seminar XIV, Lacan calls this 'all' a *One*. This One is a 'supplementary One' (*Un en plus*), so named because it is an 'additional signifier', as he puts it, 'one that is not grasped in the chain'.[91] This *Un-en-plus*, Lacan says, 'precisely explodes what is involved in the Universe of discourse, of the bubble, of the empire in question, of the sufficiency of what is closed in on the image of the imaginary whole'.[92]

---

89. See Mary Tiles, *The Philosophy of Set Theory: An Introduction to Cantor's Paradise*, Oxford, Blackwell, 1999, pp. 104-5.

90. Kierkegaard, *Either/Or*, p. 288.

91. '... by simply closing the chain, there results that each group of four [catalogues in the example Lacan is using] can easily leave outside itself the extraneous signifier, which can serve to designate the group, for the simple reason that it is not represented in it, and that nevertheless the whole chain will be found to constitute the totality of all these signifiers, giving rise to this additional unit, uncountable as such, which is essential for a whole series of structures, which are precisely the ones on which I founded, since the year 1960, my whole operation of identification', *Seminar XIV* (lesson of 23.11.66).

92. Lacan, *Seminar XIV* (lesson of 23 November, 1966).

## THE (SUPPLEMENTARY) ONE OF LOVE

Perhaps the best way to approach this One, different from the One dreamed of by the fantasies, is through Lacan's statement I referred to earlier, that love is a myth. In his seminar VIII, on the transference, Lacan cautions how 'Love as god [...] manifests itself in the real and as such we can only speak about it in a myth'.[93] Lacan presents this 'myth' in terms of a movement whereby, reaching out to grasp a desired object, one suddenly discovers the 'fruit', or the 'flower' or the 'log' mysteriously reaching back:

> [...] when in this movement of reaching, of drawing, of poking, the hand has gone far enough towards the object, if from the fruit, from the flower, from the log, a hand emerges which stretches out to encounter your hand, and that at that moment it is your hand which is fixed in the closed fullness of the fruit, the open fullness of the flower, in the explosion of a hand which bursts into flame, what is produced at that point is love![94]

Lacan employs this extraordinary image to illustrate the act of substitution that occurs in love. It arises in the context of his discussion of Plato's *Symposium*, specifically, his analysis of Phaedrus's speech where Achilles is extolled as the gods' most blessed lover. To recall briefly, in this, the first speech of the *Symposium*, Phaedrus asserts that the gods value Achilles above Alcestes because, while Alcestes died in place of her husband, it was as a lover (*erastes*) that she made her substitutive sacrifice. Achilles, however, is reserved a special place on the Isles of the Blest because, in pursuing vengeance for Patroclus who loved him, Achilles knowingly goes to his death not for the sake of his beloved (like Alcestes) but, precisely, as Patroclus's beloved (*eromenos*). And the gods, claims Phaedrus, 'are more generous with a loved one (*eromenos*) who cherishes his lover, than with a lover who cherishes the boy he loves'.[95]

In Lacan's reading, Achilles performs a 'miraculous' act when he changes position from being Patroclus's *eromenos* into an *erastes* who will stop at nothing to avenge Patroclus's death. Unlike Alcestes, as Lacan claims, 'it is not that Achilles as *eromenos*

---

93. Lacan, *Seminar VIII* (lesson of 7 December, 1960).
94. Lacan, *Seminar VIII* (lesson of 7 December, 1960).
95. Plato, 'Symposium', trans. Alexander Nehamas & Paul Woodruff, in *Plato: Complete Works*, ed., intro. & notes John M. Cooper, Indianapolis, Hackett, 1997, p. 465.

manages in some way to substitute himself for Patroclus, it is not a question of that because Patroclus is already beyond anybody's reach, anybody's attacks'. Instead, the 'miracle of love' occurs when Achilles 'who is himself the beloved', that is, the one who occupies the position of desired object, 'transforms himself into a lover' and begins, like the flaming hand in Lacan's myth, to act as a subject, and reach back.

As a myth that is intended to 'materialise' the 'phenomenon of love', what distinguishes this 'myth' of love from that other famous 'myth' with which we began this discussion, the 'first love' or mythical love of the mother? The difference between the two myths is that the former—the myth of the fruit/flower/log—is a myth that has, in Lacanian parlance, been *written*.

Typically, by 'writing' (or *écrits*), Lacan refers to the famous 'mathemes'—the $a$, the $\$$ of the signifier, A and $\Phi$—with which he represents the relations between the subject, the object of desire and the big Other in the fantasies. As a formalization, writing is accordingly 'a medium (*support*) that goes beyond speech', albeit without going beyond 'language's actual effects',[96] by which Lacan specifies that they do not represent a meta-language. Like the mathematical formulas on which they are modeled, the chief benefit of the mathemes is that they give one the ability to speak about any number of potential objects with a single 'letter'. This letter can then be assigned a specific value (or 'content') while continuing to hold onto certain established relations with the other elements in the equation. As Lacan puts it, 'formalization is nothing other than the substitution of what is called a letter for any number of ones', going on to explain how,

> when we write that inertia is
>
> $$\frac{mv^2}{2}$$
>
> [it means that] whatever the number of ones you place under each of those letters, you are subject to a certain number of laws—laws of grouping, addition, multiplication, etc. [97]

As a result of this formalization or 'writing', now in Lacan's sense, one is freed from the tyranny of always having to speak about a particular object or specific number, enabling one to talk more abstractly, about *relations* between objects. Enshrined in the formula's 'laws', these relations can then be carried over integrally

---

96. Lacan, *Seminar XX*, p. 93.
97. Lacan, *Seminar XX*, p. 130.

into any context, regardless of the specific content they may have originally been invested with.

To say that love is a myth that has been written is thus to say it has undergone just such an act of formalization, and this is also, I submit, how we must understand A's earlier description of Emmeline's love as a 'mathematical' love or now, more precisely, a mathematized love. Unlike the myth of first love as mother love so beloved of the psychoanalytic critical tradition, Emmeline's first love is a love that has seen *jouissance* formalized, 'written' through the mathemes of desire. To put this another way, the difference between the two myths is defined by how one understands the little phrase, 'that's not it', which for Lacan is endemic to all desire. From the perspective of the first myth (mother love), this disappointing discovery is registered as an object's failure to live up to some preconceived concept of 'it'—the mother or ideal One against whom we compare the beloved and find that he or she falls short, leading us to seek another possessor of the 'ring', another lover who comes closer to our vision of It. If this were in fact so, psychoanalysis would be little more than what its critics charge, that is, the contemporary iteration of an idealism that stretches back to Parmenides. But as Kierkegaard's aesthete is correct to constantly be reminding us, like Emmeline what we seek is fundamentally unknown to us. What we seek will always—must always—remain 'one station ahead' (or, in Charles' case, one station behind) because 'it' does not and never did 'exist'. The reason it does not exist is because 'it' is solely a corporealization of the limit imposed by castration, insofar as this limit and our relation to has been presented—'staged'—through the formulas of desire.

This said, it is nevertheless clear that the majority of us do at some point stop with a specific 'One', even if only for a time, since few of us possess Don Juan's insane mathematical fervor, described in one of A's earlier essays in *Either*, to try out every possible combination of his desiring fantasy to infinity.[98] Yet it is not so much exhaustion that makes us pause (although this admittedly may sometimes be part of it). When Achilles changes places with Patroclus, he stops racing against the tortoise. Something

---

98. A discusses Don Juan in an earlier essay 'The Immediate Stages of the Erotic, or the Musical Erotic'. There Don Juan is said to represent the 'third' stage, when desire is 'fully determined' as desire, desire as a 'principle' as he calls it, which seems very close in some respects to the Lacanian 'desire is the desire of the Other' or desire for desire. See *Either/Or*, pp. 83-134.

can occur that halts, at least for a time, the mathematizing fantasy and this something, just as all the traditional narratives of romance have always taught us, is 'love'. In what way does love, again quite conventionally and to the (misplaced) chagrin of lovers, reduce or even quench desire? Lacan's answer is as dense as it is precise: love changes contingency into necessity, turning the phallic signifier from something that 'stops not being written' into something that 'doesn't stop being written'.

To explain this we need to recall how in Seminar XX, *Encore*, Lacan offers the following definitions. Punning on the near homonyms between *ne pas de s'ecrire, ne cesse pas de ne pas s'ecrire* and *neccessaire*, he says the impossible, is what 'doesn't stop not being written' (*ce qui ne cesse pas de ne pas s'ecrire*). Lacan's example of such a *ne pas de s'ecrire*, such a non-writing, is the sexual relation: the sexual relation (what Badiou in the above discussion calls the void) never ceases not to be written. As impossible, it remains continually unwritten, that is to say, unrepresented and (again, like the void in Badiou) unformalized. However, once this impossibility undergoes formalization as the fantasy, the sexual relation 'stops not being written'. How does it do so? As the discussion above helps us to see, this 'stops not being written' occurs when the void is mathematized, formalized or 'written' as the 'provisional representation' (or in Badiou's terms, 'presentation') of the phallic signifier. Contrary to those who see the phallus as an instance of an implicit determination in psychoanalysis, as a *provisional* representation, the phallus is thus 'contingent', Lacan claims. 'It is as a mode of the contingent that the phallic function stops not being written'.[99] By this I understand him to mean that the formalization of the void might not have taken place (or might not have fully succeeded, as for example in the case of the psychotic and the perverse subjects).

The final step in Lacan's own 'loving formula' goes from the contingency implied by the phallus to a necessity that Lacan expresses in the phrase 'doesn't stop being written' (*ne pas de s'ecrire*). This step is taken by 'love'. All love, Lacan explains, 'subsisting only on the basis of the 'stops not being written' [that is, on the 'contingency' of the phallic 'writing', desire] tends to make

---

99. Lacan, *Seminar XX*, p. 94. The English translation is a little ambiguous here. To clarify, it is not the 'phallic function' that 'stops not being written'. It is rather the unwritable *jouissance* that stops not being written (in the form of the phallic function).

the negation shift to the 'doesn't stop being written', doesn't stop, won't stop'.[100] In a formulation whose seeming nonsense would be worthy of Emmeline, Lacan appears to be asserting that love is nothing more than a shift of a negation in a sentence about writing (and certainly at one level it's not hard to see how such nit-picking over words could have a dramatic effect on desire!). 'The displacement of the negation from the 'stops not being written' to the 'doesn't stop being written', in other words, from contingency to necessity—there lies the point of suspension to which all love is attached'.[101]

What Lacan is getting at in this distinctly unromantic sounding statement is the way love's 'doesn't stop being written' enables the subject to begin to approach the impossible *jouissance* of the sexual relation in a way that is not governed by (phallic) contingency and its imaginary stagings in the fundamental fantasies. By saying this I do not mean that love somehow by-passes or short-circuits the phallic fantasies, as is clear from the above quote. Love, it would seem, 'subsists' only on the basis of the 'writing' or formalization of *jouissance* effected by the phallic signifier. However, as the earlier example of Alcestes indicates—and which Lacan also confirms with the quote he wrote on the board during the lesson of 7 December, 1960 of Seminar VIII, *Transference*, '*Epithumian men diaplasiastheisan erota einai/ Erota de diaplasiasthenta manian gignesthai*' (A desire redoubled is love / But redoubled love becomes delusion)—love is not simply a question of desiring an object and, in certain privileged or 'miraculous' cases, of having that object desire you back. Love concerns or is 'attached' to something else, which Lacan describes in terms of a 'point of suspension'. It is to this suspension we must now look.

When desire's formalization permits *jouissance* to cease being unrepresentable and assume the form of the phallic signifier, its consequence is that an empirical lover can come to represent the 'law' of how the subject desires. That is to say, any particular lover or lovers can fill in or 'populate' the letter it corresponds to in the desiring equation with a specific 'value', while nevertheless keeping the formal relations of the subject, *a* and A intact. From one perspective, this might have a rather depressing effect, insofar as any 'choice' of one particular person over another becomes in a sense without any real difference. In this schema, anyone can be

---

100. Lacan, *Seminar XX*, p. 145.
101. Lacan, *Seminar XX*, p. 145.

the 'right' man or woman for you, for at some level a choice for one is always implicitly also a choice for 'all': the beloved object will always occupy the same structural position in the subject's pre-'chosen' fundamental fantasy. As unsentimental as it sounds, the fact is that absolutely anyone can be the subject's 'one and only true love', and in a way that is not simply the revisionist historicizing indulged in by A's former sweetheart. Despite the considerable efforts of the Western literary tradition to tell us otherwise, *who* one actually chooses is of very little importance to the subject (a point on which Kierkegaard's aesthete would surely agree). Beyond all of their unique differences, to the extent that every one of my lovers is a party in the specific pattern of how I desire, they are in some very real sense the Same.

This is true as long as we are talking about desire, however. Lacan is always careful to point out how desire's object cause—the object $a$—is not something that can be possessed by any empirical object but is always 'in you more than you': a real part of the subject that circulates in the field of the Other. The upshot is that at some level, all desire enjoys what Slavoj Žižek calls a 'masturbatory' relation with its object. The corollary to this would seem to be that the field of the Other is little more than the solipsistic projection of an idealist subject after all. However, this would again be to take the imaginary fantasy at its word and forget how the $a$ is not what completes or 'solves' the mathematizing fantasy but, precisely, what makes it fail, and this brings us now to love. With love the situation changes, and it is here in fact that the literary tradition really does begin to have something of importance to say to us. Recall how, when performed by the neurotic psychic structures, the eternal quest for the One produces a result that is not shared by the perverse and psychotic structures. Because of the way their 'infinities' are arrived at, the neurotic fantasies result in a One that is not 'counted' by the desiring operation; it is, as Lacan put it earlier, a One that is not 'grasped in the chain'. It was the $a$ that ensured that none of Emmeline's or Charles's counts to One would ever be completed, but it was also the limit thereby introduced by this $a$—the 'objective form' of the subject's castration as I described it earlier—that enabled our desiring neurotics to count 'beyond' infinity and enter the realm of what mathematicians call transfinite numbers or 'actual infinity'.

Why I say that literature has something important to say about love is because, as the privileged form of the aesthetic stage to which

A returns over and over again, literature is the Kierkegaardian discourse that is uniquely positioned to effectuate subjectivization in Badiou's precise sense. The reason is as follows: literature is uniquely placed to 'stage' the laws of desire because it treats these laws as its very subject matter. Literature—or at least stories of a certain kind, that is, romance literature, the literature of seduction—codifies the formulas of desire as narrative laws that dictate which paths a desiring character must take in order to reach the One. By 'flattening' the knot of Real, Symbolic and Imaginary into the (two-dimensional) necessities of narrative, romance literature presents these laws as resulting in an actually successful fantasy—a successful count to One. In its formulaic comic endings of marriages eventually achieved after the most unlikely of coincidences as perfected by the likes of Defoe, Austen, Trollope and of course Scribe, literature presents us with a world stripped of the topological distortion that the *a* always, in real life, introduces. This might lead one to argue, perhaps, that its chief function is to provide us a measure of Imaginary satisfaction we will never find in our own lives. Such would be its 'ideological' role, which has been rightly critiqued at length by Marxist critics of the novel.

Yet it would be a mistake to regard this aspect as what I, with Emmeline's Aunt Judith, would want to call the 'pedagogical' role of literature (or more generally of the aesthetic), since both of Kierkegaard's other two discourses, ethics and religion equally in their own ways 'stage' fantasies of a successful count to One—the fantasy of a perfectly just (that is, perversely balanced) world in the case of ethics, and the religious 'delusion' of the fallen (alienated) subject's reintegration back into the One. We must look for the educational role of literature elsewhere, namely, in the way it names its One explicitly *as another subject*. While the other two discourses similarly generate their own 'names' for love's One (the 'neighbor', in the case of ethics, and 'God' in the case of religion), in neither case is the name given to the One the name another subject. In neither of the other two discourses, then, does this naming represent the 'interventional nomination from the standpoint of the situation', as Badiou put it, by which he defines subjectivization—the subsumption of the supernumerary One beneath an immanent name extracted from the situation.[102]

What is it about the subject's proper name that distinguishes it from the (generic) naming undertaken by the other discourses?

---

102. Badiou, *Being and Event*, p. 393.

It is that, as an instance of pure, unadulterated or, as A calls it describing Emmeline, 'infinite nonsense', the proper name 'bears the trace of both the ultra-one [what we have been following Lacan in calling the supplementary One] and the multiple'.[103]

We can clarify this by stepping out of Badiou's language and returning to the question of writing. To say that love is what 'doesn't stop being written' is also to say that in love the subject's impossible *jouissance* is formalized in a way that is qualitatively different from the formalization represented by the phallic 'stops not being written'. In *Encore* Lacan calls this writing *suppléance*, an operation that 'supplements' the non-existence of the sexual relation by momentarily 'suspending' the phallic count. This is not a new idea Lacan suddenly introduces in *Encore*, for already in Seminar XIII, *The Object of Psychoanalysis* Lacan already explicitly identifies the two countermanding ways the 'excess' of the void or *jouissance*, can come to be 'written' in the Symbolic. In a discussion very pertinent to ours, Lacan comments, how 'every time we speak about something which is called the subject we make a "one" of it. However, the one to designate it is missing. What replaces it? What comes to fulfill the function of this 'one'? Several things, undoubtedly, but if you only see several very different things, the object on the one hand, for example, the proper name on the other fulfilling the same function, it is quite clear that you can understand nothing either about their distinction [...] or about the very fact that they fulfill the same function'.[104]

Both the *a* and the proper name, Lacan suggests here, are means of 'writing' the absent One, but they do so in the utterly different ways that Lacan proposes: the *a* writes the supplementary One through the failure represented as the fantasies—as 'phallic' *jouissance*. The name, on the other hand, as a signifier of 'pure nonsense' constitutes a formalization that is not in the service of the signifier—a writing, as Lacan puts it in the following lesson, that 'exists already before serving the writing of the word'.[105] Such 'writing' Lacan would go on to detect and punningly describe in Seminar XVII, in his lesson known as 'Lituraterre' where he elaborates the traces of letters carved by rivers, streams and the shadows of clouds as he flew over Siberia on the way back from a lecture in Japan. Such 'writing'—the 'gullying of the signified' as he calls it

---

103. Badiou, *Being and Event*, p. 393.
104. Lacan, *Seminar XIII* (lesson of 15 December, 1965).
105. Lacan, *Seminar XIII* (lesson of 5 January, 1966).

in that lesson—he discovers again in Seminar XX, in the lacy architecture of the spider's web, which Lacan describes there as a 'truly miraculous function to see, on the very surface emerging from an opaque point of this strange being, the trace of these writings taking form, in which one can grasp the limits, the impasses, and dead ends that show the real acceding to the symbolic'.[106] Lacan's use of the word 'miraculous' here, I think, should remind us of the previous time this word came up, in the context of his 'myth' of love. Evidently something just as 'miraculous' occurs when *jouissance* becomes capable of crystallizing around a person's name, as Kierkegaard seems to have discovered. His famous and, to some, puzzling use of pseudonyms might thus be understood in this way: as a form of 'writing' in Lacan's sense, a formalization that enabled him to surmount the seeming impasses of his three philosophical discourses. For as Kirsten Hyldgaard has explained, 'formalizations serve the purpose of presenting and talking about an experience of a paradox, an impasse, an impossibility. With the help of formulas it is possible to recognize an impossibility as an impossibility without covering it up in imaginary representations or historically variable constructions, and it is possible to know what kind of impossibility we are talking about'.[107]

To close this discussion, I would simply like to suggest that there is therefore a very good reason why Emmeline's and Charles's education was a literary one—like everyone's ought to be. Although aesthetically tempting, by this I am not suggesting that literature is responsible for the 'myth' of love—that, in a La Rochfoucauldian manner, without literature we would never have known about love. Nor am I suggesting that we should model our desiring trajectories on the comic tales of love lost and then regained at which the literary tradition excels. Emmeline and Charles would have taken the wrong lesson away from Aunt Judith's impeccable training if they believed literature was to teach them how to desire. Quite the contrary. What literature instructs us in is how to enjoy. When it invariably gives the supplementary One a proper name—Anna, Zinaida, Aaron, Mary and Charles—literature 'educates' us in the 'infinite nonsense' of a specifically linguistic *jouissance*.[108] It is thus through this 'romantic training' that we learn to better hear the nonsensical infinity—the cardinal or, as I earlier called it,

---

106. Lacan, *Seminar XX*, p. 93.
107. Kirsten Hyldgaard, *Umbr(a)*, no. 1: Identification, pp. 43-53, p. 52.
108. Kierkegaard, *Either/Or*, p. 255.

'loving' infinity in our own beloved's names. Real-izing the One in the name of another subject in this way, literature sensitizes us to better hear *jouissance's* 'transfinite infinity' encoded in every name and for this reason, as Kierkegaard well knew but the philosophical tradition around him sometimes forgets, the aesthetic should be retained as an essential pedagogical stage of everybody's—but of course also, especially, the psychoanalyst's—'life's way'.

# AFTERWORD

When infinity is imposed with a limit, it produces a new number that is mathematically 'larger' than infinity. This new number, the cardinal infinity or Aleph-zero is produced not by a count-as-One, but by what Cantor called the power set axiom. This axiom, which states the power set of x is greater than x, indicates that a number can be generated in a manner other than through a count. Cantor's *Hemmungsprinzip* or principle of limitation (which we saw Kierkegaard's aesthete A also making good use of) was one of modern mathematics' greatest breakthroughs, and it spawned literally an infinity of infinities, each with its own peculiar properties and method of generation. Among these was Paul Cohen's technique of 'forcing'. Forcing is the technique that enables one to make predictions about the contents of a non-constructible set, that is, a set that cannot be organized by the Zermelo-Fraenkel axioms such as 'well-ordering' that served to ground 'Cantor's paradise'.

In his introduction to the mathematical foundations of Badiou's philosophy, Andrew Gibson beautifully describes the infinities formed by Cantor's discovery as the 'monstrous' and 'chimerical creatures' that haunt the uninhabitable spaces and impossible times of a transcendental aesthetic lying beyond the bounds of the Zermelo-Fraenkel axioms.[1] Escaping 'numerical treatment' as he puts it, the existence of such 'large cardinals' is unprovable from within the confines of existing set theory, although this of course has not stopped mathematicians from pursuing and trying to capture them mathematically. Modern set theory is populated by the strange unthinkable beasts Gibson itemizes as the 'Mahlo, weakly compact, hyper-Mahlo, ineffable, measurable, Ramsey, su-

---

1. Andrew Gibson, *Beckett and Badiou: the Pathos of Intermittency*, Oxford, Oxford University Press, 2006, p. 12.

percompact, huge and $n$-huge cardinals',[2] a majestic pantheon that must now make room for another: the uncounted, 'literary' One of First Love.

I thus return to my initial claim that a One exists that has somehow managed to escape Badiou's 'count'. As Gibson persuasively argues, the concept of the 'actual infinity' (as these impossible cardinals are called) lies at the core of Badiou's thought. He cites Badiou's claim that number is nothing less than 'co-extensive with Being'.[3] Given this centrality of the transfinite infinity to Badiou's mathematics, how could he have missed the One of First Love? The answer, as I indicated at the start, lies in his demonstrated deep ambivalence towards language as a potential eventalsite in its own right.

What I have indicated in the foregoing is how at least one version of the Mallarméan dream of an Absolute Book or 'metapoem' might be accommodated into his philosophy without risk of relapsing into the One that lies at the foundation of philosophy's 'ruined portico'.[4] Uncounted by the count-as-One, this One of First Love is 'forced' into our consciousness (and thus acquires some measure of existence) through the extra-semantic properties of the proper name. Although carried by all words, such nonsensical 'sonant material' is nevertheless uniquely foregrounded when, under a certain repetition compulsion instated by desire, a lover silently circles around and around the beloved's magical name in the internal poem written by love.

Badiou himself indicates at different points how such a 'forcing' might be possible. As I suggested in the previous chapter, Badiou's account of subjectivization is one such point. There a proper name, Lenin, Cantor, Schoenberg, but also Simon, Bernard and Claire, was deemed capable of embodying the 'subjectivizing split'—the eventual name's self-doubling or repetition when it straddles both the border of the void and the border of the name—without falling into the 'spontaneist thesis'. Although he neglects to see it, Badiou's account of Fernando Pessoa, in the *Handbook of Inaesthetics*, is another. Titled 'A Philosophical Task', in this essay Badiou describes his experience of reading Pessoa,

---

2. Gibson, *Beckett and Badiou*, p. 12.

3. Badiou, *Le Nombre et les nombres*, Paris, Seuil, 1990, p. 175. Cited in Gibson, *Beckett and Badiou*, p, 15.

4. Alain Badiou, *Being and Event*, trans. Oliver Feltham, London, Continuum, 2005, p.23.

saying that 'when we cast our eye on a page of Pessoa, we rapidly acquire the conviction that he will always hold us captive, that it is useless to read other books, that it is *all there*'.[5] Badiou compares this positively to the Mallarméan project of the Book, claiming that 'the weakness of Mallarmé's project lay in retaining the sovereignty of the One, of the author—even if this author made himself absent from the Book to the point of becoming anonymous'. Whereas Mallarmé's anonymity 'remains prisoner to the transcendence of the author', Badiou continues, Pessoa's use of the 'heteronyms' Caiero, Campos, Resi, 'Pessoa-in-person', and Soares enables him to escape this fate and to 'establish the contingency of the multiple'.[6] Pessoa's heteronyms 'do not stake a claim upon the One or the All', which is why, in Badiou's mind, 'better than the Book, they compose a universe'.[7]

However, couldn't one just as well say that, like Kierkegaard's own use of pseudonyms, Pessoa's 'heteronyms' perform a 'writing' in Lacan's sense of a *formalization*? The reason a page of Pessoa gives the impression of being 'all there', in other words, comes as a result of the infinity of infinities opened by the *Hemmungsprinzip* that is the act of 'writing'. No matter how varied, unique and multitudinous, the sheer 'contingency of the multiple' (regarded as the infinity of ordinal numbers) cannot in any way compete with enormity of the One embodied in Aleph-Zero, as the 'first' of the transfinite infinities. Badiou's utmost conviction that he must philosophically disallow every form of the One thus prevents him from seeing what is in front of his eyes: a One exists that is not the product of a count. There is an actually existing One or perhaps better, 'some One' in whose proper name an entire infinite 'universe' is contained for the lover.

Thus the literary tradition is perfectly justified when it calls love 'first'. Love is both logically and chronologically *prior* for the irresistible reason that it is love's 'writing', the original reflexive act through which we become speaking beings, that founds a world and the infinity of objects it contains. Lacan puts it unambiguously, it is 'only once you have generated the number zero you finally lay hold of a first object'.[8]

5. Badiou, *Handbook of Inaesthetics*, trans. Alberto Toscano, Stanford, Stanford University Press, 2005, p. 44.

6. Badiou, *Handbook of Inaesthetics*, p. 44.

7. Badiou, *Handbook of Inaesthetics*, p. 44.

8. Jacques Lacan, *The Seminar of Jacques Lacan, Book XII, Crucial Problems for Psychoanalysis (1964-1965)*, unpublished seminar (lesson of 24.2.65).

In his own short story titled 'First Love', Vladimir Nabokov describes the memory of seeing Colette, his boyhood love, for the last time. The narrator mentions the presence of a small detail in her attire that he is unable to fully account for:

> The leaves mingle in my memory with the leather of her shoes and gloves, and there was, I remember, some detail in her attire (perhaps a ribbon on her Scottish cap, or the pattern of her stockings) that reminded me then of the rainbow spiral in a glass marble. I still seem to be holding that wisp of iridescence, not knowing exactly where to fit it, while she runs with her hoop ever faster around me and finally dissolves among the slender shadows cast on the graveled path by the interlaced arches of its low looped fence.[9]

It is not difficult to recognize this implacable detail, this 'wisp of iridescence', as the *Einziger Zug* that accompanies us along desire's forking paths from the earliest scene of writing which Freud called primary identification and literature, in its myriad different ways, calls 'first love'. As the double font of both the desiring count and the 'actual infinity' of the proper name, love's letter must now assume its rightful place as the cause of one of love's most peculiar but unmistakable phenomena: the way each of our multiple lovers is also always, inevitably, the One.

---

9. Vladimir Nabokov, *Nabokov's Congeries*, sel. and intro. Page Stegner, New York, Viking, 1968, p. 189.

# BIBLIOGRAPHY

Agamben, Giorgio, 'The Proper and the Improper', *Stanzas: Word and Phantasm in Western Culture*, trans. Ronald L. Martinez, Minneapolis, University of Minnesota Press, 1993.
Anzieu, Didier, 'Un Soi disjoint, une voix liante: l'écriture narrative de Samuel Beckett', *Nouvelle revue de psychanalyse*, no. 28, 1983.
Arnold, St. George Tucker, Jr., 'Eudora Welty's "First Love" and the Personalizing of Southern Regional History', *Journal of Regional Cultures*, vol. 1, no. 2, 1981, pp. 97-105.
Badiou, Alain, *Le Nombre et les nombres*, Paris, Seuil, 1990.
Badiou, Alain, 'What is Love?', trans. Justin Clemens, *Umbr(a)*, no. 1: Badiou, 1996, pp. 37-53.
Badiou, Alain, *Ethics: An Essay on the Understanding of Evil*, trans. Peter Hallward, London, Verso, 2001.
Badiou, Alain, *On Beckett*, ed. Alberto Toscano and Nina Power, Manchester, Clinamen Press, 2003.
Badiou, Alain, 'The Scene of Two', trans. Barbara P. Fulks, *Lacanian Ink*, no. 21, 2003, pp. 42-55.
Badiou, Alain, *Theoretical Writings*, ed. and trans. Ray Brassier and Alberto Toscano, London, Continuum, 2004.
Badiou, Alain, *Handbook of Inaesthetics*, trans. Alberto Toscano, Stanford, Stanford University Press, 2005.
Badiou, Alain, *Being and Event*, trans. Oliver Feltham, London, Continuum, 2005.
Badiou, Alain, *Logiques des mondes: L'être et l'événement 2*, Paris, Seuil, 2006.
Baker, Phil, *Beckett and the Mythology of Psychoanalysis*, Basingstoke, Palgrave Macmillan, 1998.
Barnard, Suzanne and Bruce Fink (eds.), *Reading Seminar XX:*

*Lacan's Major Work on Love, Knowledge, and Feminine Sexuality*, Albany, SUNY Press, 2002.

Beckett, Samuel, *First Love*, London, Calder and Boyars, 1973.

Beckett, Samuel, *Premier amour*, Paris, Les Éditions de Minuit, 1970.

Cavell, Stanley, *Pursuits of Happiness: The Hollywood Comedy of Remarriage*, Harvard University Press, 1981.

Chiesa, Lorenzo, 'Count-as-One, Forming-into-One, Unary Trait, S1', in *The Praxis of Alain Badiou*, Paul Ashton, A. J. Bartlett and Justin Clemens (eds.), Melbourne, re.press, 2006, pp. 147-76.

Clare, John, *John Clare: Major Works*, Eric Robinson, David Powell and Tom Paulin (eds.), Oxford, Oxford University Press, 2004.

Clare, John, *John Clare: Selected Letters*, Mark Storey (ed.), Oxford, Oxford University Press, 1990.

Clare, John, *The Later Poems of John Clare*, Eric Robinson and Geoffrey Summerfield (eds.), Manchester, Manchester University Press, 1964.

Clare, John, *The Prose of John Clare*, J. W. Tibble and Anne Tibble (eds.), London, Routledge and Kegan Paul, 1951.

Clare, John, *Selected Poems and Prose of John Clare*, Eric Robinson and Geoffrey Summerfield (eds.), Oxford, Oxford University Press, 1978.

Clare, John, *Selected Poems of John Clare*, ed. and intro. James Reeves, London, Heineman, 1954 (reprinted 1968).

Connor, Steven, 'Beckett and Bion', paper delivered at the *Beckett and London* conference, Goldsmith's College, London, 1998.

Copjec, Joan, 'May '68: The Emotional Month', in Slavoj Žižek (ed.), *Lacan: the Silent Partners*, London, Verso, 2006, pp. 90-114.

Copjec, Joan, *Read My Desire: Lacan Against the Historicists*, Cambridge, MIT Press, 1994.

Cronin, Richard, 'In Place and Out of Place: Clare in The Midsummer Cushion', in *John Clare: New Approaches*, John Goodridge and Simon Kövesi, Helpston, John Clare Society (eds.), 2000, pp. 133-48.

Daniels, Jonathan, *The Devil's Backbone: The Story of the Natchez Trace*, Louisiana, Pelican, 1992.

Davies, Paul, 'Three Novels and Four Nouvelles: Giving Up the Ghost to be Born at Last', in *The Cambridge Companion to*

*Beckett*, John Pilling (ed.), Cambridge, Cambridge University Press, 1996, pp. 43-66.

DeConde, Alexander, *This Affair of Louisiana*, New York, Charles Scribners' Sons, 1976.

de Kesel, Marc, 'Ontologie als katholicisme: Over Alain Badiou's Paulusinterpretatie', *Yang*, no. 1, 2004, pp. 17-32.

de Kesel, Marc, 'Truth as Formal Catholicism: On Alain Badiou, Saint Paul, La fondation de l'universalisme', *Communication and Cognition*, vol. 37, nos. 3-4, 2004, pp. 167-97.

de Landa, Manuel, *A Thousand Years of Nonlinear History*, New York, Swerve, 2000.

Dolar, Mladen, *A Voice and Nothing More*, Cambridge, MIT Press, 2006.

Dolar, Mladen, 'Vox', *Umbr(a)*, no. 1: Incurable, 2006, pp. 119-41.

Dor, Joel, *Structure and Perversions*, trans. Susan Fairfield, New York, Other Press, 2001.

During, Elie, 'How Much Truth Can Art Bear?' trans. Laura Balladur, *Polygraph*, no. 17, 2005, pp. 143-55.

Frege, Gottlob, *Die Grundlagen der Arithmetik* (1884), translated as The Foundations of Arithmetic, trans. J. L. Austin, Evanston, Illinois, Northwestern University Press, 1980.

Freud, Sigmund, 'The Disposition to Obsessional Neurosis', *The Standard Edition of the Complete Psychological Works of Sigmund Freud, vol XII (1911-1913)*, trans. James Strachey, London, Hogarth, 1968, pp. 317-26.

Freud, 'Group Psychology and the Analysis of the Ego (1921)', *The Standard Edition of the Complete Psychological Works of Sigmund Freud, vol XVIII (1920-22)*, trans. James Strachey, London, Hogarth, 1968, pp. 65-144.

Freud, Sigmund, 'Heredity and the Aetiology of the Neuroses', *The Standard Edition of the Complete Psychological Works of Sigmund Freud, vol III (1893-1899)*, trans. James Strachey, London, Hogarth, 1968, pp. 141-56.

Freud, Sigmund, 'Mourning and Melancholia', *The Standard Edition of the Complete Psychological Works of Sigmund Freud, vol XIV (1914-16)*, trans. James Strachey, London, Hogarth, 1968, pp. 243-58.

Freud, Sigmund, 'On Narcissism: An Introduction', *The Standard Edition of the Complete Psychological Works of Sigmund Freud, vol. XIV (1914-1915)*, trans. James Strachey, London, Hogarth, 1968, pp. 73-102.

Freud, Sigmund, 'Totem and Taboo', *The Standard Edition of the Complete Psychological Works of Sigmund Freud, vol XIII (1913-1914)*, trans James Strachey, London, Hogarth, 1955, pp. 1-255

Freud, Sigmund, 'Three Essays on the Theory of Sexuality', *The Standard Edition of the Complete Psychological Works of Sigmund Freud, vol. VII (1901-1905)*, trans. James Strachey, London, Hogarth, 1953, pp. 130-243.

Gaull, Marilyn, 'Clare and "the Dark System"', in *John Clare in Context*, Hugh Haughton, Adam Phillips and Geoffrey Summerfield (eds.), Cambridge, Cambridge University Press, 1994, pp. 279-94.

Gillespie, Sam, 'Giving Form to Its Own Existence: Anxiety and the Subject of Truth', in *The Praxis of Alain Badiou*, Paul Ashton, A. J. Bartlett and Justin Clemens (eds.), Melbourne, re.press, 2000, pp.180-209.

Gibson, Andrew, *Beckett and Badiou: the Pathos of Intermittency*, Oxford, Oxford University Press, 2006.

Green, André, *On Private Madness*, London, Hogarth Press, 1986.

Grimsley, Ronald, *Søren Kierkegaard and French Literature*, Cardiff, University of Wales Press, 1966.

Hallward, Peter, Badiou: A Subject to Truth, Minneapolis, University of Minnesota Press, 2003.

Hamilton, Sir William Rowan, 'Theory of Conjugate Functions, or Algebraic Couples; with a Preliminary and Elementary Essay on Algebra as the Science of Pure Time' (1837).

Harari, Roberto, *How James Joyce Made His Name: A Reading of the Final Lacan*, trans. Luke Thurston, New York, Other Press, 2002.

Haughton, Hugh and Adam Phillips, 'Introduction: Relocating John Clare', in *John Clare in Context*, Hugh Haughton, Adam Phillips and Geoffrey Summerfield (eds.), Cambridge, Cambridge University Press, 1994.

Hoens, Dominiek, 'Hamlet and the Letter a', *Umbr(a)*, vol. 2, no. 2, 2002, pp. 91-101.

Hyldgaard, Kirsten, *Umbr(a)*, 1: Identification, 1998, pp. 43-53.

Keller, John Robert, *Samuel Beckett and the Primacy of Love*, Manchester, Manchester University Press, 2002.

Johnston, Adrian, 'The Quick and the Dead: Alain Badiou and the Split Speeds of Transformation', *International Journal of Žižek Studies*, vol. 1, no. 2, 2007.

Jöttkandt, Sigi, 'Portrait of an Act: Aesthetics and Ethics in The Portrait of a Lady, *The Henry James Review*, vol. 25, no. 1, 2004, pp. 67-86.

Katz, Daniel, 'Beckett's Measures: Principles of Pleasure in Molloy and 'First Love',' *Modern Fiction Studies*, vol. 49, no. 2, 2003, pp. 246-56.

Kenner, Hugh, *Samuel Beckett: A Critical Study*, New Edition with a Supplementary Chapter, Berkeley, University of California Press, 1973.

Kierkegaard, Søren, *Either/Or*, vol. 1, trans. David F. Swenson and Lillian Marvin Swenson, revised and foreword Howard A. Johnson, New York, Anchor, 1959.

Kierkegaard, Søren, *Either/Or*, vol. 2, ed. and trans. Howard V. Hong and Edna H. Hong, Princeton, Princeton University Press, 1987.

Kierkegaard, Søren, *Works of Love*, ed. and trans. Howard V. Hong and Edna H. Hong, Princeton, Princeton University Press, 1995.

Kristeva, Julia, *Tales of Love*, trans. Leon S. Roudiez, New York, Columbia, 1987.

Lacan, Jacques, *Écrits: The First Complete Edition in English*, trans. Bruce Fink, New York and London, Norton, 2006.

Lacan, Jacques, *The Four Fundamental Concepts of Psychoanalysis*, Jacques-Alain Miller (ed.), trans. Alan Sheridan, New York, Norton, 1981.

Lacan, Jacques, *The Seminar of Jacques Lacan, Book II: The Ego in Freud's Theory and in the Technique of Psychoanalysis (1954-1955)*, Jacques-Alain Miller (ed.), trans. Sylvana Tomaselli, notes John Forrester, New York, Norton, 1991.

Lacan, Jacques, *The Seminar of Jacques Lacan, Book III, The Psychoses (1955-1966)*, Jacques-Alain Miller (ed.), trans. Russell Grigg, New York, Norton, 1993.

Lacan, Jacques, *Le Séminaire, Livre IV: La relation d'objet (1956-1957)*, texte établi par Jacques-Alain Miller, Paris, Seuil, 1994.

Lacan, Jacques, *Le Séminaire, Livre V: Les formations de l'inconscient (1957-1958)*, texte établi par Jacques-Alain Miller, Paris, Seuil, 1998.

Lacan, Jacques, *Le Séminaire de Jacques Lacan, Livre VIII, Le transfert (1960-1961)*, texte établi par Jacques-Alain Miller, Paris, Seuil, 2001.

Lacan, Jacques, *The Seminar of Jacques Lacan, Book IX, Identification*

*(1961-1962)*, unpublished seminar.
Lacan, Jacques, *The Seminar of Jacques Lacan, Book XII: Crucial Problems for Psychoanalysis (1964-1965)*, unpublished seminar.
Lacan, Jacques, *The Seminar of Jacques Lacan, Book XIII, The Object of Psychoanalysis (1965-1966)*, unpublished seminar,
Lacan, Jacques, *The Seminar of Jacques Lacan, Book XIV, The Logic of Fantasy (1966-1967)*, unpublished seminar
Lacan, Jacques, *The Seminar of Jacques Lacan, Book XV, The Psychoanalytic Act, (1967-1968)*, unpublished seminar.
Lacan, Jacques, *Le Séminaire de Jacques Lacan, Livre XVIII, D'un discours qui ne serait pas du semblant (1971)*, texte établi par Jacques-Alain Miller, Paris, Seuil, 2006.
Lacan, Jacques, *The Seminar of Jacques Lacan, Book XIX: ...ou pire (1971-1972)*, unpublished seminar,
Lacan, Jacques, *The Seminar of Jacques Lacan, Book XX: Encore, On Feminine Sexuality: The Limits of Love and Knowledge (1972-1973)*, Jacques-Alain Miller (ed.), trans. Bruce Fink, New York, Norton, 1998.
Lacan, Jacques, *Television: A Challenge to the Psychoanalytic Establishment*, Joan Copjec (ed.), trans. Dennis Hollier, Rosalind Krauss, Annette Michelson, London, Norton, 1990.
Mackey, Louis, *Kierkegaard: A Kind of Poet*, Philadelphia, University of Pennsylvania Press, 1971.
Mackey, Louis, 'Philosophy and Poetry in Kierkegaard', *The Review of Metaphysics*, vol. 23, 1969, pp. 316-32.
Marrs, Suzanne, *One Writer's Imagination: The Fiction of Eudora Welty*, Baton Rouge, Louisiana State Press, 2001.
Marrs, Suzanne, 'The Conclusion of Eudora Welty's "First Love": Historical Backgrounds', *Notes on Mississippi Writers*, vol. 13, no. 2, 1981 pp. 73-8.
McCaleb, Walter Flavius, *The Aaron Burr Conspiracy*, New York, Dodd, Mead & Co., 1903.
Mews, Constant J. (ed.), *The Lost Love Letters of Heloise and Abelard: Perceptions of Dialogue in Twelfth-century France*, trans. Neville Chiavaroli, Basingstoke, Palgrave Macmillan, 2001.
Miller, Jacques-Alain, 'On Shame', in *Jacques Lacan and the Other Side of Psychoanalysis: Reflections on Seminar XVII*, Justin Clemens and Russell Grigg (eds.), Durham, Duke University Press, 2006, pp. 11-28.

Miller, Jacques-Alain, 'Suture (Elements of the Logic of the Signifier)', *The Symptom*, no. 8, 2007.
Nabokov, Vladimir, *Nabokov's Congeries*, sel. and intro. Page Stegner, New York, Viking, 1968.
Nancy, Jean-Luc, *The Inoperative Community*, Peter Connor (ed.), trans. Lisa Garbus Peter Connor, Michael Holland, and Simona Sawhney, Minneapolis, University of Minnesota Press, 1991.
Nancy, Jean-Luc, 'Philosophy Without Conditions', *Think Again: Alain Badiou and the Future of Philosophy*, Peter Hallward (ed.), London, Continuum, 2004, pp. 39-48.
Nobus, Dany, 'Unpredictable Inevitability and the Boundaries of Psychic Life', in *The Catastrophic Imperative: Time, Subjectivity, Memory in Contemporary Thought*, Dominiek Hoens, Sigi Jöttkandt and Gert Buelens (eds.), London, Palgrave, 2009.
Norris, Christopher, *The Deconstructive Turn: Essays in the Rhetoric of Philosophy*, London, Routledge, 1989.
Pattison, George, *Kierkegaard: the Aesthetic and the Religious: From the Magic Theatre to the Crucifixion of the Image*, London, SCM Press, 1999.
Plato, 'Symposium', trans. Alexander Nehamas and Paul Woodruff in *Plato: Complete Works*, ed., intro. and notes John M. Cooper, Indianapolis, Hackett, 1997.
Poole, Roger, 'Reading Either/Or for the Very First Time', in *The New Kierkegaard*, Elsebet Jegstrup (ed.), Bloomington, Indiana University Press, 2004, pp. 42-54.
Porter, Roy, 'John Clare and the Asylum' in *John Clare in Context*, Hugh Haughton, Adam Phillips and Geoffrey Summerfield (eds.), Cambridge, Cambridge University Press, 1994, pp. 1-27.
Paulin, Tom, 'John Clare: A Bicentennial Celebration', in *John Clare: A Bicentenary Celebration*, Richard Foulkes (ed.), Northampton, University of Leicester Press, 1994, pp. 69-78.
Ricoeur, Paul, 'The Metaphorical Process as Cognition, Imagination, and Feeling', in *On Metaphor*, ed. Sheldon Sacks, Chicago, University of Chicago Press, 1979.
Storey, Mark, *The Poetry of John Clare: A Critical Introduction*, London, Macmillan, 1974.
Terada, Rei, *Feeling in Theory: Emotion after the 'Death of the Subject'*, Cambridge, MA, Harvard University Press, 2001.
Thompson, Victor H., 'Aaron Burr in Eudora Welty's "First Love"',

*Notes on Mississippi Writers*, no. 8, 1976, pp. 75-81.
Tiles, Mary, *The Philosophy of Set Theory: An Introduction to Cantor's Paradise*, Oxford, Blackwell, 1999.
Trefzer, Annette, 'Tracing the Natchez Trace: Native Americans and National Anxieties in Eudora Welty's "First Love"', *Mississippi Quarterly*, vol. 55, no. 3, 2002, pp. 419-440.
Turgenev, Ivan, *First Love and Other Stories*, trans. and intro. Richard Freeborn, Oxford, Oxford University Press, 1990.
Turgenev, Ivan, *Fathers and Sons*, intro. and notes Ann Pasternak Slater, New York, Modern Library, 2001.
Verhaeghe, Paul, *On Being Normal and Other Disorders: A Manual for Clinical Psychodiagnostics*, trans. Sigi Jöttkandt, New York, Other Press, 2004.
Vanheule, Stijn, 'Neurotic Depressive Trouble: Between the Signifier and the Real', *Journal for Lacanian Studies*, vol. 2, no. 1, 2004 pp. 34-53.
Warner, John M., 'Eudora Welty: The Artist in 'First Love',' *Notes on Mississippi Writers*, no. 9, 1976, pp. 77-87.
Welty, Eudora, *The Collected Stories of Eudora Welty*, London, Marion Boyars, 1981.
Žižek, Slavoj, 'A Plea for Ethical Violence', *Umbr(a)*, no. 1: War, 2004, pp. 75-89.
Zupančič, Alenka, *Ethics of the Real*, London, Verso, 2000.
Zupančič, Alenka, 'The Fifth Condition', in Peter Hallward (ed.), *Think Again*, London, Continuum, 2004, pp. 191-201.
Zupančič, Alenka, *The Shortest Shadow: Nietzsche's Philosophy of the Two*, Cambridge, MIT Press, 2003.

www.ingramcontent.com/pod-product-compliance
Lightning Source LLC
Chambersburg PA
CBHW022103160426
43198CB00008B/330